The Teacher's Little ...ok

Published by QG
With advertising ...
Red Kite Minibuses

Project Directors: [...ell Clarke.

Chief Editor: Dr Chri ... OBE.

Executive Co-Editors: Richard Bird, Alice Cunliffe.

Specialist Editors: Michael Howells, Stephen Szemerenyi OBE.

Consultant Editor for SEN Issues: Gail Treml.

Project Manager for QGP Ltd: Elizabeth Reed.

Panel of contributors and reviewers: David Brierley; Russell Clarke; Bob Hargreaves; Max Hill; JL Associates; Samantha Gibbs; Rona Tutt; Peter Whitlam.

We wish to thank our partners and advertisers for their invaluable support.

British Library Cataloguing
ISBN 978-0-9561095-1-4
First published 2004   Second Edition 2005
Third Edition 2006   Fourth Edition 2008
Fifth Edition 2009   Sixth Edition 2010

Designed by McCormick Creative Ltd
Printed by Core Publications

Copyright TLPB © 200? Chris Lowe.

QGP Ltd., The College Business Centre
Uttoxeter New Road, Derby DE22 3WZ. Tel: 01332 869240
website: www.qgpsolutions.com.

Introduction & Foreword

Law making has continued to proceed apace. At the time of writing (January 2010) one Education Act (the **Apprenticeships, Skills, Children and Learning Act 2009 (ASCLA 2009)**) has just received Royal Assent and the Children School and Families Bill is now before Parliament. If it is passed in its existing form it will introduce legal guarantees for parents, new complaints procedures and a licence to teach. At the time of writing, however, it may be lost in the pre-election crush. This sixth edition of *The Teacher's Little Pocket Book* includes notes on all enacted legislation and guidance since the previous edition as well as a complete table of the new teacher salaries and summary of the changes to teachers' conditions of service: including the new threshold arrangements. The SEN section has been revised and extended. We have also included a number of important new court cases that will be of interest (and instruction) to all teachers, leadership teams and governors.

Differences in guidance for Wales are shown in red. We also refer to documents that form part of the QGP Quick Guides for School Management in purple. Please see the QGP website at www.qgpsolutions.com for further details of our CM SYSTEM. Quick Guides School Management Documents provide model policies, guidance, checklists and model letters and the explanation of the law in five divisions: School Government; School Organisation; Management of Staff; Management of Pupils and Management of Health and Safety.

The *Teacher's Little Pocket Book* is not a definitive publication since the law and its implications changes all the time. For a complete understanding of the legal requirements you will need to go to the Acts of Parliament, Regulations and government guidance. To enable you to learn more, we have included a comprehensive index, a list of contact details and websites. We urge you to consult these as appropriate. They will help you develop your understanding of the complex business of being a teacher in 2010.

Foreword by Samantha Gibbs

I am now into my second year of teaching, having had an exhilarating but extremely hard first year, in common with most new teachers. It has been a real challenge to establish myself in my new school with both pupils and staff, not to mention keeping on top of the copious amounts of lesson planning, marking and making sure we meet seemingly impossible targets!

But a year in, teaching my subject is very much only part of the responsibilities to be grappled with from day to day as a teacher, and it never ceases to amaze me the variety of issues that arise; from dealing with parents, child protection, health and safety risk, to employment issues; all kinds of different and often difficult issues. I seem to get a never-ending supply of all sorts of legal information and guidance from the trade unions and the school, but with the hours I'm working and the demands on my time, I find I never have a spare moment to absorb it all. This is where the *Teacher's Little Pocket Book* has continued to be invaluable to me! Right from the start of my career it has been an instant life-saver, packed full of snappy practical advice in one neat compact pocket book, which is perfect when you're run off your feet and need answers fast!

Personal Details

NAME:	
School:	
School address:	
Tel. number:	
Fax number:	
Internal numbers:	
School email address:	
School website:	
School DCSF number:	
Examination Board reference number:	
Designated teacher for child protection:	
Health and safety representative(s):	
Union representative:	
Union learning representative:	
Other:	
GOVERNING BODY:	
Chair of the governing body:	
Staff governors:	
Nominated governor for child protection:	
Clerk to the governing body:	
LOCAL AUTHORITY:	
Key contacts:	
Local Learning & Skills Council (LLSC):	

Personal Details

TERM DATES:
Summer 2010
Begins:
Ends:
Half term:
Autumn 2010
Begins:
Ends:
Half term:
Spring 2011
Begins:
Ends:
Half term:
Summer 2011
Begins:
Ends:
Half term:

NOTES:

Contents

EXPLANATION:

The law, guidance and comment is in black.
Information exclusive to Wales is in red.
Places to go for further information are in ***black bold italics.***
Websites and email addresses are black underlined.
References to QGP Quick Guides documents are in purple.

Inspection coming up?
Struggling to update your policies?

Let QGP take the strain!

QGP provides summarised guidance, model policies, checklists and procedures to ensure that you do not fall foul of the Law. Areas covered include:

- health and safety; risk assessment and child protection;
- management of staff and pupils; school organisation and governance.

- **Access** our content-managed CM SYSTEM of 400 documents (with differences for Wales highlighted throughout)
- **Download** and adapt our model policies to your own situation
- **Purchase** our *Teacher's Little Pocket Book* and *Support Staff Little Pocket Book* – vital sources of information on all school related matters.

Find out more at: www.qgpsolutions.com
Email: qgp@qgpsolutions.com

QGP LTD

School Governance and Management

A SCHOOL GOVERNANCE AND MANAGEMENT

A1 WHO IS YOUR EMPLOYER?

Note: Under the **Children Act 2004** Local Education Authorities (LEAs) were to be replaced by Children's Services Authorities (CSAs). However, from February 2010 the terms LEA and CSA have been removed from primary legislation and replaced with the term 'local authorities' (LAs).

Your employer is:
For **community and controlled schools**
- the local authority (LA) through the Children's Services Department of the local authority but governors exercise most direct employment powers.

For **foundation and voluntary aided schools**
- the governing body.

For **independent schools**
the governing body or proprietor.

For **city technology colleges (CTCs)**
- the governing body.

For **academies**
- the governing body or the sponsoring trust.

For **'trust' schools (i.e. foundation schools with a trust behind them)**
- the governing body.

Education Act 1996.
Standards and Framework Act 1998 Education (Modification of Enactments Relating to Employment) (England) (Amendment) Order 2004. Education and Inspections Act 2006.

A2 TYPES OF SCHOOL

Note: 'maintained schools' are those whose funding comes through the local authority which has powers of intervention and control, depending upon the school type. Academies receive their funding through central government. Under the *Apprenticeships, Skills, Children and Learning Act 2009 (ASCLA 09)* this will be routed via the *Young Peoples Learning Agency*.

Community schools: the LA owns the buildings and land and holds the employment contract.

Voluntary controlled schools: the land is owned by a voluntary body (usually a Church), but the school is controlled by a LA. Employment as for community schools.

Voluntary aided schools: the land (but not necessarily all the buildings) are owned by a voluntary body; but the capital and maintenance costs are shared with the DCSF and the LA. A majority of governors is appointed by the voluntary body. The voluntary body employs the staff and determines its own admission policy.

Foundation schools: they determine their own admission

School Governance and Management

arrangements, own their own buildings and land, and employ the staff, but are subject to LA financial regulations.

'Trust' schools: were created by the *Education and Inspections Act 2006.*
In law they are foundation schools with voluntary aided governance arrangements, i.e. a majority of the governing body is appointed by the trust body behind them. A trust may be responsible for a single school or a number of schools. They are able to form links with external partners; employ their own staff; set their own admission arrangements; and be eligible for additional flexibilities.

Specialist schools/colleges: this is a status open to all categories of school by acquiring a specialism, (e.g. technology or sports or languages etc), recognised by the Specialist Colleges and Academies Trust, www.specialistschools.org.uk. Regulations in 2005 made it easier for successful secondary schools in England to become foundation schools.
Education (School Organisation Proposals) (England) Regulations 2005.

Central government funded academies: 'independent' schools created under legislation. Supported by 'sponsors' who have control of the governing body. Sponsors may control several schools. The DCSF directly provides running costs. The rules of governance are established through the 'Funding Agreement' with the DCSF. They vary but increasingly mirror the rules

governing all maintained schools. They are required to cooperate with other neighbouring schools and the LA in matters of admissions but employ their own staff outside the statutory framework for teacher's pay and conditions.

City technology colleges (CTCs): independent schools funded by the government. They differ from academies in that they have no funding agreement or other restrictions on their operation.

Outside the public system - independent schools: these schools are fee-paying institutions whose relationships are governed by a contract with parents and (in most cases) charitable foundations. They are subject to inspection on matters of children's welfare by Ofsted.

A3 SCHOOL GOVERNANCE

All governing bodies of maintained schools in England and Wales consist of 9-20 members, determined by the current governing body, and include parent, staff, LA and community governors. Foundation, partnership, and sponsor governors may replace community governors in foundation schools; foundation and sponsor governors in voluntary-aided schools. The regulations set out the format for the Instrument of Government and give flexibility to the terms of office for governors. Regulations provide that almost all decisions can be delegated to a committee or individual governors.
Governing bodies may collaborate to discharge jointly

School Governance and Management

any of their functions. They may enter into formal federation in which case the federation has a single governing body (of up to 29 members). Each school in the federation may have a headteacher or a single headteacher may be appointed from the whole governing body. Key governors are appointed on the stakeholder principle by the federated schools. A federation can consist of up to 5 schools. In these cases governing bodies may exceed the number of 20. Each headteacher is a member of the federated governing body.

The governance of academies is regulated by the Memorandum and Articles of Association of the company which entered the funding agreement.
The School Governance (Federations) (England) Regulations 2007 School Governance (Constitution) (England) Regulations 2003 at www.governornet.co.uk.
The School Government (Terms of Reference)(Wales) Regulations 2000.
The School Government (Terms of Reference) (Amendment) (Wales) Regulations 2002. The Government of Maintained Schools (Wales) Regulations 2005.

A4 NURSERY SCHOOLS

All maintained nursery schools in England and Wales have governing bodies since 1 September 2006. *Laying the Foundations: Guidance for Governing Bodies in Maintained Nursery Schools 2003 (DfES 0425/2003).*

A5 REGISTRATION OF INDEPENDENT SCHOOLS

Independent schools are required to register. It is a criminal offence to operate an unregistered independent school. There are now precise requirements on information to go to parents. Under the *Education and Skills Act 2008* registration and inspection of independent schools includes schools which offer short-time or part-time education. Academies and CTCs are also independent schools and subject to the regulations.
Education (Independent Schools) (Standards) Regulations 2003.

The reporting and registration requirements are summarised in *The Independent Schools Council (ISC) Bulletin No.13*, along with a checklist of policies required by the regulations. In particular, there is a requirement to have a parental complaints policy. The ISC has published model policies.
The Education and Inspections Act 2006 contains the provisions relating to trust schools.
Quick Guides GOV7 Independent Schools: Registration.

Academies and CTCs do not exist in Wales, nor do trust schools.

A6 SCHOOL FUNDING

Recurrent funding
Funding of schools in England comes through the LA but is 80% (approximately) resourced by national government. The remainder of LA spending on

School Governance and Management

education is funded by council tax. Money that is spent in schools is the Dedicated Schools Grant (DSG). This includes money delegated to individual schools in the Individual Schools Budget (ISB) and money controlled by the LA but spent in schools (e.g. SEN funding). It also includes specific grants and LSC funding for post-16 education.

An individual school has a delegated budget, calculated in accordance with a locally-determined formula agreed by the local Schools Forum, which the governors may spend for 'any of the purposes of a school': including 'extended activities' if they are directly related to the purposes of the school (e.g. catch-up classes). The Secretary of State sets out the framework for funding. The Secretary of State has determined that English LAs should 'passport' a set increase to schools. Post-16 funding in England is the responsibility of the Learning and Skills Council which provides funding against planned numbers of students weighted according to the priority and cost of courses. However, this will pass to local authorities in October 2011. In the meantime LAs and the LSC are to plan together for coherence 14-19.

This system does not apply in Wales where funding is at the discretion of the local authority.

In order to exercise effective control of school finances, and deploy resources effectively, senior managers in schools can access the following:

- **Financial management standard and toolkit for schools** - intended to help schools evaluate the quality of their financial management and to aid in training staff to become better financial managers. The toolkit puts sixty guidance documents in one place accessible through the standard to support leadership teams in achieving the standard.

- **Schools financial benchmarking** - allows schools to compare income and expenditure information with similar schools. The website currently holds CFR data from around schools in England together with school level context and attainment information and is available to all schools, LAs and governors. All DCSF guidance and toolkits available at:
www.teachernet.gov.uk/management/schoolfunding/schoolfinance.
Avail provide a DCSF-funded free consultancy service for individual schools:
www.consultancyforschools.co.uk.

- **Financial management in schools from the National College**
A wide variety of professional development and materials set up to help schools' budget management and the development of expertise in staff, with the aim of creating greater financial stability for schools, are available through the National College for Leadership of Schools and Children's Services. Workshops for schools and LA staff, and consultancy

School Governance and Management

support is available. *See all the financial programmes at*: www.nationalcollege.org.uk.

The Welsh Assembly Government does not fund schools directly except for grants that are earmarked for particular purposes such as capital buildings, implementation of the Foundation Phase and Sixth Forms.

Schools in Wales are funded by local authorities from a block grant called the Revenue Support Grant. With council tax these funds provide income for a range of services including education. A local authority sets a council budget which includes an Education Budget. The Education Budget has three parts: LA Budget (pays for central functions); Schools' Budget (pays for services provided to schools); and Individual Schools Budget (formula driven, based on the *School Budget Shares (Wales) Regulations 2004* and delegated to the school).

Capital funding

In England, funding for capital comes either from LA recurrent funding (Capital Expenditure from Revenue Account - CERA) or from central government grant. This has now been devolved to a government agency - Partnerships for Schools. Capital funding has three streams: Devolved Formula Capital (DFC) which is devolved to schools; Local Authority Devolved Capital; and money for the Building Schools for the Future scheme which is designed to rebuild or refurbish all secondary schools and which is controlled by Partnerships for Schools.

Funding major projects

Maintained schools may borrow with permission from the LA as long as that borrowing is contained within the LA's borrowing limits. Schools may also 'save up' from their revenue budgets. This is controversial and controls have been placed on the level of retained balances that may be carried forward.

A7 OFSTED INSPECTIONS

Under section 5 of the *Education Act 2005* and the *Education and Inspections Act 2006*, schools are required to be inspected at prescribed intervals for:

1. the quality of the education provided in the school;
2. how far the education meets the needs of the range of pupils at the school;
3. the educational standards achieved in the school;
4. the quality of the leadership in and management of the school, including whether the financial resources made available to the school are managed effectively;
5. the spiritual, moral, social and cultural development of the pupils at the school;
6. the contribution made by the school to the well-being of those pupils (especially in relation to the five Every Child Matters outcomes); and
7. the contribution made by the school to community cohesion.

So as to encourage schools to:
- improve;
- be user-focused; and
- be efficient and effective in the use of resources.

School Governance and Management

Under the current Ofsted Framework inspectors pay particular attention to:

- promoting improvement: inspectors make specific recommendations based on their diagnosis of the school's strengths and weaknesses;
- evaluating the achievement and wider well-being of pupils as a whole and of different groups of pupils, and assessing the extent to which schools ensure that all pupils, including those most at risk, succeed;
- evaluating learning and teaching: inspectors spend a high proportion of their on-site inspection time in the classroom;
- assessing how well schools promote equality of opportunity, and how effectively they tackle discrimination;
- checking schools' procedures for safeguarding – keeping children and young people from harm;
- fostering the engagement of headteachers, schools' staff and governors in the process of inspection so that they understand the judgements made;
- gathering, analysing and taking into account the views of parents and pupils;
- assessing how effectively schools work in partnership with other providers in order to promote better outcomes for pupils.

The revised Framework, puts a greater emphasis on safeguarding and attainment. An additional half day of inspection time has been allocated to scrutinise safeguarding provisions.

Judgements on safeguarding appear in the specific leadership and management section, but two of the seven outcomes also include safeguarding aspects:

- To what extent do pupils feel safe? and
- Pupils' behaviour.

To ensure safer recruitment practice, appropriate checks must be made and a comprehensive record of what the school has done must be stored centrally permitting immediate access.

In a secondary school, inspectors look at KS4 attainment indicators of the last three years, KS4 attainment indicators for groups (average and capped average points scores) and attainment indicators for key subjects (English, maths, specialist school subjects and subjects with very high levels of entry). Contextual Value Added (CVA) tables of performance are seen as the strongest achievement indicator. However, the government has introduced a threshold (currently 30% 5 A* to C grades, including English and maths), below which schools are subject to the National Challenge additional support programme.

Inspectors are required to consider any limiting judgements which may lead to an overall judgement of inadequacy in the areas of: pupils' achievement and the extent to which they enjoy learning, the quality of the school's procedures for safeguarding and/ or the extent to which the school promotes equality and tackles discrimination.

All school inspections carried out by Ofsted use the same grading scale:

School Governance and Management

Grade 1: outstanding
Grade 2: good
Grade 3: satisfactory
Grade 4: inadequate.

If a school's overall effectiveness is judged inadequate, inspectors decide whether it requires:

a) **Special measures**: the school is failing to give its pupils an acceptable standard of education, and the persons responsible for leading, managing or governing the school are not demonstrating the capacity to secure the necessary improvement in the school.

b) **Notice to improve**: the school requires significant improvement, because either:
   - it is failing to provide an acceptable standard of education, but is demonstrating the capacity to improve, or
   - it is not failing to provide an acceptable standard of education but is performing significantly less well than it might in all the circumstances reasonably be expected to perform.

All schools that are judged to be satisfactory and inadequate receive monitoring visits without notice.

Schools are given between zero and two working days' notice of an inspection. The lead inspector usually contacts the school as soon as possible after notification (and always within 24 hours). Inspections do not usually last more than two days, but the number of inspectors involved varies according to the size and nature of the school. In a primary school it is likely that one inspector will visit the school for one day.

All schools must be inspected every five school years. Schools judged to be good or outstanding will usually be inspected at five-year intervals unless: concerns have been raised in the interim; they are, for example, part of an annual cycle selected to ensure that HMCI's report reflects evidence from a fair cross-section of schools; or they are a special school, a PRU, a school with residential provision or one providing for 0-3 year-olds. Schools judged satisfactory will be inspected every three years. Schools judged to be inadequate are monitored regularly and reinspected after a specified period.

You would not normally expect to be observed by an inspector unless the school has identified your teaching area as one of outstanding practice or weakness. The emphasis is on teaching areas rather than individual teachers and on outcomes rather than on intention. The onus is on school leadership teams to ensure that policies, practices and processes are evident and that key staff are aware of these and how they should impact on the school.

The school self-evaluation form (SEF) is the key document in evaluating the quality of leadership and management. The SEF is intended to enable schools to evaluate their progress against the inspection schedule, set out the main evidence on which the evaluation is based, identify school strengths and weaknesses and explain what

School Governance and Management

action the school is taking to address the weaknesses and develop the strengths. Schools are encouraged to update their SEF regularly (an online version is available) and to submit their SEF each time it is updated.

Ofsted reports are presented in draft form to the governors by the end of the week of the inspection visit for a factual check. The school has one working day in which to comment on the draft. The final report is signed off by an HMI and published on the Ofsted website within 15 working days of the end of the inspection. The governing body must send a copy of the report within five working days of receiving it to all registered parents and carers of pupils at the school (a brief letter to pupils is supplied as an appendix to the report). Following the report schools feed their intended actions into their school development/improvement plans.

The content of c**ollective worship and denominational education in schools** that are designated by the Secretary of State as having a religious character is inspected separately under section 48 of the Education Act 2005. The governing body, in consultation with its associated faith body, is responsible for arranging a section 48 inspection – and will often seek to arrange this at the same time as the school's section 5 inspection.

Early years registered provision is inspected under section 49 of the *Childcare Act 2006*. Where the provision is managed by the school, the section 49 inspection is carried out concurrently with the section 5 inspection and the quality of the provision reported in a single inspection report. However, where registered provision on a school's site is managed by a private, voluntary and/or independent provider, it is inspected separately under the *Childcare Act 2006*; in these circumstances the inspection is scheduled to take place at the same time as the school's section 5 inspection, whenever possible.

Education Act 2005. Education and Inspections Act 2006.
Ofsted Direct is a termly online newsletter, which provides the latest inspection information together with tips and advice.
Further details on the changes in Ofsted arrangements are available by registering on the Ofsted Direct site, which can be accessed through: www.ofsted.gov.uk.
Ofsted reports can be accessed on: www.ofsted.gov.uk/reports
Quick Guides SO4 Ofsted Inspections: England.

ESTYN

Its purpose is to inspect quality and standards in education and training in Wales. Estyn is responsible for inspecting:
- nursery schools and settings maintained by LAs;
- primary, secondary and special schools, further education, adult community based learning, youth support service, LAs, teacher training elements of job centre plus; and
- careers and related services.

Estyn also:
- provides advice and quality and standards in education and

School Governance and Management

training in Wales to the Welsh Assembly Government; and
- makes public good practice based on inspection evidence.

There are proposed changes to the inspection and training in Wales from September 2010. More emphasis will be placed on provider self-evaluation and the inspectors will base their "lines of enquiry" on the information and assessment provided to them in the self-evaluation report. Currently Estyn is working with DCELLS to align the quality indicators in the *Common Inspection Framework (CIF)* in the requirements of the *School Effectiveness Framework (SEF)* and the *Quality and Effectiveness Framework (QEF)*.

Current schedule for implementation
Easter 2010
Publication and launch of new Common Inspection Framework.
Summer 2010
Publication of self-evaluation toolkits (provisional). Training of inspectors.
September 2010
New six-year cycle begins.

Quick Guides SO5 School Inspections: Wales.

A8 LOCAL AUTHORITY POWERS OF INTERVENTION

Local authorities have the duty to intervene if a school they maintain is:
- operating its finances in an unlawful or reckless fashion;
- neglecting the school estate; or

- if standards of achievement are low (i.e. lower than:
  ◊ reasonably expected;
  ◊ previous performance;
  ◊ comparable schools); or
- if there is a breakdown in management or governance likely to prejudice the standards attained by students; or
- if the safety of staff or students is threatened.

*(Under **ASCLA 2009** an LA will also be able to intervene if a school is failing to implement part of the School Teachers Pay and Conditions Document.)*

They may issue a warning notice describing:
- action expected from the governors;
- the period within which this action must be taken;
  action to be taken otherwise.

Governors may appeal to the chief inspector against a warning notice.
Following the warning notice a LA may compel a school to:
- contract for advice and support;
- enter into collaborative arrangements with another school;
- enter into federation with another school or schools; or
- appoint additional governors;
- replace the existing governing body with an Interim Executive Board; and
- suspend delegation.

*(Under the **ASCLA 2009** the Secretary of State takes the power to order an LA to intervene if he considers it should.)*

School Governance and Management

The school year for pupils in maintained schools consists of 190 days. There must be a break in the middle of the day, making 380 school sessions. Teachers other than those on the leadership scale are required to be available in school on further five days at the reasonable direction of the headteacher up to 1265 hours a year. For community, community special schools and voluntary controlled schools the LA sets the term and holiday dates. Governing bodies control the dates for foundation and voluntary aided schools.

The school day
Governors of all schools set the timings of the school day, bearing in mind government recommendations, and the advice of the head, and after consultation with parents. *(Three months' notice are required for start and finish times; six weeks for session times)*. Independent schools will have their own arrangements.
Education (School Day and School Year) (England) Regulations 1999.

A10 THE STANDARD SCHOOL YEAR

The traditional school year consisted of three terms with half terms of varying duration. The Local Government Association proposed a six-term year (now called the Standard School Year), set out in **The Rhythm of Schooling**. It includes a fixed Easter, a shortened summer holiday, two terms before Christmas separated by a two-week break, and four terms from January. A number of LAs have introduced variations of this; others continue to operate the traditional year.
Note: Where a 'term' is referred to in regulations or guidance it refers to a 'traditional term' unless otherwise stated. Where doubt may arise, a number of school days is generally quoted. Some CTCs operate other patterns: e.g. a year of five equal terms.

A11 INFORMATION TO PARENTS

A communication or document authorised to be published under the **Education Act 1996** can now be made by electronic means as well as being delivered to the named person or being left at the last known address, or sent to that address. Parents must consent in writing to any information being sent by electronic means.
The Education (Pupil Information) (England) Regulations 2005 Electronic Communications Order 2004.
Information from: www.teachernet.gov.uk/management/atoz/p/pupilrecords.
Quick Guides GOV16 Annual Report and Parents' Meetings.

A12 FREEDOM OF INFORMATION

Parents, the press or the general public can ask to see information held by the school. Data held by the school includes electronic data and CCTV materials. It includes all memos and emails. Maintained schools/colleges (and also CTCs and academies)

School Governance and Management

have to comply with **Freedom of Information** legislation, which applies to all public authorities.

Processing

Anyone who requests a maintained school or a college for information, including personal information, must be informed whether the school/college holds that information or not and, if it does, it must supply the information. Much of the information held by schools and colleges is already made public e.g. Ofsted reports, school prospectuses, homework policies, home/school agreements. The Act applies to information which already exists. A school is not required to collect or re-process information. It may refuse to supply information if that information will be published in due course anyway. Some information of a particularly sensitive nature can be withheld, but even if a disclosure is not required by the law the school/college must consider whether it should be released in the public interest. It can only be withheld if the public interest in withholding it is greater than the public interest in releasing it. Confidential material must be evaluated in the same way.

LAs and schools are required to establish a publication scheme that will set out how it intends to publish details of the different classes of information it holds and whether it will charge for supplying information. Your school will need a management system to facilitate the retrieval of information and will need to consider the charging policy, staff training and how best to publicise the service.

Guidance from the Information Commissioner and the DCSF for schools on the handling and management of the requirements has been published and a notice to all schools in England, Wales, and Northern Ireland is on the Information Commissioner's website: www.ico.gov.uk. *There is also a telephone help line. Further advice is available on Teachernet, including Freedom of Information Act 2000 Summary Guidance for Governing Bodies.*

Also available are guidelines from **The Records Management Society of Great Britain.** These are guidelines about the retention of information and documents in schools. They help schools decide what to discard and what to keep.

The Welsh Assembly Government has published a model scheme - *Freedom of Information Act 2000 – Model Publication Scheme for Schools - Circular 9/2004.*

Quick Guides DA3 Freedom of Information: Points of Law; DA3A A Guide for Maintained Schools on the Full Implementation of the Freedom of Information Act from January 2005; DA3B Freedom of Information: Checklist for Action on receipt of a Request for Information.

A13 COPYRIGHT

Modern technology makes copying material very easy, but much of what you want to copy will be covered by copyright. Someone will have the legal

School Governance and Management

right to decide whether a piece of writing, or film or music or computer software or photographs or other material from the internet can be reproduced by someone else. Although the law allows you limited rights to copy for learning purposes, you will have to rely on licensing schemes for most of your copying purposes. Your school should make sure that up to date guidance is easily available.
Intellectual Property Office at: www.ipo.gov.uk.

Copyright licensing

The Copyright Licensing Agency runs a scheme for copying books, periodicals and journals. Each maintained school should be licensed through the LA and possess a copy of the agreement. You must not ignore the requirements of the licence. Schools have been successfully sued for doing so. The Copyright Licensing Agency website has a 'Copywatch' where someone could blow the whistle on your illegal copying! The Copyright Licensing licence does not apply to CD-ROM DVD-based learning materials which are sold with a publisher's licence explaining what printing and copying of material on the disk is allowed.
Copyright Licensing Agency Limited, Saffron House, 6-10 Kirby Street, London, EC1N 8TS; tel: 0207 400 3100; www.cla.co.uk; **e-mail:** cla@cla.co.uk.

Recording TV programmes in schools

The **Educational Recording Agency Ltd (ERA)** operates a licensing scheme for the UK education sector which allows

recordings of broadcasts to be made for non-commercial educational use. This covers broadcasts on:
• BBC television and radio;
• ITV network services;
• Channel Four and E4;
• Five television; and
• S4C.

You can make recordings on site or at home onto video or audio tape, DVDs or CDs and your recordings can be copied provided this is for educational use and there is no commercial element. Recordings can also be made and stored in digital form for access through computers or to use on white boards. The recording must be labelled or marked up with:
• date of recording;
• name of broadcaster;
• programme title; and
• the wording 'This recording is to be used for educational and non-commercial purposes under the terms of the ERA licence'.

Most schools are covered by the ERA licence either individually or as part of a blanket licence. Licences are renewable annually. ERA licensees can take out an additional licence so that licensed ERA recordings can be accessed by students and staff online, either on school premises or at home. This is the 'ERA Plus' licence.
ERA, New Premier House, 150 Southampton Row, London, WC1B 5AL – Tel: 020 7837 3222, www.era.org.uk, **e-mail:** era@era.org.uk.
Quick Guides DA11 Copyright Licensing.

Employment and Performance

A14 PERFORMANCES IN SCHOOL

Public performances of plays/musicals on school premises, whether school plays or plays performed by visiting companies, require a licence. Since 2004 all licences for public entertainment now come under the LA. The school can apply for a premises licence or a temporary licence for a single event. Performances of a school play just to parents, families, staff and pupils are not likely to constitute a 'public performance', and, therefore, no licence would be necessary. If alcohol is to be sold at any school function, a licence must be obtained.

If you are in charge of the school play, you must apply and pay for permission to perform a play under copyright. Even a 400-year-old Shakespeare play will require permission if the edition you use is itself under copyright. It is advisable to find out from the company which provides your copies of the play. You would not require permission to perform a play, or use extracts from books, purely for educational purposes in the school.

A15 LETTING SCHOOL PREMISES

School premises are under the control of governors and may be hired out by them. The LA may require that premises be let to them, subject to a fair charge, in the case of all but foundation schools. Alcohol can be sold or supplied at school events on school premises up to a maximum of 12 times a year (on a maximum of 15 days). Local authories have the responsibility for issuing licenses.
Licensing Act 2003.
Quick Guides PR14 Licensing Law and Schools.

B EMPLOYMENT AND PERFORMANCE

B1 BECOMING A TEACHER

If you have the necessary qualifications (see below), you can apply for an Initial Teacher-Training (ITT) course. The Training and Development Agency for Schools (TDA) website has details of courses. *Further information at:* www.tda.gov.uk/recruit.

Employment-based training

Alternatively you can apply to a school to join the Graduate Teacher or Registered Teacher programmes if you are aged 24 or over. You would be employed as an unqualified teacher, and be given a programme leading to Qualified Teacher Status (QTS). You can be paid on the main scale or the unqualified teachers' scale. You need GCSE mathematics and English at grade C or above, find a school which will take you on and, for the GTP, have a degree or equivalent, or for the Registered Teacher programme, have completed two years higher education resulting in at least 240 CAT points under the Credit Accumulation Transfer Scheme. The school (or LA) acts as the 'recommending body' (RB), assessing you against the

Employment and Performance

standards required for QTS. A training grant is paid to the RB for each employment-based trainee.

School-centred ITT

School-centred initial teacher training (SCITT) is a postgraduate initial teacher training (ITT) programme run in and by schools. All SCITT courses lead to QTS and many, not all, award the Post Graduate Certificate in Education (PGCE).

Teach First

'Teach First' is a programme run by an independent organisation which takes high-quality graduates and places them for two years in schools in Greater London, Greater Manchester and the Midlands. They are given leadership training and internships and work experience in commercial firms and at the end of the two years are awarded QTS. The aim is that they can go either into a commercial career or remain in teaching. www.teachfirst.org.uk.

Qualified Teacher Status (QTS)

If you complete an initial teacher training (ITT) programme successfully you will gain Qualified Teacher Status (QTS). You need this in order to teach in maintained schools and non-maintained special schools in England and Wales. On becoming a qualified teacher you must then successfully complete an induction year in a maintained school or non-maintained special school or an approved independent school, within five years of becoming qualified.
For information about QTS contact The Training and Development Agency for Schools: Tel: 020 7925 3700. Website at: www.tda.gov.uk/Recruit/becomingateacher/waysintoteaching.aspx – *for routes into teaching.* www.tda.gov.uk - *for information for schools and universities.*

Overseas Trained Teachers (OTTs)

If your qualification is from a country within the European Economic Area, it may be recognised under EU mobility legislation. You should check with the GTC *(see below under Assessing Qualifications).* If you are coming from a country from outside the EEA you will need a Work Permit to teach in England and your employer will need to help you to get one. You will not be admitted to work in Britain without a sponsor. The sponsorship will be limited to certain categories and, in teaching, to shortage subjects. The rules change and it will be important for you and the school to check with the Border agency as to what the current rules are. Your potential employer may have to 'test the market' by advertising in a local Job Centre plus before he can offer you a post.

If you are qualified from outside the European Economic Area (EEA) you can work as a temporary unqualified teacher for up to four years without QTS. However, you are expected to work towards QTS through the Overseas Trained Teachers Programme. **You may not work for more than four years without gaining QTS.** The DCSF has produced a very useful leaflet on OTTs, updated as at October 2008, which is available on: www.

Employment and Performance

teachernet.gov.uk/wholeschool/overseastrainedteachers.

In England suitably qualified overseas trained teachers can be assessed for QTS without further training, and in some circumstances can be exempted from the requirement to serve an induction year after qualifying.

Assessing qualifications

To have your qualifications assessed for recognition as QTS contact the **General Teaching Council for England (GTCE) on + 44 870 001 0308 or email:** info@gtce.org.uk **or visit the GTC website at** www.gtce.org.uk.

The Education (School Teachers' Qualifications) (Wales) Regulations 2004 specify the requirements to be met by anyone before they can become a qualified teacher in Wales. It also sanctions an employment-based teacher-training scheme, enabling persons to train to be teachers whilst employed. All intending teachers must be checked for their fitness to teach.

Under the **Education (Specified Work and Registration) (Wales Regulations 2004)**, only qualified teachers and other people in certain circumstances can carry out specified work – teach at a school maintained by a LA, or non-maintained special school in Wales. There are two routes operating in Wales through which people can meet requirements needed to become qualified teachers: complete an ITT Course, or undertake an employment-based teacher training scheme while at a school. In both cases the requirements must be met

by persons assessed meeting 'specified standards'.

The Graduate Teacher Programme (GTP) is an employment-based route to gain QTS. Under the Graduate Teacher Programme, graduates who do not have QTS may be authorised by the Welsh Assembly Government to undertake training in a school following an approved training programme. The GTP allows people to teach in a school while following an approved training programme. **Graduate Teacher Programme (Wales) Guidance on the Employment Based Teacher Training Scheme 2006** provides information on the employment based route into teaching that leads to the gaining of Qualified Teacher Status (QTS).

The revised **Qualified Teacher Status (QTS) Standards** incorporate technical amendments to reflect the revised curriculum in Wales. The **Qualified Teacher Status Standards Wales 2009 (2009 No. 25)** will apply to all trainees on all ITT courses or employment-based programmes starting on or after 1 September 2009. Changes are restricted to the Standards which have been altered and to adding references to new or replacement Welsh Assembly Government policies and related guidance materials which have been introduced in Wales since the previous circular was published in 2006.

Statutory requirements for ITT courses.

No changes have been made to the Requirements, but the supporting text in the

Employment and Performance

replacement Circular has been updated to cover statutory changes and updated guidance references.

Handbook of guidance

Contains non-statutory guidance aimed at helping everyone involved in ITT (including trainees) understand the aims and scope of both the Standards and Requirements. *Welsh Assembly Government Circular No: 017/2009 - Becoming a Qualified Teacher: Handbook of Guidance.* This revised version of the *Becoming a Qualified Teacher – Handbook of Guidance* replaces circular No: 41/2006. The document provides updated information on the aims and scope of the revised QTS Standards.

Since September 2006 General Teaching Council for Wales (GTCW) not only awards QTS and Induction Certificates but also administers the funding for mentoring and development opportunities.

Training to teach in Wales

A new bilingual website has been launched that will make it easier to find out about initial teacher training opportunities in Wales. It is: www.teachertrainingwales.org The website provides comprehensive information for anyone considering taking any of the different routes into teaching including flexible and employment-based routes.

In Wales contact the General Teaching Council for Wales on 029 20 55 0350 or email: registration@gtcw.org.uk or visit their website: www.gtcw.org.uk.

The GTC for Wales (Cyngor Addysgu Cyffredinol Cymru)

In respect of Initial Teacher Training the GTCW is responsible for the following:

- confirming QTS following initial teacher training;
- persons wishing to teach in Wales, with teaching qualifications gained in Scotland, N. Ireland, and the European Economic Area (EEA); and
- persons recommended for QTS by the States of Guernsey Education Council.

The Welsh Assembly is responsible for the award of QTS gained through the Graduate and Registered Teacher programmes and certain teachers with FE or independent school experience.

The Council also has the power to recognise EU professional qualifications.

The Council can also give information and advice to the public about the acceptability in Wales of teachers' qualifications obtained in relevant European states. The Council commenced the piloting of a Chartered Teacher Programme in Wales from September 2007 until 2009. Teachers with at least five years' experience are eligible to become involved in the Chartered Teacher pilot modules. The Council is piloting two routes to Chartered Teacher:

- a programme (taught) route; and
- an accreditation route.

CPD/Masters

Following some very successful Chartered Teacher pilot modules, from September 2009 to February 2010 the Council offered teachers

Employment and Performance

with five full years' teaching experience the opportunity to take part in three more fully funded modules (all fees, supply costs, additional travel costs, additional care costs and a book allowance included). Teachers successfully completing a module will gain 20 Masters Degree credits.

For details of proposals there is a Welsh Assembly Government Document that can be downloaded from GTC (Wales) website entitled *Professional Development, Recognition and Accreditation July 2006.* For information about QTS in Wales contact the *Registration and Qualification team: General Teaching Council for Wales, 4th Floor, Southgate House, Wood Street, Cardiff CF10 1EW. Tel: 029 205 503 50. Fax: 029 205 503 60.* Email: registration@gtcw. org.uk.

B2 RETURNING TO TEACHING

(only applies to England)
If you go on a TDA-funded returners course, you will receive a training bursary. You may also get childcare support for every child up to the age of five years old and, for every child aged between 5 and 14 years, for a maximum of 12 weeks.
For information on childcare in your area call *Childcare Link on 0800 096 02 96 at* www. tda.gov.uk then use the index on the home page. For further information on training bursaries or childcare support, please contact the *Returning to Teach line on 0845 6000 993,* or email: helpline@kit-tta.co.uk.

You could be eligible for a Career Development Loan. This is a DCSF sponsored programme to assist those who wish to undertake vocational training. *Further information is available via a free phone number: 0800 585 505. For general information about funding for returners courses go to:* www.tda.gov.uk and then use the index on the home page.

B3 INDUCTION OF NEWLY-QUALIFIED TEACHERS (NQT)

As a newly-qualified teacher you must complete an induction period of three school terms in a maintained school, FE college, non-maintained special school or prescribed independent school, if you wish to work in a maintained school or non-maintained special school in England or Wales. If the school you are working in operates a six-term year you must complete 6 terms. If some other pattern is operated in your school you must complete three continuous periods of 63 days. You may complete your induction year in supply teaching or part-time teaching but the amount of continuous teaching must amount to the same: i.e. 190 days if in school 189 if in an FE college. The school has the power to reduce the qualifying period by up to 29 days where you are absent.
You cannot do your induction year in a school or college which has been found by Inspectors to be in need of intervention unless you began there before the inspectors reported or the chief inspector certifies that the department in which you are working is

Employment and Performance

capable of working with you. An independent school must be teaching the national curriculum for the phase of education that you are preparing to work in.

The induction period will contain an individualised programme of monitoring and support based in part on the Career Entry Profile (CEP). You should not be asked to teach for more than 90% of the hours taught by the substantive teachers at the school. You will have an induction tutor, and your performance will be assessed periodically during the period culminating in a final assessment. Those responsible for your induction should be positive in their support and encouragement. The period will include at least three lesson observations (1 per term) covering literacy, numeracy and one other subject in primary.

Most LAs provide a local induction programme for NQTs. Money is available for NQT professional development. You should also be given the opportunity to see others teach, possibly in other schools. The TDA have published guidance to support the induction process. This is in the form of a booklet which will enable you and your induction tutor to work through the 'Core Standards' (**see B16**) which you have to reach in order to pass your induction period. They have been arranged thematically so that a particular area of a teacher's professional life and the standards associated with it can be explored on your own or with your tutor through a series of prompt questions. During the induction period you will not be subject to the performance review process. For England the standards you are expected to reach are laid down in **DCSF Guidance: The Induction Support Programme for Newly Qualified Teachers DfES/0458/2003.** See also: **Supporting the Induction Process – TDA 2007,** www.tda.gov.uk/

The Education (Induction Arrangements for School Teachers) (Consolidation) (England) (Amendment) Regulations 2007.

Education (Induction Arrangements for School Teachers) (England) Regulations 2008. Statutory Guidance on the Induction of Newly Qualified Teachers in England 2008.

Failure to complete the induction satisfactorily

If you fail to complete the induction period satisfactorily you will not be able to teach in a maintained school or non-maintained special school. Your school would have to dismiss you within 10 working days, unless you decide to appeal to the General Teaching Council. If there is an appeal, the school can continue to employ you but your duties will be restricted. If the appeal fails the school must dismiss you within 10 working days. It is more usual, however, for the teacher to resign rather than be dismissed.

The school's responsibility

The head is responsible directly for ensuring an appropriate programme and appointing an induction tutor, with the necessary skill and experience who has considerable contact with the NQT and the head. The tutor's key functions are:

Employment and Performance

- to make rigorous and fair judgements; and
- to provide co-ordinated guidance and effective support for the NQT's professional development.

The head recommends to the LA (or in the case of independent schools it can be the Independent Schools Council Teacher Induction Panel) whether the requirements have been satisfactorily met.

The guidance (which is identified below) gives guidance on the monitoring and support, assessment arrangements, and the action to be taken if the NQT is showing signs of unsatisfactory performance. The induction period can be extended if the teacher has been absent for 30 days or more and an NQT on maternity leave can choose to request an extension.

Other teachers' responsibilities

Responsibility for planning and managing ITT and induction programmes lies with the school management (and any higher education institution which is collaborating with the school). You are only obliged to participate in these schemes if you have any contractual responsibility or if what is requested of you lies within your normal management or teaching responsibilities. It is possible to be paid for any extra duties associated with ITT (but not if it is part of your Advanced Skills Teacher's (AST) duties).
DCSF Guidance: Statutory Guidance on Induction for Newly Qualified Teachers in England.

Wales
Professional development for teachers

The Welsh guidance summarises the arrangements for the completion of a period of induction by newly qualified teachers if they wish to work in a maintained school or non-maintained special school in Wales. The guidance also covers the arrangements for the extension of an induction period before completion and the appeal arrangements (to the GTC Wales) if a teacher fails assessment against End of Induction Standard.
Induction for Newly Qualified Teachers in Wales (Revised August 2005) Circular 24/2005.

Induction and Early Professional Development Handbook

Provides the framework for the induction and early professional development arrangements in Wales and offers support and guidance for newly-qualified teachers. *This handbook should be read in conjunction with the Guidance Circular 24/2005 above.*

Mentoring and development opportunities

From September 2006 GTCW not only awards QTS and induction certificates but administers the funding for mentoring and development opportunities.
Quick Guides ST7 Induction of Newly-Qualified Teachers.

Names of staff responsible for induction:

Employment and Performance

B4 FAST TRACK TEACHERS/ ACCELERATE TO HEADSHIP

The Fast Track programme came to an end on 31 August 2009. The National College for Leadership of Schools and Children's Services, however, is developing an Accelerated Leadership programme to meet the changing needs and challenges of leadership in today's schools to replace the Fast Track programme from September 2010. The application window opened in January 2010.

Under the **STPCD 2009**, fast track teachers are subject to the working time provisions of classroom teachers – 195 days and 1265 hours. All references to such teachers have been removed from the Document, except for the provision that fast track teachers who were assessed as meeting the standards under an earlier Document and who are first placed on the main scale under the 2009 Document must be given an additional point on the scale. Any points awarded previously will be retained, but henceforth fast track teachers will not be given an additional point. The Fast Track programme was not available in Wales and there are currently no plans to introduce such a programme. *Quick Guides PAY19 Fast Track Teachers.*

B5 APPOINTMENTS

All schools must respect the laws on discrimination in making appointments.

Schools may not discriminate on grounds of religion or belief, gender, sexual orientation, race, disability or age. Schools with a religious character can give preference in employment matters to teachers whose religious beliefs are in accordance with the tenets of the relevant faith where this is a Genuine Occupational Requirement (GOR) of the post. *See below Section C - Equal Opportunities and Discrimination.*

If your appointment is on 'Burgundy Book' conditions your appointment and salary will run (if you start at the beginning of the term) from 1 September (or the first day of the autumn term if earlier than 1 September); 1 January; or 1 May (or the first day of the summer term if this is earlier than 1 May). If you join a school mid-term then your appointment and salary will run from the day you start work.

Independent schools
Independent schools can appoint staff in their own way so long as they do not offend the discrimination laws.

Maintained schools teaching posts
For temporary posts the procedures are the same for all maintained schools. The school may make a temporary appointment for up to four months without engaging the full procedure.

For a permanent post (other than the head or deputy) in **community and voluntary controlled schools** the governors determine a specification for the post and send it to the LA (normally a copy of an advertisement suffices). The head, or a committee of

Employment and Performance

governors and the head, then makes the selection. The LA must appoint the person unless the staff qualifications are not met i.e. the candidate is not qualified or fit to teach. The school would then have to recommend someone else. Under the *School Staffing (England) Regulations 2009* staffing regulations, the governing body can determine that appointments other than for deputy headship may be made by the head acting alone.
Quick Guides Appointments (AP) Section.

Foundation and aided schools make their own appointments subject to the fitness of candidates. They may grant the LA 'advisory rights' but do not have to. The LA can apply to the Secretary of State to be granted these rights but only if the school has no equivalent effective source of advice.
'Trust' schools, which are essentially foundation schools with VA governance, follow the same process as other foundation schools.

Appointment of heads and deputies
Procedures for the appointment of heads and deputies are different. According to the regulations, such posts must be advertised *'in such a manner as the governing body considers appropriate unless it has good reason not to'*. Normally the advertising for deputies should be in the national press, unless there are exceptional reasons (e.g. reorganisation where deputies are already in post). The guidance suggests that the governing body should consider the best way to reach its target audience, taking into account the type of media to be used and the level of exposure the advertisement will receive. It is recommended that advice is sought from the LA and/or the diocesan authority before a decision not to advertise is taken. The governing body must appoint a selection panel of at least three governors, who will make the choice. The governing body approves the selection, and recommends the appointment to the LA. The LA must appoint the recommended person unless the staff qualifications are not met.

Academies
They have complete freedom of appointment to all posts (subject to the *Transfer of Undertakings (Protection of Employment) Regulations (TUPE)* where they are the 'successor school' to a school that closes) and to equality and discrimination laws.

Position of aided schools viz discrimination
VA schools with a religious foundation may discriminate in appointing staff on the basis of faith where faith is for a genuine operational requirement so long as no racial group, nor individual, within the faith, is discriminated against either directly or indirectly.
(See C5).
School Staffing (England) Regulations 2009.

Regulations
The *School Staffing (England) Regulations 2009* cover the appointment and dismissal of school staff. For further information refer to: *Guidance on Managing Staff Employment in Schools DCSF 2009.*

Employment and Performance

In Wales there are similar but not identical regulations: *The Staffing of Maintained Schools (Wales) Regulations 2006; The Staffing of Maintained Schools (Miscellaneous Amendments) (Wales) Regulations 2007; The Staffing of Maintained Schools (Wales) (Amendment) Regulations 2009; The Staffing of Maintained Schools (Wales) (Amendment 2) Regulations 2009. The Education (Miscellaneous Amendments relating to Safeguarding Children (Wales) Regulations 2009 and The Education (Independent Schools) (Unsuitable Persons) (Wales) Regulations 2009.*
Quick Guides Appointments AP Section.

Support staff posts

Maintained schools, like independent schools, can select and appoint support and administrative staff. Current legislation and guidance allows schools where the LA holds the contract of employment to place support staff on any point on a current local government scale. This is not affected by the Single Status Agreement but such schools are expected to consult, and have regard to, the views of the local authority. Foundation and voluntary aided schools may pay staff any appropriate salary, but this will alter with the establishment of the SSSNB *(See D20)*.

In a test case the Employment Appeals Tribunal (EAT) accepted that voluntary aided schools are run by the governing body (GB) as a separate entity, operating autonomously in terms of engaging staff as employer and being responsible for staff terms and conditions, the cost of which must be met from their delegated budgets. The EAT went on to hold that, because the power to determine terms and conditions of employment for staff rested with the GB, the LA was not the 'single source' contended for by the Claimants. Therefore, there was no single source that could restore equal treatment. **Dolphin v Hartlepool Borough Council.**

The *School Staffing Regulations (England) 2009* specify that the governing body must complete the following checks before an appointment may be made:

- the identity of the person;
- that the person meets al the relevant staff qualification requirements; and that the person has a right to work in the UK;
- that the person is not on the barred persons list held by the Independent Safeguarding Authority.

The governing body must, moreover, obtain an enhanced criminal record certificate in respect of any such person before or as soon as practicable after his/her appointment.

Since 1 January 2010, the governing body must ensure that any person who interviews an applicant for any post under the 2009 regulations has completed the safer recruitment training or in cases where a panel has been established for appointment purposes that at least one member of that panel has completed

Employment and Performance

the safer recruitment training. The guidance recommends that the person who has undergone safer recruitment training should be involved at all stages of an appointment process.

The DCSF issued guidance on safe recruitment in January 2007 which has been updated in 2010. *Safeguarding Children and Safer Recruitment in Education.*

The document constitutes statutory guidance and is to be taken as the basis for Ofsted limiting judgements in inspection. Failure to apply these processes or ones that are equally valid, could be a basis for a claim for negligence and may be grounds for the Secretary of State to take action against an LA, governing body, or promoter.

Application

The guidance applies to the appointment of every person who:

- works in an educational setting (for children under 18); and
- is likely to be perceived by children as a trustworthy adult.

It includes all school staff but also staff employed to work in the school setting by contractors (e.g. on a PFI contract) and volunteers. Criminal Records Bureau (CRB) checks are now mandatory for all new appointments to the school workforce of individuals who have not worked in a school, FE institution or LA education service in the last 3 months. Teacher agencies are required to have a CRB Disclosure for all staff who work in schools. Failure to comply may mean a fine at level 5 (£5000) or imprisonment on conviction. It is an offence to apply to work or work in regulated activity if you are barred from it. **The full document can be downloaded from the DCSF website at:** www.everychildmatters.gov.uk and copies ordered from: www.teachernet.gov.uk/publications.

List 99 and the Independent Safeguarding Authority (ISA)

List 99 was the list of those individuals subject to a bar on their employment in school. Following intense media spotlight on some anomalies in List 99 procedures, as from September 2009 all other lists have been replaced by a barred list maintained by the new ISA. Within 5 years of November 2010 all members of staff involved in 'regulated work' and volunteers and work experience supervisors will have to gain registration with the Authority. This will begin with new entrants to the 'children's workforce.' Your employer may register an interest with the ISA which will mean that any change in your status will be passed to your employer in real time.

Regulated work is any work which involves 'regular' or 'intensive' contact with young people which may lead to a building up of trust or which gives control over the recruitment of staff who have this contact. All work in schools is regulated work. The definition of regular work is work with the same group four times in a month and for intensive work more than once a week.

Controlled work is any work where there is incidental access to young people or access to young people's data.

Employment and Performance

To check the regulations and to contact the Independent Safeguarding Authority: www.isa-gov.org.uk.

As stated above, all appointment panels must now have at least one person on them who has successfully completed a course in safer recruitment approved by the Secretary of State. If a person is interviewing alone, he/she must have successfully completed the course.

Your school must have a named person responsible for safeguarding for you to consult if you suspect that a child is in danger of harm.

B7 CONTRACTUAL DETAILS

You will be given a contract and statement of particulars on appointment. However, all contracts of employment have 'implied terms' as well as 'express terms' i.e. those agreed at interview, or written into a letter of appointment, or contained in a staff handbook. In maintained schools reference will be made to the fact that the post is subject to the pay and conditions set out in the *School Teachers' Pay and Conditions Document*. Independent schools should point out to you before appointment the terms on which you will be appointed. Most maintained schools include the conditions of employment in the *'Burgundy Book' (Conditions of Employment for School Teachers in England and Wales)* in their contracts for teachers. Your contract may only be altered by consent between you and your employer, though it is lawful for an employer to dismiss with

notice and then to re-employ on new terms.

Implied terms

These are things which are not articulated but form part of the contract by implication. A breach of these can terminate the contract.

The employer's implied duties include:

- to provide work;
- to be a good employer;
- to pay for work done;
- to take care for employees' safety and well-being; and
- to maintain the employment relationship.

The employee's duties include:

- to be loyal to the employer;
- to show good conduct;
- to be obedient;
- to take care at work; and
- to maintain the employment relationship.

DBERR/DBIS Websites dealing with employment rights at: www.berr.gov.uk and http://payandworkrightscampaign.direct.gov.uk/index.html.

Quick Guides Appointments (AP)Section.

B8 WRITTEN STATEMENT OF TERMS AND CONDITIONS

All employees are entitled to a written statement of terms and conditions of employment within the first two months of service. You should normally receive two copies from the LA/school/college: one for signing and returning, and one for you to retain. Do read your contract.

Employment and Performance

Remember, too, that every time you receive a pay rise or other promotion a new contract technically comes into being and you should receive another statement.

s1 Employment Rights Act 1996.

B9 PART-TIME AND FIXED-TERM CONTRACTS

Part-time

Teachers engaged on part-time and fixed-term contracts must not be treated less favourably than comparable full-time or permanent employees, unless the employer can justify the discrimination on objective grounds. This is because part-time staff are predominantly women so that discrimination against part-time staff is an indirect form of sex discrimination. The regulations cover not only unfair dismissal rights, but other rights, such as access to training, consideration for promotion, crossing the threshold, performance management and any other rights and benefits. Your part-time job description should specify not only the days and times you are expected to be in school, but also the pro rata teaching and non-teaching duties expected of you and your allowance of time for planning preparation and assessment (PPA).

In a landmark case a part-time adult education tutor sued Manchester City Council for operating a negotiated agreement which meant that if cuts had to be made in teaching hours, then part-time staff would lose hours before full-time staff. The courts found that this was unlawful discrimination. **(Sharma v Manchester City Council)**

Job sharing

Job sharing is simply two part-time teachers sharing a full-time post. Your school is not obliged to comply with a request for a job-share (any more than any other form of flexible working) but must consider it fairly. If you are contemplating job sharing you will need to ensure that the arrangements for the situation when one of the job sharers leaves is clearly spelled out. You should seek your union's advice.

In a 2006 case an hourly paid part-time lecturer won a settlement against Leeds Metropolitan University. The lecturer worked more hours than full-time colleagues, but was paid up to £10000 less. In addition she did not receive annual increments and was not paid for bank holidays. Part of the settlement consisted of a cash amount (£25000), plus a contribution to MA fees and a transfer to a full-time contract.

Fixed-term

If you are on a fixed-term contract you have the right not to be treated less favourably than a permanent employee in relation to promotion, training, pay, and conditions of service. After a series of fixed-term contracts over a four-year period your contract will automatically become permanent. Fixed-term contracts should only be used where there is a genuine requirement for a fixed-term contract such as an illness or maternity leave or, for

Employment and Performance

example, to teach an SEN pupil who will be leaving school within the year.

If you are on a part-time or fixed-term contract and feel that you are being treated less favourably you should approach the head and notify your union.

In 2005 a tutor of excluded pupils argued that she had continuous employment with Cornwall County Council even though she had no on-going contract and worked with individuals as the need arose and there were breaks in between (from August to September). The Court of Appeal decided that the gaps were merely 'temporary cessations' and there was sufficient mutuality for a contract of service to exist so that she did have continuity of employment. **(Prater v Cornwall County Council)**

In 2007 the Scottish Court of Session heard the case of a part-timer who worked on Wednesdays, Thursdays and Fridays was not allowed time off in lieu for public holidays even though his colleagues who worked on Mondays got the day off. This was not less favourable treatment of a part-timer.

In 2008 the EAT ruled that a part-timer on a fixed-term contract had been unfairly dismissed even though his fixed-term contract had ended. Though this case had specific factors in it that make it an uncertain authority, great care has to be taken in such cases **(Dorset v Labarta)**

Employment Act 2002. Part-time Workers (Prevention of Less Favourable Treatment) Regulations 2000. Fixed-Term Employees (Prevention of Less Favourable Treatment) Regulations 2002.

DBERR Booklets: Fixed-term work: a guide to the regulations (PL512), and Fixed-term work: a guide to the regulations (PL512). (www.berr.gov.uk)

Quick Guides AP10 Specimen Letter for a Fixed-Term Teaching Appointment; ST10A Part-Time and Fixed-Term Staff: Points of Law.

B10 SUPPLY TEACHERS

Normally supply teachers would be expected to have QTS, but exceptions can be made for trainees on the Graduate Teacher Programme (GTP), instructors or teachers trained overseas. As a supply teacher, you will usually have a contract with the LA or a school governing body, and will be subject to a check on your:

- qualifications;
- health;
- being barred from teaching;
- reported misconduct; or
- being subject to child protection procedures or investigation.

Although the regulations relating to QTS do not, in general, apply to independent schools, the checks on a person's employment status must still be carried out. There are regulations in both England and Wales limiting periods during which a person who has not served an induction period may be employed as a supply teacher.

Employment and Performance

Wales
The General Teaching Council for Wales (Associated Functions) (Amendment) Order 2005.

Agency workers
Sometimes you may be engaged through an agency. In this case you will still be subject to the checks by the agency. An agency commits a criminal act if it supplies a teacher who has not been checked. Employment agencies are expected to check that the teachers they provide have the qualifications required, are medically fit and are not barred from being employed as teachers. The government has made agencies responsible for making the checks on the staff they employ. Schools will seek assurances from the agency that such checks have been carried out and that overseas teachers have permission to work in this country and keep records of these assurances.

As a result of a case in 2008 (**James v Greenwich**) it has been established that agency workers are the employees of the agency unless the arrangement is manifestly a sham and so may be removed from a school at the request of the school with no notice. The government, the CBI and the TUC have come to an agreement to ensure that agency workers are not employed on less favourable terms than other workers in an enterprise but this will not extend to employment rights. The consequence of this case is that a school may ask for you to be removed without notice and without giving any reason.

The Conduct of Employment Agencies and Employment Business Regulations 2003 came into force in 2004. The Regulations establish a framework for minimum standards that clients, work-seekers and hirers can expect. Agencies must have written terms of business, and cannot charge a work-seeker for finding a job.
There is a guide on the agency regulations www.berr.gov.uk . Guidance on the employment of supply teachers is provided in *Circular 7/96 Use of Supply Teachers.*
Supply staff can be covered by the *Part-time Workers (Prevention of Less Favourable Treatment) Regulations 2000*, which enhance the rights of these members of staff, requiring them not to be less favourably treated than permanent full-time staff. *The Fixed Term Employees Regulations 2002* apply only to employees, however, not to agency staff. *See the government's supply teaching website:* www.teachernet.gov.uk/supplyteachers.
Quick Guides ST1 Conditions of Employment, ST2 Managing Staff: Changing Contractual Terms; ST10 Managing Staff: Supply Teachers: Points of Law.

B11 REGISTRATION

All qualified teachers, including supply teachers, wishing to teach in a maintained school, non-maintained special school or pupil referral unit, are legally required to register with their General Teaching Council (The General Teaching Council for England (GTCE) or the General Teaching Council for Wales (GTCW)).

Employment and Performance

Teachers' fees

In order to maintain their registration status, teachers pay an annual registration fee. The fee year runs from 1 April to 31 March each year. The fee in 2009-10 was £33 in England and £45 in Wales. In England, if you are employed as a teacher by an LA or a maintained school you will be entitled to receive an allowance of £33 towards the cost of your registration fee.

Contact: GTC website: www.gtce.org.uk.

Your personal details

The school/LA has to tell the GTC your address, teacher reference number, national insurance number, date of birth and which school you are employed at (this only applies to teachers in maintained schools or non-maintained special schools).

Contact: The General Teaching Council for England (GTCE): 0370 0010308 or email: info@gtce.org.uk *or visit the GTC website at:* www.gtce.org.uk. *General Teaching Council for Wales: Tel: 029 205 503 50 or website at:* www.gtcw.org.uk.

Wales

The GTCW requests an enhanced CRB check when determining the suitability of a person to be a registered teacher.

Quick Guides ST13 The General Teaching Council for England (GTC(E))and for Wales (GTC(W)).

> **B12 THE GENERAL TEACHING COUNCILS FOR ENGLAND (GTCE) AND FOR WALES (GTCW)**

The Councils include registered teachers, both directly-elected and appointed, for example from the trade unions. GTCE members also include nominees from other bodies concerned with education, for example representing employers, parents and higher education, and people appointed through the public appointments system.

The Councils' prime function is to promote high professional standards of teaching. They exercise disciplinary powers over registered teachers. All qualified teachers are eligible to join, but registration is only compulsory for teachers working in maintained schools and non-maintained special schools. Teachers can only work in these schools if they are registered.

In Wales only those teachers who are required to be registered are eligible for election or appointment to the council. It also makes it clear under Regulation 3 that all Council members (whether elected or appointed) are to act as individuals and not as representatives of any organisations to which they belong or which nominated them for appointment. Regulation 4 includes the amendment to the category of elected members which comprise heads and deputies, to now include assistant heads.

The General Teaching Council for Wales (Constitution) (Amendment) Regulations 2007. The General Teaching Council for Wales (Constitution) (Amendment) Regulations 2009 amend the 1999 regulations mainly as a consequence of the coming into force of provisions of the *Safeguarding Vulnerable Groups Act 2006.*

Employment and Performance

The GTCE also:
- maintains a register of qualified teachers in England;
- regulates the profession in the public interest;
- raises the standing of the teaching profession; and
- provides advice to the government and other agencies on key issues affecting the quality of teaching and learning.

Wales
The GTC (Wales) functions include:
- establishing and maintaining a register of teachers;
- issuing a Code of Practice laying down the standards of professional conduct and practice;
- exercising disciplinary powers in relation to registered teachers and those applying for registration; and
- giving advice about teaching issues to the National Assembly of Wales.

It is also the designated authority for recognition of the professional qualifications from members of the European Community, Iceland, Norway, Liechtenstein and Switzerland. GTCW also has to maintain records about persons who are first employed as a supply teacher, and whether a person is permitted to continue in employment as a supply teacher.

The General Teaching Council for Wales (Functions) (Amendment) Regulations 2009 amend the *General Teaching Council for Wales (Functions) Regulations 2000.* Among these regulations the new duty is that The General Teaching Council will now have to determine the question of suitability afresh, essentially whether the person is subject to monitoring under the *Safeguarding Vulnerable Groups Act 2006* or, if not, whether the Secretary of State has ceased monitoring.

GTCW manages the Welsh Assembly Government CPD (Continuing Professional Development) programme. Initial grants of £500 annually are available for individual teachers to apply to use CPD. Since 1 April 2006, a scheme allows for a group of teachers in the same school to apply for a group bursary to work on a CPD project. GTCW is discussing with the Privy Council the possibility of the body becoming chartered so that it will be possible to recognise teachers with a chartered teacher status.

Professional development
The Teacher Learning Academy, which is led by the GTCE and delivered by Cambridge Education, helps teachers to improve their skills and gain professional recognition. Find out more at www.teacherlearningacademy.org.uk The GTCE also has a network for linking teachers nationally and puts them in touch with the latest research and evidence. See www.gtce.org.uk/networks.
The GTCW runs a CPD programme on behalf of the Welsh Assembly Government.
For GTCE activities at www.gtce.org.uk *and for* *GTCW go to* www.gtcw.org.uk.

Code of Conduct and Practice
Teaching's new code, adopted by the GTCE in October 2009, makes

Employment and Performance

a powerful positive statement about contemporary teaching. It shows how teachers encourage learning and how they work with colleagues, other professionals and parents.

These eight principles, which set out a shared picture of teacher professionalism, lie at the heart of the code.

Registered teachers:

1. Put the well-being, development and progress of children and young people first.
2. Take responsibility for maintaining the quality of their teaching practice.
3. Help children and young people to become confident and successful learners.
4. Demonstrate respect for diversity and promote equality.
5. Strive to establish productive partnerships with parents and carers.
6. Work as part of a whole-school team.
7. Co-operate with other professional colleagues.
8. Demonstrate honesty and integrity and uphold public trust and confidence in the teaching profession.

To find out more, go to: www. gtce.org.uk/teachers/thecode

There is also a statement of Professional Values and Practice in Wales at: www.gtcw.org.uk.

The GTCE and teacher misconduct

Employers must refer a teacher to the GTCE when a teacher has a criminal conviction, or appears to be guilty of unacceptable professional conduct, and the circumstances do not raise any issue of the safety of under-19 pupils. The GTCE has a duty to inform the Secretary of State where the safety or welfare of pupils under-19 is at issue, or where a prohibition order has been made. It can also investigate issues raised by the general public. The Council investigates the allegations against a teacher and decides whether the case should be heard by a committee of the Council. Teachers are entitled to a fair hearing before the committee and can be represented.

Teacher incompetence

The GTCE has a duty to investigate cases of alleged serious professional incompetence. This means a level of incompetence which falls seriously short of what is expected of a teacher. It can include failings in management and leadership roles, as well as the classroom role. The procedure is the same as for misconduct and the teacher has the same rights. Employers have a legal obligation to inform the GTCE of teachers who are subject to dismissal or would have been had they not resigned in anticipation of dismissal proceedings.

In Wales the Council must maintain a register of teachers, including a Code of Practice, laying down standards of professional conduct and practice expected of registered teachers; exercising disciplinary powers in relation to registered teachers and persons applying for registration; and giving advice about teaching issues to the National Assembly for Wales. LAs, governing bodies, independent school proprietors and employment agencies must notify the National Assembly for

Employment and Performance

Wales (and in certain cases the GTCW) when any employee in the education field is dismissed, or leaves in circumstances which might have led to his/her dismissal, if the grounds for the departure are his/her unsuitability to work with children or his/her misconduct and/or if his/her health is causing concern. If the teacher departs because of incompetence the matter is referred only to the GTCW. Refer to *The Education (Supply of Information)(Wales) Regulations 2009 and The General Teaching Council for Wales (Disciplinary Functions) (Amendment) Regulations 2009 and The General Teaching Council for Wales(Additional Functions) Regulations 2009.*

Both the English and Welsh Councils have the power to take away a teacher's registration, or qualify the registration in cases of professional misconduct or incompetence. *Quick Guides D7 The General Teaching Council (GTCE and GTCW): Responsibilities for Discipline.* Regulations and guidance in Wales are also incorporated in the QGP documents.

B13 TEACHERS' PROFESSIONAL DUTIES

Your professional duties as a teacher, which must be carried out under the reasonable direction of the head (see below), are set out in Part XII of the STPCD, which is published annually. If you consider that you are being asked to teach or do other duties unreasonably, you should seek the advice of your union. Do not refuse to do the duties without receiving advice.

Teaching
This includes:
- planning and preparing courses/lessons;
- promoting the development of the abilities and aptitudes of the pupils in any class or group assigned to the teacher;
- teaching pupils according to their educational needs (including setting and marking of work); and
- assessing, recording and reporting on the development, progress and attainment of pupils.

Other activities
- promoting the general progress and well-being of individual pupils and groups assigned to the teacher;
- the provision of advice and guidance on educational and social matters (e.g. careers);
- making records of and reports on the personal and social needs of pupils;
- communicating and consulting with parents;
- communicating and co-operating with outside agencies;
- attending meetings related to the above and to the school's curriculum, administration/organisation and pastoral arrangements;
- contributing to oral and written assessments, reports and references relating to individual pupils and groups;
- reviewing teaching methods and programmes of work;
- participating in CPD, particularly with regard to

Employment and Performance

needs identified in appraisal objectives/statements (cf. under performance management);

- advising, both orally and in writing, and co-operating with the head and other colleagues in the preparation of courses, teaching materials, teaching programmes and assessment methods;
- maintaining good discipline and safeguarding pupils' health and safety;
- covering rarely for absent colleagues in circumstances that are not foreseeable (this does not apply to teachers who are wholly or mainly employed to provide cover);
- participating in arrangements for preparing pupils for public examinations (including assessment, recording and reporting);
- contributing to the development of other teachers, including the induction and assessment of new teachers;
- helping the head to carry out threshold assessments (in the case of teachers for whom the teacher has a management responsibility);
- participating in the administrative and organisational duties associated with the above (but not routinely to undertake tasks of a clerical or administrative nature which do not require a teacher's professional skills and judgement – cf. the tasks listed in **Annex 5 of the STPCD**); and
- attending assemblies; registering the attendance of pupils and supervising pupils (before, after or during school sessions).

Quick Guides Managing Staff (ST) Section.

The right to teach your own subject

In 2004 an employment appeal tribunal found that a sixth form college employer who had insisted that a health studies teacher should teach religious studies had unilaterally changed her contract, and consequently had constructively dismissed her. The employer could not rely on the catch-all phrase 'any duties.....which may be reasonably assigned to you.' The teacher, said the tribunal, was not employed as a generic teacher but as a teacher with specific skills suitable for the job she had been employed to do. There were particular circumstances in this case and it is not clear whether it will have wider application. **(Josiah Mason College v Parsons)**

B14 WORKING TIME

If you are a teacher in an **independent school** your working time will be defined by your contract within the boundaries of the Working Time Directive.

If you are in a **maintained school,** your working time is defined by statute and regulations. Teachers in maintained schools must be available to work for 195 days, of which 190 are days when they may be required to teach pupils in addition to carrying out other duties, in any school year. Teachers must be available to perform such duties at the times and in the places as prescribed/

Employment and Performance

directed by the head for 1265 hours in any school year. Time spent travelling to and from the place of work does not count against the 1265 hours. Teachers are also required to work such reasonable additional hours beyond the 1265 hours as may be needed to carry out their professional duties.

Teachers are not contractually obliged to undertake midday supervision and must be allowed a reasonable break between school sessions (or between 12.00 and 2.00 pm). The 195 days and the 1265 hours do not apply to members of the leadership group or ASTs.

The Working Time Regulations 1998 apply to teachers in maintained schools in respect of the working week, but in practice have little impact because the termly pattern of working means that they are very unlikely to exceed the 48-hour limit averaged out over 17 weeks. However, where a teacher's daily working time is more than 6 hours, he/she is entitled to an uninterrupted rest break of at least 20 minutes, and a daily rest of 11 consecutive hours. There is a requirement that a worker should be given an uninterrupted break of 24 hours every week or an uninterrupted break of 48 hours once every fortnight. This has particular implications for boarding schools.

B15 RAISING STANDARDS AND TACKLING TEACHER WORKLOAD

The open-ended nature of the teacher's contract caused difficulties and a National Agreement to reduce teacher workload was signed on 15 January 2003 and subsequently given statutory expression in the *School Teachers' Pay and Conditions Document (STPCD) 2003, 2004, 2005, 2006, 2007, 2008 and 2009.* The main legal provisions are set out below.

Cutting workload

You are not routinely required to carry out the 21 clerical and administrative tasks, listed in *Annex 3 of the STPCD 2009,* which are:

- collecting money from pupils and parents;
- investigating a pupil's absence;
- bulk photocopying;
- typing or making word-processed versions of manuscript material and producing revisions of such versions;
- word processing, copying and distributing bulk communications, including standard letters, to parents and pupils;
- producing class lists on the basis of information provided by teachers;
- keeping and filing records, including records based on data supplied by teachers;
- preparing, setting up and taking down classroom displays in accordance with decisions taken by teachers;
- producing analyses of attendance figures;
- producing analyses of examination results;
- collating pupil reports;
- administration of work experience (but not selecting placements and supporting pupils by advice or visits);

Employment and Performance

- administration of public and internal examinations;
- administration of cover for absent teachers;
- ordering, setting up and maintaining ICT equipment and software;
- ordering supplies and equipment;
- cataloguing, preparing, issuing and maintaining materials and equipment and stocktaking the same;
- taking verbatim notes or producing formal minutes of meetings;
- co-ordinating and submitting bids (for funding, school status and the like) using contributions by teachers and others;
- transferring manual data about pupils not covered by the above into computerised school management systems; or
- managing the data in school management systems.

Though 'not routinely' is not defined, it clearly cannot mean 'never'. Heads, therefore, are able to ask you to undertake such tasks in emergencies, provided that they have appropriate systems and policies in place for support staff to carry out these tasks under normal circumstances.

You may, however, be asked to carry out tasks, which require a teacher's professional skills and judgement, for example:

- using analyses of attendance;
- using analyses of examination and test results;
- making the initial entry of pupil data into the school's management information system;
- communicating action points from meetings; and
- contributing to the content of records.

Similar provisions apply to members of the leadership group: i.e., their responsibilities should be focused on weighty teaching and learning dimensions and they should not be asked to carry out tasks of a clerical or administrative nature that could beneficially be transferred to support staff.

Work/life balance

Heads are under a statutory duty (in addition to their existing responsibilities in common law and under health and safety legislation) to have regard to the work/life balance of all teachers at their school. They need to ensure that:

- the hours worked by teachers over and above their annual directed time limit of 1265 hours are reasonable; and
- the overall hours worked by members of the leadership group and ASTs, who are not subject to an annual limit of 1265 hours, are also reasonable.

One of the main objectives of the Workload Agreement is to exert downward pressure on workload and over time to reduce the average number of hours worked by teachers during term-time from 52 to 45, as recommended by the STRB.

A 'no-detriment' clause applies, but when considering 'no-detriment', teachers should focus on the overall effect of the adjustments that schools have made, not just on individual items that might seem to increase

Employment and Performance

workload. The entitlement to a reasonable work/life balance applies equally to heads and governing bodies should take appropriate measures to ensure that this is the case.

Leadership and management time

All teachers, including members of the leadership group, with leadership and management responsibilities must be given a reasonable allocation of time within school sessions (this is not the same as the time-tabled teaching week) to support the discharge of their responsibilities. The allocation should be in reasonable blocks (not 10 or 20 minutes).

A no-detriment clause applies and teachers in receipt of leadership and management time, which was unaffected by the transfer of the 21 tasks to support staff, should not have had their allocation reduced as a result of contractual change.

Cover

From 1 September 2009 you should only be asked to cover rarely for absent colleagues in circumstances which are not foreseeable. 'Foreseeable circumstances' include events that are foreseeable on the basis of historic experience, events that are foreseeable in the normal local experience and events that may be expected as part of the evolving pattern of provision. This would imply that schools now need to make alternative provision to cover the kinds of absence that teachers have traditionally covered. The contractual entitlement applies to all teachers except those who are employed wholly or mainly to undertake cover.

Heads are statutorily bound to ensure that cover is shared equitably among all teachers, but this will, in practice, be extremely difficult to achieve as the coincidence of teachers' availability for cover and the incidence of unforeseen circumstances is not likely to be under the head's control. The member of staff responsible for administering cover should keep an accurate record of the amount of cover undertaken by each teacher.

Schools must not enter into any voluntary cover arrangements, however attractive and appealing they may appear. Schools should continue with whatever arrangements they have adopted thus far for covering the absence of form tutors in registration. To ensure that their system for managing cover is robust, schools should publish a calendar and a timetable for each school year after consultation with staff and union representatives. They should endeavour to plan any changes year-on-year well in advance. The calendar sets out the activities scheduled to take place in the academic year (e.g., learning outside the classroom, meetings, parental consultation evenings and INSET days). The timetable depicts the school's provision for teaching and learning in the school's timetabled teaching week. The guidance allows schools some flexibility in their planning for the year and in the management of cover, for example:

Employment and Performance

- the pattern of the timetable may vary across the year (i.e., schools may accommodate activities during the year by having a timetable that follows the same pattern for 35 weeks and a different pattern for the other 3 weeks; where the pattern is different, teachers' individual timetables will also be different;
- whatever timetabling pattern may pertain, it is the absence of the person timetabled to take a class or group that is the trigger for cover;
- teaching timetables are not frozen in time and there may be variations year-on-year (teachers may, therefore, be asked to teach more in one year than another and can be given a higher teaching load in a particular year than in the previous year);
- in-year variations are also permissible, for example, in the case of a long-term absence or a significant educational development, but these should not be a frequent occurrence.

It is still expected that long-term cover will be carried out by qualified supply teachers. For short-term absence schools have a range of options at their disposal, including supply teachers, higher level teaching assistants (HLTAs), cover supervisors, floating teachers and teachers at the school. If support staff undertake cover supervision, heads will need to be careful as to whether the work undertaken is 'specified work' or not. Heads are obliged to have regard to the HLTA standards if support staff work with whole classes.

Gained time occurs when teachers are released from their time-tabled teaching commitments because their pupils are away on a planned educational trip or visit, on study leave or sitting an examination. Teachers' use of gained time for professional activities is under the direction of the head. The guidance in the **STPCD 2009** contains an agreed list of such activities, including:

- developing curriculum/subject materials;
- working on schemes of work, lesson plans, policies etc. in preparation for the next year;
- helping select pupils with coursework;
- taking groups of pupils to provide additional learning support (or double-staffing some classes); and
- assisting colleagues in appropriate, planned team teaching activities.

Invigilation

Teachers cannot routinely be asked to invigilate external examinations. They may, however, still be required to:

- conduct oral and practical examinations in their own subject area and to undertake the preparation of pupils and those aspects of assessment, recording and reporting associated with external examinations which require their professional input; and
- supervise internal tests where these are arranged in their normal time-tabled teaching time.

If a school reorganises its timetable for 'mock' examinations to replicate the public examination process, teachers should not

Employment and Performance

be asked to invigilate. In the context of a teacher's professional expertise it is considered reasonable for a teacher to be present at the beginning of an external examination in his/her subject area to check the paper and to ensure that there are no problems with it. It would also be reasonable to be on call during the examination to enable support staff, who are invigilating, to refer professional matters that may arise. The guidance also states that it may be appropriate for teachers to be present at the end of an external examination to ensure its efficient conclusion.

Planning, preparation and assessment (PPA) time

All teachers have a contractual entitlement to planning, preparation and assessment time (PPA) to ease workload pressures and to raise standards. PPA time:

- should amount to at least 10% of a teacher's time-tabled teaching time (i.e., if a teacher teaches 21 periods out of a 25 hour teaching week, he/she is entitled to a minimum of 2.1 periods for PPA time);
- is guaranteed and must not be encroached upon under any circumstances;
- is for the teacher to determine how it will be spent (within the parameters of PPA-type activities);
- should appear on a teacher's timetable; and
- must be allocated in blocks of no less than 30 minutes.

A no-detriment clause applies and teachers already in receipt of more than the minimum 10% specifically for PPA time before the implementation of contractual change should not have had their allocation reduced. Heads and members of the leadership group who have a teaching commitment are similarly entitled to guaranteed PPA time.

PPA time is the only non-contact time that may not be used for cover.

Dedicated headship time

Governing bodies are obliged to ensure that heads have dedicated headship time within school sessions (not necessarily the time-tabled teaching week) having regard to the school's resources to assist them in the discharge of their leadership and management responsibilities.

Reducing the workload

In England there is an Implementation Review Unit (IRU) charged with advising on how bureaucracy can be reduced in order to lessen the workload on teachers.

In Wales the School Workforce Advisory Panel (SWAP) is equivalent to the IRU.

Quick Guides PAY12 Tackling Workload.

B16 PROFESSIONAL STANDARDS

You are expected to meet professional standards which have been developed by the Training and Development Agency (TDA) in conjunction with the Rewards and Incentives Group (RIG). **Note: These professional standards apply only in England and are available on the TDA website** (www.tda.gov.uk.) The Welsh Assembly Government remains responsible for the development

Employment and Performance

of professional (non-pay) standards in Wales.

Professional standards, which are statements of a teacher's professional attributes, skills and knowledge and understanding, clarify the expectations at each career stage and depict what progression looks like. They will also help you identify your professional development needs (e.g., the next level(s) of the framework provides a reference point for future development). The standards are cumulative and progressive; where the standards are only defined at one career stage (i.e. where there is no further progression), they continue to apply at all subsequent career stages and you must continue to meet them if you want to progress to the next or to a different career stage, as well as meeting the standards for that career stage and fulfilling the relevant eligibility criteria. For example, if you want to apply for AST assessment, your head must be satisfied that you have continued to meet:

- as a main scale teacher, the core standards;
- as a post-threshold teacher, the core and the post-threshold standards; and
- as an ET, the core, post-threshold and ET standards.

All the standards are underpinned by the five key outcomes for children and young people set out in **Every Child Matters** and the six areas of the **Common Core of Skills and Knowledge for the Children's Workforce.**

The standards provide the backdrop to discussions about how your performance should be viewed in relation to your current career stage or the one you are approaching. The introduction to the framework has been re-produced in **Section 1 of the STPCD 2009**. It is non-statutory and applies only in England.

ALL TEACHERS
All teachers should:
Professional attributes
Relationships with children and young people

- Have high expectations of children and young people including a commitment to ensuring that they can achieve their full potential and to establishing fair, respectful, trusting supportive and constructive relationships with them.
- Hold positive values and attitudes and adopt high standards of behaviour in their professional role.

Frameworks

- Maintain an up-to-date knowledge and understanding of the professional duties of teachers and the statutory framework within which they work, and contribute to the development, implementation and evaluation of the policies and practice of their workplace, including those designed to promote equality of opportunity.

Communicating and working with others

- Communicate effectively with children, young people and colleagues.
- Communicate effectively with parents and carers, conveying timely and relevant information

Employment and Performance

about attainment, objectives, progress and well-being.

- Recognise that communication is a two way process and encourage parents and carers to participate in discussions about the progress, development and well-being of children and young people.
- Recognise and respect the contributions that colleagues, parents and carers can make to the development and well-being of children and young people, and to raising their levels of attainment.
- Have a commitment to collaboration and co-operative working where appropriate.

Personal professional development

- Evaluate their performance and be committed to improving their practice through appropriate professional development.
- Have a creative and constructively critical approach towards innovation; being prepared to adapt their practice where benefits and improvements are identified.
- Act upon advice and feedback and be open to coaching and mentoring.

Professional knowledge and understanding

Teaching and learning

- Have a good up-to-date working knowledge and understanding of a range of teaching, learning and behaviour management strategies and know how to use and adapt them, including how to personalize learning to provide opportunities for all learners to achieve their potential.

Assessment and monitoring

- Know the assessment requirements and arrangements for the subjects/curriculum areas they teach, including those relating to public examinations and qualifications.
- Know a range of approaches to assessment, including the importance of formative assessment.
- Know how to use local and national statistical information to evaluate the effectiveness of their teaching, to monitor the progress of those they teach and to raise levels of attainment.
- Know how to use reports and other sources of external information related to assessment in order to provide learners with accurate and constructive feedback on their strengths, weaknesses, attainment, progress and areas for development, including action plans for improvement.

Subjects and curriculum

- Have a secure knowledge and understanding of their subjects/curriculum areas and related pedagogy including: the contribution that their subjects/curriculum areas and other relevant can make to cross-curricular learning; and recent relevant developments.
- Know and understand the relevant statutory and non-statutory curricula and frameworks, including those provided through the National Strategies, for their subjects/curriculum areas and other relevant initiatives across the age and ability range.

Employment and Performance

<u>Literacy, numeracy and ICT</u>
- Know how to use skills in literacy, numeracy and ICT to support their teaching and wider professional activities.

<u>Achievement and diversity</u>
- Understand how children and young people develop and how the progress, rate of development and well-being of learners are affected by a range of developmental, social, religious, ethnic, cultural and linguistic influences.
- Know how to make effective personalised provision for those they teach, including those, for whom English is an additional language, or who have special educational needs or disabilities, and how to take practical account of diversity and promote equality and inclusion in their teaching.
- Understand the roles of colleagues such as those having specific responsibilities for learners with special educational needs, disabilities and other individual learning needs, and the contributions they can make to the learning, development and well-being of children and young people.
- Know when to draw on the expertise of colleagues, such as those with responsibility for the safeguarding of children and young people and special educational needs and disabilities, and to refer to sources of information, advice and support from external agencies.

<u>Health and well-being</u>
- Know the current legal requirements, national policies and guidance on the safeguarding and promotion of the well-being of children and young people.
- Know the local arrangements concerning the safeguarding of children and young people.
- Know how to identify potential child abuse or neglect and follow safeguarding procedures.
- Know how to identify and support children and young people whose progress, development or well-being is affected by changes or difficulties in their personal circumstances, and when to refer them to colleagues for specialist support.

Professional skills
<u>Planning</u>
- Plan for progression across the age and ability range they teach, designing effective learning sequences within lessons and across series of lessons informed by secure subject/curriculum knowledge.
- Design opportunities for learners to develop their literacy, numeracy and ICT thinking and learning skills appropriate within their phase and context.
- Plan, set and assess homework, other out-of-class assignments and coursework for examinations, where appropriate, to sustain learners' progress and to extend and consolidate their learning.

<u>Teaching</u>
- Teach challenging, well-organised lessons and sequences of lessons across the age and ability range they teach in which they:

Employment and Performance

◊ use an appropriate range of teaching strategies and resources, including e-learning, which meet learners' needs and take practical account of diversity and promote equality and inclusion;

◊ build on the prior knowledge and attainment of those they teach in order that learners meet learning objectives and make sustained progress;

◊ develop concepts and processes which enable learners to apply new knowledge, understanding and skills;

◊ adapt their language to suit the learners they teach, introducing new ideas and concepts clearly, and using explanations, questions, discussions and plenaries effectively; and

◊ • manage the learning of individuals, groups and whole classes effectively, modifying their teaching appropriately to suit the stage of the lesson and the needs of the learners.

• Teach engaging and motivating lessons informed by well-grounded expectations of learners and designed to raise levels of attainment.

Assessing, monitoring and giving feedback

• Make effective use of an appropriate range of observation, assessment, monitoring and recording strategies as a basis for setting challenging learning objectives and monitoring learners' progress and levels of attainment.

• Provide learners, colleagues, parents and carers with timely, accurate and constructive feedback on learners' attainment, progress and areas for development.

• Support and guide learners so that they can reflect on their learning, identify the progress they have made, set positive targets for improvement and become successful independent learners.

• Use assessment as part of their teaching to diagnose learners' needs, set realistic and challenging targets for improvement and plan future teaching.

Reviewing teaching and learning

• Review the effectiveness of their teaching and its impact on learners' progress, attainment and well-being, refining their approaches where necessary.

• Review the impact of the feedback provided to learners and guide learners on how to improve their attainment.

Learning environment

• Establish a purposeful and safe learning environment which complies with current legal requirements, national policies and guidance on the safeguarding and well-being of children and young people so that learners feel secure and sufficiently confident to make an active contribution to learning and to the school.

• Make use of the local arrangements concerning the safeguarding of children and young people.

• Identify and use opportunities to personalise and extend learning through out-of-school

Employment and Performance

contexts where possible making links between in-school learning and learning in out-of-school contexts.

- Manage learners' behaviour constructively by establishing and maintaining a clear and positive framework for discipline, in line with the school's behaviour policy.
- Use a range of behaviour management techniques and strategies, adapting them as necessary to promote the self control and independence of learners.
- Promote learners' self-control, independence and co-operation through developing their social, emotional and behavioural skills.

Team working and collaboration
- Work as a team member and identify opportunities for working with colleagues, managing their work where appropriate and sharing the development of effective practice with them.
- Ensure that colleagues working with them are appropriately involved in supporting learning and understand the roles they are expected to fulfil.

POST-THRESHOLD TEACHERS
Post-threshold teachers should:
Professional attributes
Frameworks
- Contribute significantly, where appropriate, to implementing workplace policies and practice and to promoting collective responsibility for their implementation.

Professional knowledge and understanding
Teaching and learning

- Have an extensive knowledge and understanding of how to use and adapt a range of teaching, learning and behaviour management strategies, including how to personalise learning to provide opportunities for all learners to achieve their potential.

Assessment and monitoring
- Have an extensive knowledge and well-informed understanding of the assessment requirements and arrangements for the subjects/curriculum areas they teach, including those related to public examinations and qualifications.
- Have an up-to-date knowledge and understanding of the different types of qualifications and specifications and their suitability for meeting learners' needs.

Subjects of the curriculum
- Have a more developed knowledge and understanding of their subjects/curriculum areas and related pedagogy including how learning progresses within them.

Health and well-being
- Have sufficient depth of knowledge and experience to be able to give advice on the development and well-being of children and young people.

Professional skills
Planning
- Be flexible, creative and adept at designing learning sequences within lessons and across lessons that are effective and consistently well-matched to learning objectives

and the needs of learners and which integrate recent developments, including those relating to subject/curriculum knowledge.

Teaching

- Have teaching skills which lead to learners achieving well relative to their prior attainment, making progress as good as or better than, similar learners nationally.

Team working and collaboration

- Promote collaboration and work effectively as a team member.
- Contribute to the professional development of colleagues through coaching and mentoring, demonstrating effective practice and providing advice and feedback.

EXCELLENT TEACHERS
Excellent teachers should:
Professional attributes
Frameworks

- Be willing to take a lead role in developing workplace policies and practice and in promoting collective responsibility for their implementation.

Personal professional development

- Research and evaluate innovative curricular practices and draw on research outcomes and other sources of external evidence to inform their own practice and that of colleagues.

Professional knowledge and understanding
Teaching and learning

- Have a critical understanding of the most effective teaching,

learning and behaviour management strategies, including how to select and use approaches that personalise learning to provide opportunities for all learners to achieve their potential.

Assessment and monitoring

- Know how to improve the effectiveness of assessment practice in the workplace, including how to analyse statistical information to evaluate the effectiveness of teaching and learning across the school.

Subjects and curriculum

- Have an extensive and deep knowledge and understanding of their subject/curriculum areas and related pedagogy gained for example through involvement in wider professional networks associated with their subject/curriculum areas.

Achievement and diversity

- Have an extensive knowledge on matters concerning equality, inclusion and diversity in teaching.

Professional skills
Planning

- Take a lead in planning collaboratively with colleagues in order to promote effective practice.
- Identify and explore links between subjects/curriculum areas in their planning.

Teaching

- Have teaching skills, which lead to excellent results and outcomes.

Employment and Performance

- Demonstrate excellent and innovative pedagogical practice.

Assessment, monitoring and giving feedback
- Demonstrate excellent ability to assess and evaluate.
- Have an excellent ability to provide learners, colleagues, parents and carers with timely, accurate and constructive feedback on learners' attainment, progress and areas for development that promotes pupil progress.

Reviewing teaching and learning
- Use local and national statistical data and other information in order to provide:
  ◊ a comparative baseline for evaluating learners' progress and attainment;
  ◊ a means of judging the effectiveness of their teaching; and
  ◊ a basis for improving teaching and learning.

Team working and collaboration
- Work closely with leadership teams, taking a leading role in developing, implementing and evaluating policies and practice that contribute to school improvement.
- Contribute to the professional development of colleagues using a broad range of techniques and skills appropriate to their needs so that they demonstrate enhanced and effective practice.
- Make well-founded appraisals of situations, upon which they are asked to advise, applying high-level skills in classroom observation to evaluate and advise colleagues on their work and devising and implementing effective strategies to meet the learning needs of children and young people leading to improvements in pupil outcomes.

ASTs
ASTs should:
Professional attributes
Frameworks
- Be willing to take on a strategic leadership role in developing workplace policies and practice and in promoting collective responsibility for their implementation in their own and other workplaces.

Professional skills
Team working and collaboration
- Be part of or work closely with leadership teams, taking a leadership role in developing, implementing and evaluating policies and practice in their own and other workplaces that contribute to school improvement.
- Possess the analytical, interpersonal and organisational skills necessary to work effectively with staff and leadership teams beyond their own school.

In Wales the end of induction standards are the equivalent of the core standards in England. In order to meet the end of induction standards in each of the four areas set out below NQTs must:

Professional characteristics
- conduct themselves with integrity and apply their knowledge and skills within their professional work;

Employment and Performance

- reflect on and act to improve their professional practice, taking shared responsibility for their own professional development and learning;
- work collaboratively and co-operatively with those who contribute toward the work of the school;
- demonstrate commitment to equal opportunities, social justice and inclusion.

Knowledge and understanding

- demonstrate an understanding of practice and the broader educational perspective in Wales when engaging in professional dialogue;
- demonstrate a detailed working knowledge of their sector, the schools in which they teach and their related professional responsibilities;
- demonstrate secure knowledge and understanding of the theory and practical skills in the curriculum area or subjects taught;
- deliver the common requirements of the National Curriculum in Wales; that is communication, mathematical, problem-solving, creative and information technology skills; Cwricwlwm Cymreig and personal and social development.

Planning, teaching and learning and class management

- plan effectively to meet the needs of all pupils, including, where applicable those with identified special educational needs, gifted and talented pupils and those with English or Welsh as an additional language;

- demonstrate increasing proficiency in selecting and using a broad range of teaching and learning strategies and available resources, which they evaluate critically in terms of pupils' learning;
- be able to justify their approach in terms of the curriculum, learning objectives of schemes of work and the learning needs and abilities of their pupils;
- secure a good standard of pupil behaviour through establishing rules and high expectations in order to achieve positive relationships; purposeful activity; and an appropriate environment for learning taking due account of school policy.

Monitoring, assessment, recording and reporting

- recognise the level a pupil is achieving and make accurate formative and summative assessments, independently, against attainment targets, where applicable, and performance levels associated with other tests and qualifications relevant to the subject(s) or phases taught;
- record and use the results of day-to-day assessment to modify their teaching, and secure progression in pupils' learning by identifying appropriate learning targets for individuals and groups of pupils;
- provide reports on pupils' progress and achievements, identifying appropriate targets and learning goals, and providing guidance to enable parents/carers to support their children's learning.

Employment and Performance

The regulations

The revised performance management regulations **(The Education School Teacher Performance Management (England) Regulations 2006)** for teachers and heads came into effect for pay progression purposes from 1 September 2008. Accompanying guidance has been issued by the Rewards and Incentives Group (RIG).

The regulations are only applicable in England. They apply to all teachers employed on a contract of one term or more, but not to NQTs who have not completed their induction, to teachers subject to capability procedures or to daily supply teachers or agency staff. The new professional standards for classroom teachers will serve as the backdrop to the performance management review process.

The School Teacher Appraisal (Wales) Regulations 2002

The regulations provide for the appraisal of the performance of school teachers (including unqualified teachers) at community, voluntary, foundation, community special or foundation special schools other than teachers employed under a fixed-term contract for less than a year. The governors and the head must ensure that that the performance is appraised regularly. The appraisal cycle lasts for a year. The governing body decides on the procedures for appraisal, that is, it establishes a policy setting out how the performance management at the school is implemented. The appraiser must observe the school teacher on at least one occasion in the cycle. Before the policy is implemented the governors must ensure that all teachers in the school are consulted. For NQTs an induction year became a statutory requirement from Sept 2003.

The School Teacher Appraisal (Amendment) (Wales) Regulations 2009 came into force on 1 September 2009. These regulations bring within the scope of the 2002 regulations the appraisal of the performance of school teachers (including nursery school teachers) who are employed by local authorities for more than one school term and teachers employed by local authorities who are not attached to one particular school or who teach outside school settings. For all school teachers within the scope of the 2002 regulations, the appraisal review must determine whether there has been a successful review of overall performance. **The School Teacher Appraisal (Wales) (Amendment No 2) Regulations 2009** clarify that a teacher employed at two schools whether or not the LA is the employer must be appraised by both schools.

Main features performance management policy

The governing body will have formulated a performance management policy (or to adopt one formulated by the head) after consulting with all teachers at the school and after seeking to agree the policy with recognised unions, having regard to the outcome of that consultation. (In the event of a failure to secure agreement, the decision of the governing body prevails).

Employment and Performance

The policy should:
- specify the outcomes it is intended to achieve and how these will be measured;
- link performance management arrangements with the school improvement plan and school self-evaluation processes;
- show how the school will endeavour to achieve consistency of treatment and fairness between teachers with similar experience or levels of responsibility;
- set out the timing of the PM cycle;
- include a classroom observation protocol;
- include arrangements for appeals; and
- make provision for PM training.

Head's role
The head will usually be expected to draft the school's PM policy for the governing body to consider, modify and adopt (subject to consultation and seeking to secure agreement with recognised unions). In addition, the head is required to:
- report annually to the governing body on the operation of the school's PM policy and the effectiveness of the school's PM procedures and on teachers' training and development needs (in general, not teacher-specific, terms);
- appoint reviewers and act as a reviewer;
- retain copies of all planning and review statements (for 6 years) and provide access to others as appropriate;
- take account of review outcomes in school improvement;
- produce an effective plan for CPD;
- establish a protocol for classroom observation within the PM policy;
- pass on evidence on request if a teacher moves in mid-cycle;
- evaluate standards of teaching and learning and ensure that proper standards of professional practice are established and maintained; and
- intervene and change a statement if necessary (cf. below).

If you move in mid-cycle, and request it in writing, PM evidence will be passed on. This is likely to prove particularly important if you are coming up for threshold assessment (because you will need evidence of meeting the standards) or you have completed one year or part of a year since you last moved up the upper pay spine (as progression is normally biennial).

Performance cycle
Performance is assessed annually with regard to the previous academic year. In secondary schools, it will be difficult to carry out the review before September/ October because examination results and comparative data, on which some assessments of pupil progress are likely to depend, are not available before then. Pay progression decisions need to be made by 31 October (backdated to 1 September) in accordance with the provisions of the STPCD for all teachers other than the head (for whom the deadline is 31 December) and, consequently, assessments of performance must be completed in advance of that

Employment and Performance

date to permit pay progression decisions to be made by 31 October.

Appointment of reviewer

Head

The governing body is required to appoint two or three governors to carry out the review of the head's performance. In schools with a religious character, at least one of the two/three governors appointed must be a foundation governor. In voluntary aided schools, where two governors are appointed, one of them must be a foundation governor and, where three are appointed, two must be foundation governors. The governing body must use the services of a school improvement partner (SIP), whom the LA has appointed for that school to provide the appointed governors with advice and support in relation to the head's performance review. No governor who is a teacher or any other member of staff may be appointed to review the head's performance.

Other teachers

The head shall be the reviewer for all other teachers at the school. In cases where the head is not a teacher's line manager, he/she may delegate the responsibility in its entirety to your line manager. The 'in its entirety' requirement means that it is not permissible for heads to delegate the task partially (e.g., by retaining pay progression decisions).

Where a teacher has more than one line manager, the head should delegate the responsibility to the line manager he/she considers best placed to carry out the teacher's review. Where the reviewer is not the teacher's line manager, he/she must have an equivalent or higher status in the school's staffing structure than the teacher's line manager.

Alternative reviewer

In exceptional circumstances and for professional reasons (e.g., where such relationships have become very strained), you may ask the head in writing to appoint an alternative reviewer (of comparable or higher status in the staffing structure than the original reviewer). The head may make a similar request of the chair of governors if he/she feels that one of the appointed governors is unsuitable for professional reasons.

If your request is refused, the head (the chair of governors in the case of the head) should notify you of his/her decision in writing giving the reasons for the refusal and, if asked to do so, attach the original request and the notification of rejection to the PM statement for that cycle.

Preparation for the planning and review meeting and self-evaluation

The performance management process is essentially a professional dialogue and both parties should be ready to engage fully in the process. In preparation for the meeting, the reviewer should ensure that all the relevant contextual documentation is available for the meeting and has been shared with you. The documentation would include:
- a copy of the revised professional standards;
- the pay progression criteria in the STPCD, including the

Employment and Performance

clarification of the application of the criteria (if you are eligible for progression);

- in England, the post-threshold standards (if you are on point M5 or M6 and are soon to be eligible for threshold application);
- the reviewee's job description (portfolio of job descriptions); and
- the school's improvement priorities. The reviewer should also be aware of your career aspirations and have consulted with relevant third parties with direct professional knowledge of you and other line managers on, for example, appropriate objectives for the next cycle, performance/success criteria, evidence to be collected and any support that might be provided.

You should also prepare properly for the meeting and ensure that you have copies of any relevant documentation/evidence. Self-evaluation has an important part to play in the process, but schools may not require any formal or written input. You should have reflected on:

- your achievement in the cycle and the progress made against the agreed performance (success) criteria;
- the impact of any CPD undertaken;
- any issues relating to support that had been promised;
- what you would like to achieve in the next cycle;
- the pay progression criteria in the STPCD (if eligible);
- any professional development needed; and
- your professional/career aspirations.

Planning and review meeting

Planning

At the beginning of the cycle you and your reviewer should meet to consider
and determine:

- your objectives;
- the performance/success criteria for each objective/activity;
- the arrangements for classroom observation (e.g., how many hours, the duration of visits);
- any other evidence that will be taken into account for assessing your overall performance (and the source);
- the support to be provided (if any);
- the timescale;
- any CPD provision;
- your professional aspirations and what you might wish to achieve in the next cycle;
- any pay progression considerations (you are eligible for); and
- how progress will be monitored during the year.

Review

The outcomes of the planning meeting should serve as the agenda for the assessment of performance (unless the statement has been amended as a result of a mid-year meeting). Judgements of performance should be securely based and firmly rooted in evidence. At the review meeting, you both should seek to agree an assessment of the progress made towards the achievement of your objectives and your overall performance against the performance criteria agreed/set at the beginning of the cycle. It is important that the impact of any CPD undertaken

Employment and Performance

is assessed. Where agreement cannot be reached, the reviewer's judgement prevails.

Planning and review statement

The statement is effectively in two parts: the planning component and the assessment of performance. Within five days of the planning and review meeting, the reviewer is required to:

- prepare a draft statement covering the outcomes of the review, an assessment of your performance and any recommendation on pay progression and the items set out as bullet points under 'planning' above;
- include in a separate annex your training and development needs; and
- pass on the draft statement to you.

The statement should be a fair and accurate summary of what took place at the meeting and changes should only be made at this stage if the statement does not convey this properly or where the wording is capable of misinterpretation. Within ten days of the meeting, the reviewer must produce a final version signed by both parties and give a copy to you. You may add your comments. Where this happens, it is the revised statement which must be passed to the head (to the chair of governors (though the regulations state 'to the governing body'), if you are the head) and to you. You may also appeal.

A copy of the training and development annex should be given to the person responsible for planning the training and development of teachers at the school. The statement should be completed by 31 October (31 December in the case of the head).

Objectives

The revised performance management regulations no longer require objectives to be set/agreed in relation to 'school leadership and management' and 'pupil progress' for heads and 'improving and developing professional practice' and 'pupil progress' in the case of classroom teachers. The only proviso is that the teacher's objectives shall be such that, if they are achieved, they will contribute to improving the progress of pupils at the school.

Objectives should be rigorous, challenging, but achievable, time-bound, fair and equitable in relation to teachers with similar roles/responsibilities and experience and reflect the need for a satisfactory work/life balance. The regulations have not imposed a limit on the number of objectives that should be set/agreed, but this should be reasonable. It would be sensible to take the degree of difficulty or challenge entailed in an objective into account when determining the number in particular cases. Similarly, there is no limit on the number of teachers whom a reviewer may performance manage, but this, too, should be reasonable.

The performance management cycle is annual, but it is possible to set/agree objectives over a longer time span. In such a case, the milestones towards the objective to be achieved during the first

Employment and Performance

year should be recorded in the review statement. You should not be held accountable for failing to make good progress towards an objective when the support which had been promised has not materialised.

Though an assessment of overall performance needs to be made at the end of the cycle, objectives cannot be expected to cover the full range of a teacher's roles/ responsibilities. They should only focus on priorities. It must be assumed that those aspects of a teacher's roles/ responsibilities (e.g., the requirements of their job description, the relevant duties and the appropriate professional standards, as well as the pay progression criteria set out in the STPCD in the case of those eligible for progression) that are not covered by the objectives are being carried out satisfactorily. Where during the cycle this proves not to be the case, a meeting should be held to discuss the concerns raised, which could lead to a revised statement, with additional objectives being set/agreed that reflect those concerns.

Performance criteria for each objective must be provided. These should be able to make it clear to you what success against the objective looks like (i.e. what the reviewer is expecting to be achieved and what he/she will take into account at the end of the cycle when making a judgement of progress). Evidence may only be sought from persons (which might include support staff) with a direct professional knowledge of your work. The most important dimension is that you should be fully aware from the outset of what is expected of you, the evidence that will be taken into account and the basis on which judgements will be made at the end of the cycle.

It is good practice for the reviewer and you to agree objectives, but, where this cannot be achieved, the reviewer's decision is final. When objectives are imposed, you will still be expected to do your best to make good progress against the objective set.

Classroom observation

Schools are required to formulate a protocol for classroom observation and to include it in their performance management policy (after due consultation with teachers and unions). All classroom observation should be carried out in accordance with the provisions of the protocol. All such observation should be supportive and developmental and be capable of being used for a variety of purposes (e.g., monitoring and school self evaluation). Observation should reflect your circumstances and be proportionate to individual need, as well as taking account of the school's needs. Observation should have a clear and agreed focus, but this does not prevent some other issues or concerns that emerge during an observation from being properly addressed. Not all of the observations undertaken need to be carried out by the reviewer, but only those with appropriate professional expertise should do so.

A maximum of three hours is specified in the regulations in any single review cycle. This does not

Employment and Performance

mean three observations, as the length of observations is for the school to determine. There is no requirement for all of the three hours to be used, though schools should take care to ensure that both individual and school needs can be met from the amount determined. Peer observation or observation carried out for coaching and mentoring, for example, where teachers work together voluntarily to improve and develop their practice do not count towards the three hours' maximum. Observation carried out by Ofsted (Estyn) or by local authorities by virtue of their statutory powers of intervention also lies outside the scope of the PM regulations.

Heads have a statutory obligation to evaluate the standards of teaching and learning and to ensure that proper standards of professional performance are established and maintained. They, therefore, have the right to drop in on lessons to monitor the quality of teaching and learning in their schools. In large schools this duty may also be delegated to one or more members of the leadership group (who have a responsibility for quality assurance). Where schools feel that their statutory responsibilities can be accommodated within the three hours of observation agreed for performance management, the need for drop-ins may not arise.

If concerns that are serious, but not so serious as to warrant the invocation of capability procedures, emerge during the three hours' observation or drop-in monitoring visits, additional classroom observation that exceeds the three hours within the PM cycle may be determined. Where this happens, the determination should be recorded in a written addition to the review statement following a meeting. You should be provided with oral feedback on the outcomes of all observation within 24 hours and written feedback within 5 days. This should apply to drop-ins, too, though written feedback may only be necessary if the concerns raised are such as to trigger additional observation.

Feedback should summarise the outcome of the observation, any learning points and possible follow-up actions. Judgements of performance should be made in all cases, but how these are graded is for schools to determine.

Heads should ensure that all observers are properly trained and have the skills to provide constructive feedback and support.

Moderation of plans and scope for heads to intervene and change the planning and review statement

Heads are under a statutory duty to ensure that the PM processes and procedures are applied fairly and consistently throughout the school and to have due regard to equal opportunities considerations. How this will be achieved should be spelled out in the school's PM policy and reviewers should be made fully aware of their responsibilities in the matter. As part of the procedures for monitoring and moderating the plans set out in the planning and review

Employment and Performance

statement, heads may review planning and review statements within 10 days of their completion and, where necessary, instruct the reviewer to prepare a new statement prior to it being finalised. Such intervention may only occur at the outset of the process (e.g. with regard to the objectives set/agreed and not in relation to any judgements that may be made at the end of the cycle). Where this happens, following discussions with you, the reviewer should produce a revised statement within 10 days of being asked to do so by the head. You are entitled to add any comments you might wish to make or to appeal against one or more of the entries as with the original statement.

The usual grounds on which the head might insist on a revised statement are that the statement:

- is not consistent with those for other teachers with similar experience and/or similar levels of responsibility; or
- is not in line with the school's PM policy or improvement plan. Heads are not obliged to review planning and review statements – it is their decision – but there is likely to be a greater need for such intervention in the early years of the new arrangements. Moderation might cover all review statements or just a sample.

Mid-year review
There should be a professional dialogue between the reviewer and you throughout the year as a matter of routine, though there is no formal requirement for meetings between the

reviewer and you to be held. It may, however, be necessary to review what has been agreed in the review statement during the cycle when, e.g.:

- your post and/or responsibilities have changed;
- in the event of difficulties in accessing support;
- if you are on maternity leave or on long-term sick leave and some of the entries in the plan are no longer appropriate;
- where concerns (short of capability) about your performance have been registered; or
- where reasonable adjustments are required under the provisions of the **Disability Discrimination Act.**

In such cases, if either the reviewer or you seek a mid-year meeting, it must take place. Any changes to e.g., the objectives, success criteria, classroom observation, the support to be provided or the evidence to be collected must be recorded as a written addition to the review statement (you can make any comments in writing or appeal as in the case of the original statement). Where your responsibilities have changed during the cycle, the head (or the governing body in the case of the head) will determine whether the cycle should begin again and whether to appoint a new reviewer.

Pay recommendations
Any recommendation on pay progression by the reviewer should be passed on unaltered by the head to the governing body, who will continue to be responsible for discretionary pay progression decisions. Such a recommendation only affects the pay of:

Employment and Performance

- post-threshold teachers;
- members of the leadership group; and
- ASTs.

Threshold assessment remains the responsibility of the head and progression on the main scale is not performance-related (you must receive an increment unless you are subject to capability procedures), except in the case of double-jumping, when the reviewer should make a recommendation. Reviewers will need to be properly trained to assume and to discharge such responsibilities and their job descriptions might need to be changed.

Confidentiality
The whole performance management process and in particular the review statements should be treated with confidentiality at all times. Under the new arrangements, your line manager or line managers, in cases where you have more than one line manager, may be given access to the head's copy of the review statement, where this is necessary to enable him/her to carry out his/her line management responsibilities. Line management is defined as 'the direction, management and professional responsibility for staff on a daily basis' and in this context many teachers are likely to have more than one line manager. 'Staff' may include teachers and support staff e.g. a head of science may line manage teachers and technicians. In cases where in a large department/faculty a teacher's reviewer is someone other than the head of department (HOD) or faculty

(HOF), the HOD/HOF will in future, unlike now, be able to access your review statement (as will the non-reviewer HOD/HOF if you work in two or more areas). The governing body or the committee charged with the responsibility for pay decisions shall be provided with access to the review statements when making such decisions.

Head's report
The head is required to produce an annual report for the governing body on the following:

- the operation of the school's performance management policy;
- how effective the school's PM procedures have been during the year; and
- the training and development needs of teachers at the school (the information provided should ensure that no individual can be identified).

Appeals
You may appeal against any of the entries in your statement (or amended statement) in accordance with the school's grievance procedures. Where you wish to appeal on more than one entry, this would still constitute one appeal (i.e., all of the points cited should be heard at the same appeal meeting). The guidance suggests that any appeal should be deferred until after the moderation process has been completed. Simple disagreement should not be regarded as grounds for an appeal. The usual grounds (the list is not intended to be exhaustive), which would reflect a flawed process in some measure, would be similar to

Employment and Performance

those set out in the DCSF model pay policy:

- failure to have proper regard for the regulations;
- incorrect application of the regulations or the provisions of the school's PM policy;
- failure to take proper account of relevant evidence;
- undue reliance on irrelevant or inaccurate evidence;
- bias; or
- unlawful discrimination.

Quick Guides PM1 Performance Management.

B18 DATA PROTECTION

Schools generate and keep a great deal of information about you and about pupils. Data includes any information held whether it is in paper or electronic form, including photographs and CCTV footage. You have a right to know what personal information is being kept about you by the school and/or the LA/DCSF – either on paper or electronically. So do your pupils. Any expressions of opinion about a teacher, or any recorded intentions by the head towards a teacher, count as data for the purposes of the Act.

Principles

The data protection principles, to which all schools must adhere, are that personal data:

- should be processed lawfully and fairly;
- should be held for one or more specified purposes;
- should not be disclosed in any manner incompatible with the purposes for which it is held;
- should be held in such a way that is adequate, relevant and

not excessive for the purposes for which held;

- should be accurate and up-to-date; and
- should not be held longer than necessary. You should be informed regularly by the head about the data being kept about you. You should also be given access to the information, and are entitled, where appropriate, to have any data corrected or erased. If you want a copy of it you should request it in writing and be prepared to pay an appropriate fee (a current maximum of £10). If the school fails to comply with a request for details of the information held, you could seek a court order requiring the school to do so. You should involve your professional association if difficulties arise. You do not have to consent to the information being held, unless it is 'sensitive' material. In this case you must give permission. You must observe the same principles in respect of any information you hold on pupils or contribute to pupils' records.

The school should be taking security measures to guard against unauthorised access to, or alteration to, disclosure or destruction of personal data and against accidental loss or destruction of such personal data. Each school (or LA), as a data user, has to nominate a named person who is responsible for compliance with the provisions.

Damage and distress

You have a right to require the school, in certain cases, not to

Employment and Performance

keep personal details about you, on the grounds that it is likely to cause you or another person substantial unwarranted damage or distress.

Confidential references

Heads can still write confidential references for specified purposes, such as for training or employment. You cannot demand access to these. However, you can access the material on which the reference is based if kept on file. In addition, the head to whom a confidential reference for a job is sent must consider giving access to the information if requested to by the applicant, though it may not be released if the duty of confidentiality prevents it.

Pupil records

Pupils are entitled to the same protection as anyone else and the same care should be taken with their files. Pupils have the right of access to examination marks no later than 5 months from the date of their request, or 40 days from the announcement of the results, whichever is shorter. The practice of returning candidates' examination papers has clearly added to the whole move towards transparency of personal information.

Monitoring at work

The monitoring at work section of the *Information Commissioners' Code of Practice* does not prevent employers from monitoring their workers' activities e.g. telephone calls and access to the internet, but sets out to regulate them. The underlying intention is to protect employees from unnecessary or unfair intrusion.

In a case decided by the European Court of Human Rights in 2007 **(Copland v United Kingdom),** it was ruled that the right to respect for private life of an FE College employee had been violated by the monitoring of her emails and phone calls. However, at the time when this was done there was no British legislation to allow monitoring by employers and part of the ground for the decision was that it was not 'in accordance with law.' Since the case began there has been such legislation and an employer is now entitled to monitor provided that it is for a legitimate purpose (e.g. to prevent employees from misusing the employer's equipment) and so long as employees are told that monitoring may be undertaken and they therefore have no expectation that their communications will be private.

Computer misuse

It is a criminal offence to access computer material without authorisation and to modify any material held on a computer without authorisation.

National Pupil Database (NPD) in Wales

The Assembly Government introduced a programme in 2005 aiming to develop the use of information systems for school management and administration. The database links pupil data collected through the *Pupil Level Annual School Census* (PLASC) with data on pupil attainment to create educational profiles of the school population to promote the recognition and the sharing of good practice to support self-evaluation and development and encourage the appropriate use of data to raise standards.

Data Protection Act 1984 and 1998. Data Protection (Subject Access Modification) (Education) Order 2000 – provides that individuals do not have a right to access some records. The Code of Practice and other information can be viewed at: www.ico.gov.uk . ***The Computer Misuse Act 1990.***

The DCSF has issued for LAs and schools **Guidance on the collection and recording of data on pupils' ethnic background** (in compliance with the Data Protection Act) - ***DfES 0002/2002.***

Quick Guides DA2A Data Protection and Confidentiality Policy.

B19 PARENTS' EVENINGS

You are obliged to attend parents' evenings so long as these form part of your directed time (i.e. within your 1265 hours of time to be worked under the direction of the head). Part-time teachers should determine with the head at the time of appointment contract what the expectation is. Parents now have access to a DCSF website suggesting questions that they might ask at parents' evenings, such as 'does my child's behaviour give cause for concern?' at www.parentcentre.gov.uk.

B20 LEAVE OF ABSENCE

Whichever type of school and college you work in you are entitled to statutory time off for specific purposes. There is a national agreement for schools where the LA is the employer called 'the Burgundy Book.' This may have transferred to schools where the LA is not the employer under the TUPE Regulations. In addition LAs, schools and colleges can have their own policies for additional discretionary leave of absence. *(For sick leave see B24 and sick pay see B25).*

Quick Guides Leave of Absence (LA) Section .

....WITH PAY

Trade union duties

Reasonable time off work for office holders (below) to perform trade union duties and to undergo training for trade union duties should be provided.

Although the time off is a right, the requests must be 'reasonable'. The school is not bound to grant a request, if the absence will cause damage to the service provided by the school, which could be avoided if permission was given for the time off to be taken at a different time.

Union learning representative

A union learning representative (ULR) is a category of union representative. They are trained in advising members on learning needs and opportunities. They are entitled to reasonable time off with pay to carry out their duties and to take part in relevant training.

Elected employee representatives

An elected employee representative (whether a member of a trade union or not) must be allowed time off with pay to perform his/her function if

Employment and Performance

there are proposed redundancies or transfer of undertakings.

Employees made redundant

If you have been continuously employed for two years or more and are made redundant, you must be given reasonable time off to arrange training or look for a new job. Seeking work can include perusal of newspapers in a local library, attending careers interviews, or even a door-to-door search.

Ante-natal care

A pregnant woman who has made an appointment to receive ante-natal care on the advice of a registered medical practitioner, registered midwife, or registered health worker, has the right to take time off to attend the session, provided that, if her employer requests it, she produces evidence of the appointment, and except for the first appointment, produces a certificate stating that she is pregnant.

....WITHOUT PAY

The law requires that 'reasonable' time off without pay should be granted in the following circumstances:

Trade union activities

Members of recognised trade unions are entitled to reasonable time off without pay during working hours to take part in union activities. The *Employment Rights Act 1996* does not specify what constitutes 'union activity', except to say that industrial action is not included. But union meetings are probably included, although the purpose for the time off need not be directly connected with school business.

Other trade union activities might be:

- taking out a grievance according to the school's procedures;
- membership of an employment tribunal;
- taking part in a union conference; or
- taking part in a union election.

ACAS Code of Practice on Time Off for Trade Union Duties and Activities gives guidance on the question of how much time off, and the problem of what might constitute union activity (for example, voting on industrial action) at: www.acas.org.uk.

Public duties

The following must be allowed reasonable unpaid time off to perform their duties:

- Justices of the Peace;
- Members of LA councils;
- Members of boards of prison visitors;
- Members of a police authority;
- Statutory tribunal members;
- National Rivers Authority members;
- Health Authority members;
- Members of National Health Service Trust; and
- Members of school, college or higher education corporation governing bodies.

Duties include attendance at meetings or any other occasion approved by the body for the purpose of discharging their duties.

Reasonable time

The amount of time off that an employer must allow depends on what is reasonable in the circumstances, having regard to:

- how much time is required;

Employment and Performance

- how much time off the employee has had previously both under this heading and also for any trade union duties and activities; and
- the school's or college's circumstances.

See DBERR booklet: Time off for public duties (PL 702).

Jury service

You can be called on for jury service and must be allowed time off. Pay is at the discretion of the school. Members of juries are entitled to allowances and expenses. In common with everyone else, school employees can ask to be relieved of the duty. Courts will only grant exemptions for good reasons. They are usually sympathetic if the summons is at a sensitive time when the absence of a teacher might cause particular damage to children's education.

These are minimum statutory requirements. National and local agreements can enhance these: e.g. **Burgundy Book paragraphs 9.3 to 9.6 and Appendices IV and V. Appendix V of the Burgundy Book** define what schools should consider, as do other locally-negotiated agreements. Further guidance is available in the **ACAS Code of Practice on Time Off for Trade Union Duties and Activities. Employment Rights Act 1996. Quick Guides Leave of Absence (LA) Section.**

B21 PARENTING RIGHTS

Maternity leave

All pregnant women regardless of length of service are entitled to 26 weeks' ordinary maternity leave (OML), so long as they have given the required notice, and a further entitlement to 26 weeks' unpaid leave (AML). Pregnant employees are entitled up to 39 weeks' statutory maternity pay (SMP). Statutory maternity pay (SMP) was due to increase to 52 weeks by 2010. This has been postponed indefinitely. The employee must give written notice to the school by the end of the 15th week before the expected week of childbirth (EWC):

- that she is pregnant;
- the date of the EWC;
- the date she intends to start maternity leave and her last day at work; and
- the fact that she wishes to be paid SMP.

All maternity, paternity and adoption rights are now available to same-sex couples.

Maternity pay for teaching staff

The current arrangements for maternity pay for teachers in maintained schools where the LA is the employer (based on the Burgundy Book) are as follows:

- Teachers with less than one year's continuous service at the beginning of the 11th week of EWC (expected week of confinement) are only entitled to SMP (statutory maternity pay).
- Teachers who have completed not less than one year's continuous service at the beginning of the 11th week before the EWC are entitled to maternity pay as follows:
  ◊ a teacher eligible for SMP will have the payments made in the first six weeks of absence offset against the payments mentioned below;

Employment and Performance

◊ for the first four weeks' absence – full pay, offset against payments made by way of SMP or maternity allowance (MA) for employees not eligible for SMP: provided that the total weekly payment shall not be less than 9/10ths of a week's salary reduced by the flat-rate maternity allowance;

◊ for the next two weeks' absence – 9/10ths of a week's salary, offset against payments made by way of SMP or MA for employees not eligible for SMP;

◊ for the next 12 weeks of paid absence, half pay without deductions except by the extent to which the combined pay and SMP (or, if not eligible for SMP, maternity allowance and any dependants' allowances) exceeds full pay; and

◊ no pay for any remaining period of absence up to the date of return to work notified by the teacher.

In the event of the teacher not being available, or being unable, to return to her job for the required period following the leave, she must refund such sums as the employer at their discretion may decide. A woman with at least two years' continuous service is entitled to retain the first six weeks' payment. (Payments made by way of SMP are not refundable).

A woman with at least two years' continuous service as a teacher, who does not return to duty for 13 full-time equivalent weeks following maternity leave has the right to retain only the first 6 weeks' payments i.e. the 12 weeks' half pay could be recovered including any NI and tax.

Note: Burgundy Book conditions only apply in schools where the LA is the employer if continuous service has been in a school or schools where the LA is the employer.

See the booklet **Maternity rights (PL958)** available from **DBERR Publications, Tel: 08701502500 or visit** www.berr.gov.uk/publications/ and go to: www.direct.gov.uk/en/Parents/Moneyandworkentitlements/work and families/pregnancyandmaternityrights/index.htm.
The Maternity Alliance also offers advice: **Tel: 020 7490 7638.**

Adoptive parents
Adoptive parents have similar rights as the above where a child is newly placed. Adoption leave can be taken by either parent, and same-sex parents.
Statutory adoption pay (SAP) is paid for the first 39 weeks, followed by an entitlement to an additional 13 weeks' unpaid leave. You must have had 26 weeks' service with the employer by the week in which the approved adoption agency matches the employee and child. The rate for SAP changes annually on 1 April – **check the benefits section of** www.direct.gov.uk The rate is as stated, or 90% of gross average weekly pay, whichever is the lower.
Booklets: Adoptive parents: rights to leave and pay - a guide for employers and employees

Employment and Performance

(PL518), and, *Adoptive parents; rights to leave and pay – a basic summary (PL515)*. www.berr.gov.uk .

'Keeping in touch' days

The Work and Families Act 2006 introduced 'keeping in touch days'. Employees on maternity or adoption leave can undertake up to 10 days' paid work by agreement with the employer during their leave period without terminating it. Work includes training or any other activity to help the employee keep in touch with the workplace. The employer cannot require the employee to work this way and the employee cannot be penalized for not doing so. *The Work and Families Act 2006* also allows reasonable contact between employer and employee during maternity leave. There may be important information to be shared or return to work arrangements to be discussed.

Paternity rights

New paternity rights are available to fathers who have had 26 weeks' service at the 15th week before the expected week of the mother's confinement. Paternity leave is up to two weeks' paid leave, in addition to the current entitlement to 13 weeks' unpaid parental leave. It can only be taken for the purpose of caring for the new-born or adopted child and supporting the mother. The rate for statutory paternity pay changes annually on 1 April – *check the benefits section of* www.direct.gov.uk. The rate is as stated, or 90% of gross average weekly pay, whichever is the lower. In 2009 the government consulted on draft regulations to introduce additional paternity leave for fathers of children due on or after April 2011. This will be up to six months' extra leave which can be taken once the mother has returned to work.

Parental leave

If you are a parent of a child under 5 (under 18 if disabled, or within 5 years of adoption) you are entitled to have 13 weeks' leave of absence to care for the child, spread over five years. You can take it in blocks of no less than one week or more than four weeks in a calendar year. You can, in fact, take just one or two days off school, but any period less than a week will count as one week of your entitlement. If you have more than one child under 5 the right is the same for each child. The employer can also postpone the leave up to six months if there is a good reason for doing so, unless the leave immediately follows a birth or adoption. Whether or not it is paid leave will depend on your employer. These are the minimum rights. Schools can negotiate better entitlements with the staff. *Employment Relations Act 1999.*
Quick Guides LA5 Parental Leave: Points of Law.

Dependants' leave

You are also entitled to take 'reasonable' time off during working hours:

- to look after a dependant who falls ill, is injured or gives birth;
- to deal with an unexpected incident involving your child; or
- to deal with the death of a dependant. A dependant is defined as a spouse, child, parent or person who lives in

Employment and Performance

the same household (other than as a tenant or lodger or boarder or employee).

A court has determined that this time off is intended to be for emergencies. It is not a substitute for effective childcare arrangements. The right does not stretch to mending leaking pipes! Such leave of absence for personal emergencies is at the discretion of the school.

In a significant case a Mrs Harrison worked part-time for a bank. Her childminder told her that she would not be available. Mrs Harrison tried to make other arrangements. She failed. When she took the time off, she was given a verbal warning to lie on her record for 6 months and her appeal against that failed. The EAT found there was no justification to import the word 'sudden' to qualify 'unexpected'. Mrs Harrison had not previously taken so much time that this one day could make her time off amount to 'unreasonable time'.

Employment Relations Act 1999. Work and Families Act 2006.
www.direct.gov.uk.
Quick Guides LA4 Dependants' and Carers' Leave: Points of Law.

B22 FLEXIBLE WORKING

If you look after a child under 17 (or up to 18 in the case of disabled children), you are able to ask the school to consider changing your working arrangements to enable you to take care of the child. This right is not necessarily just for one of the parents. It could be a grandparent, who looks after a child. Employers must give serious consideration to any request for a change in hours of work, times of work, whether they can work at home, or any other aspect of the conditions of service. If granted this will be a change of contract and permanent. There is now a similar right for an employee who wishes to care for a sick, elderly or disabled adult, who is a spouse, or partner, a near relative (e.g. parents, grandparents or sibling) or someone who is living at the same address as the employee. There is no minimum level of care required to qualify. It can include personal care, or help with mobility.

Process
You must apply to the head in writing, detailing the work pattern that you wish to adopt, and explaining the effect that the changes might have. You must also state whether a previous application has been made and when. The head may have the delegated power to deal with the request, or might have to refer it to the governing body. The school has 28 days in which to arrange to meet you to discuss the request. The meeting should explore the relevant issues, and any alternatives. If the application is rejected it can only be for a permitted reason with an explanation. The permitted reasons are:

- the burden of additional costs;
- detrimental effect on ability to meet customer demands;
- inability to re-organise work among existing staff or recruit additional staff;

Employment and Performance

- detrimental impact on quality or performance;
- insufficiency of work during the periods the employee proposes to work; and
- planned structural changes.

You have a right of appeal within 14 days.

In a landmark case the European Court of Justice ruled that a parent with a disabled child had been discriminated against on grounds of disability because she had been harassed and otherwise discriminated against for taking time off to look after him. This judgement, which establishes discrimination by association with a person who is disabled, suggests that caring for any person where that person may be protected by discrimination law will be protected and widens the range of flexible working claims. **(Coleman v Attridge Law)**

Employment Act 2002. Employment Relations Act 1999 for parental leave rights and dependants' rights. Flexible Working (Eligibility, Complaints and Remedies) Regulations 2002. Flexible Working (Procedural Requirements) Regulations 2002. DBERR booklet: Flexible working: The right to request and the duty to consider (now only available in internet copy form) *at*:
www.berr.gov.uk/whatwedo/employment/employmentlegislation/employment -guidance/page35663.html.

For advice from ACAS tel: 08457 474747, or refer to their website at: www.acas.org.uk.
Quick Guides LA6 Family Friendly Rights: Maternity, Paternity, Adoption; LA4 Dependants' and Carers' Leave: Points of Law.

B23 CAPABILITY

Teachers, like all other employees, have to be capable of doing the job they are contracted to do. This means, to begin with, holding the relevant qualifications for teacher status (QTS), and maintaining your capability while you are in work - by appropriate training, studying or experience. Teachers are expected to:

- be able to communicate effectively;
- possess sound judgment and insight;
- remain alert at all times;
- be able to respond to pupils' needs rapidly; and
- be able to manage classes.

If your capability to perform your duties is called into question the school must do what it can to help and support you. But in the end it is you that must make the improvement. Consequently it is likely that the school will invoke the capability procedures. These will have been set by the governing body (usually based on the LA's recommended policy), and must be made known to the staff.

In 2000 the government in co-operation with the teaching unions produced a model policy. LAs, church authorities and maintained school governing

Employment and Performance

bodies must have regard to this guidance when constructing or reviewing their policies and when dealing with any lack of capability in teaching staff in maintained schools. Independent schools may publish their own procedures.

School Staffing (England) Regulations 2009. Model Capability Procedures (Guidance 0125/2000).
For Welsh Regulations refer to Regulations Section in B5.
Quick Guides Capability Procedures (C) Section.

B24 SICK LEAVE

A teacher absent from school is deemed to be absent without leave until he/she notifies the school. Teachers must 'self-certify' a sickness absence which lasts more than 3 days. A doctor's certificate will be required for illnesses lasting longer than 7 calendar days. It should be sent to the school on the eighth day of absence. If your absence from a maintained school continues into a school holiday period you must notify the school when you are fit again. This enables the employer to make statutory sick pay (SSP) adjustments. If you teach in an independent school you may be subject to the same rule in your contract.

On return to work after a prolonged illness you should hand to the school a medical certificate to say that you are fit for work. A teacher has to meet standards of health to be permitted to teach. These apply before joining the profession and once employment has begun. If you have a prolonged single absence, or have many short but frequent absences, you may be required to submit to a medical examination at the employer's initiative to ensure that you are still fit to teach. There is no definition of 'prolonged', but it is likely to be required after a three-month absence.

Governing bodies and LAs may also refer teachers to the Occupational Health Service. Teachers, too, may refer themselves to the Occupational Health Service.

There is a duty on the employer to make reasonable adjustments to enable disabled teachers to continue to teach but if none can be made the teacher may be dismissed. *(See below B29 Fitness to Teach; and C7 Disability.*
Quick Guides Absence through Ill Health (AB) Section includes a model policy.

B25 SICK PAY

All employers must pay statutory sick pay (SSP) for periods up to 28 weeks.

Teachers in maintained schools, and many independent schools, have arrangements that are better than the statutory minimum. According to the agreement between local authorities and unions set out in the Burgundy Book (conditions of service of school teachers in England and Wales), available in all maintained schools, a teacher is entitled to the following in any period of one year:
- 1st year of service: full pay for 25 days, and after completing

4 calendar months' service, half pay for 50 working days;

- 2nd year of service: full pay for 50 working days and half pay for 50 working days;
- 3rd year of service: full pay for 75 working days, half pay for 75 working days;
- 4th and successive years: full pay for 100 working days, half pay for 100 working days. The rate for statutory sick pay changes on 1 April annually. **See the benefits section of** www.direct.gov.uk .

To calculate average earnings for statutory sick pay purposes monthly paid employees should add the payments made in the two monthly pay periods before the beginning of the period of incapacity for work (PIW), multiply by six and divide the total by 52. This will be the basic sick pay, to which should be added any earnings from an occupational pensions scheme. An employee reaches the maximum entitlement to SSP in one spell of incapacity when he/she has been paid 28 times the rate i.e. the rate from 2 April of the year in question. *Quick Guides Pay (PAY) Section.*

B26 MISCONDUCT AND DISCIPLINARY PROCEDURES

You are expected to meet professional standards appropriate to your responsibilities and experience and to behave in a professional manner. All schools must have disciplinary procedures. Many LAs will recommend procedures to maintained schools but it has to be the governing body which adopts them as it exercises disciplinary

powers. All procedures will be based on those recommended by the Advisory, Conciliation and Arbitration Service (ACAS) in its **Code of Practice on Disciplinary Practice and Procedures at Work**. The minimum discipline/grievance and dispute resolution procedures introduced via the **Employment Act 2002** were abolished and replaced by a revised ACAS Code of Practice from April 2009. If an employer does not comply with the Code reasonably this may lead to a 25% uplift in an award at Employment Tribunal. **Employment Act 2009.**

> **The school's procedures will include information on the following:**
> - oral warnings;
> - written warning;
> - final written warning;
> - consideration of dismissal;
> - facilities for appealing against any of the warnings; and
> - what constitutes gross misconduct.

Responsibilities for exercising disciplinary procedures in maintained schools can now be delegated by the governing body, to the head alone, or a committee of governors, or to named governors.

Suspension

In maintained schools the head and governing body have the power to suspend a teacher without loss of pay, where in their opinion, the exclusion is necessary because there is an allegation of gross misconduct which needs to be investigated or 'good and urgent cause.'

Employment and Performance

Suspension is often stated to be a neutral act (not statement of belief of guilt) pending the completion of an investigation. However, in a judgement in the Court of Appeal the judges agreed that this was not so. If you are in danger of suspension you should immediately contact your union. The investigation should be concluded as soon as it is reasonably practicable. A suspension can only be ended by the governing body. In general suspension is only justified where the person concerned might otherwise do harm to person or property; destroy or corrupt evidence; or otherwise prevent a fair investigation.

School Staffing Regulations (England) 2009.
For Welsh Regulations refer to Regulations Section in B5.
Quick Guides Discipline (D) Section.

Sexual offences

The **Sexual Offences Act 2003** covers sexual offences by a teacher, or any other person who works in a college/school, who is a person in a 'position of trust, i.e. 'who looks after children under 18 who are receiving education at an educational institution where the victim is receiving education and the offender is not receiving education'. 'Sexual offences' have been widely interpreted by the courts. **Sexual Offences Act 2003.**
Quick Guides Discipline (D) Section.

B27 POWERS OF DISMISSAL

An employer or employee may terminate a contract with notice. An employer may terminate a contract with notice and offer re-employment on different terms. **Fair dismissals can only be on the grounds of:**

- retirement;
- redundancy;
- capability;
- misconduct;
- contravention of a statutory duty; or
- some other substantial reason.

Under the 2003 regulations the governing body of a maintained school can determine that either the head or a committee of governors advised by the head can terminate a teacher's employment at the school. Appeals can be made to a governing body's Appeals Committee. The school dismissal policy will generally allow the Appeals Committee to uphold the decision, or to substitute a lower penalty, or quash the decision entirely, but cannot substitute a higher penalty.

Retirement

Employers can fairly retire employees at or above age 65 provided they follow a statutory retirement procedure which enables the employee to request to continue working beyond the intended retirement date.

Independent schools

It is usual for the disciplinary procedures to be delegated to the head, with an appeal to the governing body. The school's procedures must be conformable with the ACAS code of Practice.

Employment and Performance

Right to be accompanied

The teacher is entitled to be accompanied by a suitably trained and certified trade union official, or fellow worker at any of the hearings concerned with a disciplinary issue. This does not apply to investigatory meetings. The companion may address the hearing but cannot answer questions on the employee's behalf. The hearing can be postponed if the companion is unavailable. The teacher must offer an alternative date within 5 working days of the original date.

In 2002 the dismissal on the grounds of gross misconduct of a teacher who had worked in a hair salon during school time was upheld by the Court of Appeal. The teacher had telephoned the school on a Friday to say that she was ill but would return to school on the Monday following. The head was suspicious and with another colleague saw the teacher at the salon where she was working. Dismissal followed further investigation and disciplinary proceedings. The teacher contended that the tribunals had not given sufficient consideration to alternative sanctions that the governing body might have applied, but the Appeal Court said that it was sufficient for the tribunals to consider what the governing body did and not what it might have done. The Appeal Court held that the governing body's decision (that the woman's misconduct was a sufficient reason for dismissal) fell within the range of reasonable responses permitted to the employers.

A music teacher, who had caused an injury to a girl pupil when ejecting her from his classroom, was dismissed by the governing body for gross misconduct. The Employment Tribunal to which he took his case held that the dismissal was unfair as it did not fall in the 'range of reasonable responses' that could be expected of the governing body. The law entitled the music teacher to use reasonable force to uphold discipline, and this right had not been prohibited by the governing body, which it could have been. The LA's appeal to the EAT failed.

In a landmark case the Appeal Court ruled that where the governors' hearing meant a reference to a barring body without further consideration of the evidence, a teacher is entitled to legal representation in the governors' hearing. **(R v Governors of X School).** This has been reinforced in a similar case involving the medical profession.

Education (School Government) Regulations 1999. s10 Employment Rights Act 1999 Right of the teacher's representative to speak at hearings. The School Staffing (England) Regulations 2009 allow the governing body of a maintained school to delegate discipline and dismissal of staff to the head or a committee of governors.
For Welsh Regulations refer to Regulations Section in B5.

Quick Guides Discipline (D) Section contains a summary

Employment and Performance

of requirements and model procedures.

Also see www.cesew.org.uk and navigate from the home page**.**

In 2004 a primary school head, who had been head of the school for some ten years, was sacked after critical Ofsted and LA inspection reports. She was dismissed without notice. The LA, it was reported, even changed the locks on the doors of the school to keep her out. An employment tribunal decided that dismissing a head, against whom there had been no previous criticism over a ten-year period, was unreasonable. In addition the LA had not followed its own dismissal procedures. The tribunal chair said that it was extremely unusual for an employer to dismiss an employee without first telling an employee of its concerns and giving a warning of the possibility of dismissal, and an opportunity to improve performance.

After dismissal or resignation before dismissal
What happens to those deemed unsuitable to work with children?

A teacher or other school employee who has a criminal conviction or caution will appear on the CRB check-list. If a teacher has been dismissed for misconduct, or has resigned in circumstances where misconduct was an issue, he/she will be reported to the GTC and/or the ISA and might be placed on the barred **List of Persons Considered Unsuitable to Work with Children**. It is a criminal offence for an independent school as well as maintained schools to employ a person who is on the list. **(See section B6 above).**

Role of the General Teaching Councils

The GTCE and GTCW are responsible for the registration of teachers and can withdraw the registration on the grounds of unacceptable professional conduct or serious professional incompetence or where a teacher has been convicted of a relevant offence.

The Secretary of State and the Welsh Assembly are responsible for taking action when the misconduct involves the safety and welfare of children.

The GTCs can stipulate that teachers receive some form of support. Their menu of orders ranges from outright prohibition to a conditional registration order which can include, for example, a requirement for psychiatric help or extra training. The GTCs can also issue reprimands, which stay in place for two years, and may be taken into account if the teacher reappears before a council disciplinary panel. In England, employers have a duty to refer cases direct to the GTC that fall within its remit. Those cases of misconduct that are not to do with the safety and welfare of children are passed to the GTCs.

The GTCE appoints a panel of three, two teachers plus one lay person, to hear the cases. They are advised by a legal expert, but the panel makes the decision, based on the teacher's professional experience balanced

Employment and Performance

by the lay input. The GTCW has a similar constitution.

A teacher who was often absent from school without leave, planned her lessons inadequately and failed to organise an inter-school sports event which ended in chaos, also left a student teacher in charge of her class. Eventually she resigned after she had not met targets to improve attendance and lesson planning. She was found guilty by the GTCE of unacceptable professional conduct. She was given a two-year registration order, which means that she has to make reports on her attendance and planning to the head and GTCE every term.

A deputy head who failed to plan lessons or mark pupils' books was also found guilty of unacceptable professional conduct by the GTCE. He was given a conditional registration order, banning him from holding a school management position for two years. He must also report to the GTCE once a term for six terms with evidence of improvement in planning, meeting deadlines, monitoring assessment, and IT skills.

A teacher who failed to meet performance targets was found by the GTCE not to be guilty of professional incompetence. The school claimed that failings were found in her lesson delivery, planning and attainment. The school's doubt about her performance was also confirmed by Ofsted. The GTCE panel felt that although she failed to meet the criteria for effective learning she did not fall below the level required for a teacher. The panel concluded that the facts did not amount to serious professional incompetence. The teacher had, however, resigned before the school had completed the capability proceedings against her.

A teacher who viewed internet pornography during working hours in a unit for difficult pupils was found guilty by the GTCE of unacceptable professional conduct. The material was of, and for, consenting adults, and was not, therefore reported to the police. But the material was considered by the school to be 'pretty offensive'. He resigned from his post, but the matter was reported, as required by the regulations, to the GTC. He was given a conditional five-year registration order. If he returns to teaching, any employer must monitor his internet use and send an annual report to the GTC.

Quick Guides Termination of Employment (T) Section.

B28 WHISTLEBLOWING

You may come into possession of information which you believe suggests that a crime is being committed in school or the school is not fulfilling its legal obligations. You are entitled to raise this with your line manager or to go above him or her if you believe that they will do nothing or destroy evidence. The *Public Interest Disclosure Act 1998* sets out to protect individuals who make certain disclosures of information

Employment and Performance

in the public interest. It is known popularly as 'the whistleblowers' charter'. Your school should have a policy and it should have been brought to your attention. If you go beyond your line manager or outside the school you must make the disclosure in good faith (i.e. not for personal spite) and not for gain and must reasonably believe that it is substantially true and that the law is being broken.

Implications for schools

The legislation leaves heads and governing bodies open to unfounded allegations, but the Act makes clear that 'whistleblowers' have to be squeaky clean or relief by a court will be denied them. All LAs should now have 'confidential reporting policies' which must be observed by community and controlled schools. Foundation and aided schools, city academies and city technology colleges, and independent schools can follow LA policies or develop their own.

In 2004 a teacher reported his deputy head for smoking in classrooms to the head. He claimed that the head did nothing to remedy this and he was subsequently made redundant. He claimed unfair dismissal and, although an employment tribunal upheld the school's decision, an appeal tribunal considered that the original decision was flawed and recommended that a fresh tribunal should re-hear the case.

In 2006 a technology teacher in an ICT department complained that the computer system was insecure and put the school in breach of the Data Protection Act. To prove that he had a valid case, he deliberately broke into the system. The school had to shut it down at a cost of around £1000. The teacher was disciplined and resigned in protest. The court said that the whistleblowing legislation protects employees from discrimination after a disclosure, but it cannot sanction what would have otherwise been misconduct or illegality by a member of staff looking to justify whistleblowing. In a case in Derbyshire an employee of an unemployed workers centre was refused protection because the EAT decided that she had been driven by malice and not by public interest.

Public Interest Disclosure Act 1998. Public Concern at Work, is based at **Suite 301, 16 Baldwin Gardens, London EC1N 7RJ; Tel: 0207404 6609; Fax: 020 74046576,** www.pcaw.co.uk *Redress* is an organisation that provides personal support for teachers. **Tel: 01405 764 432.**
Circular 36/07 Procedure for Whistleblowing in Schools and Model Policy.
Quick Guides DA5 Example of a Policy on Public Interest Disclosures: A Whistleblowing Policy.

B29 FITNESS TO TEACH

In addition to the qualifications to teach, teachers must also be fit to teach. Schools and LAs have a statutory responsibility to safeguard teachers' health, safety and welfare and to conduct risk assessments. Teachers, as employees, are also required to do what they can to maintain their

Employment and Performance

own fitness to teach. This means that teachers should:

- have the health and well-being necessary for their specific teaching responsibilities and associated duties;
- not constitute a risk to health or safety of the children in their care; and
- be enabled, where there is a disability, to meet these criteria by reasonable adjustments where these are possible.

There is no obligation on the employer to employ you if no reasonable adjustment can be made to enable you to continue to teach.

Responsibilities

The qualifications and fitness to teach in a community or voluntary controlled school is the responsibility of the LA. In other schools it is the governing body's responsibility.

Referral

When a school is concerned about a teacher's fitness, a referral should be made to the Occupational Health Service (OHS) or a medical adviser, who will make an assessment and report on the person's fitness to continue teaching. The OHS or medical adviser will advise the school on the likely duration of any absence, and whether the teacher will be able to resume full teaching duties or whether there will be permanent or temporary restrictions. The aim should be to produce a report, which will benefit the individual and the school. It is up to the governing body to make decisions about the employment of the teacher based on the advice received.

Suspension on medical grounds

Governing bodies and heads have the power to suspend teachers on medical grounds, but must first seek advice from the medical adviser, unless the circumstances dictate that emergency action has to be taken without the advice.

Barring on the grounds of ill-health

The Secretary of State can make directions barring a teacher from teaching, or impose restrictions, on medical grounds.

Retirement on the grounds of ill-health

The Teachers' Pension Scheme's criteria require that retirement on the grounds of ill-health can only be granted to teachers who are 'permanently unfit'. The DCSF makes the decision on the basis of a recommendation from a panel of independent medical advisers.

Supply teacher agencies

The agency is responsible for determining the medical fitness of teachers.

Circular 4/99: Physical and Mental Fitness to Teach of Teachers (guidance on procedures for assessing the physical and mental fitness to teach). Fitness to Teach Guidance DCSF 2007. www.teachernet.gov.uk.

Quick Guides Discipline (D) Section contains a summary and model procedures.

B30 GRIEVANCES

If you are concerned about how you have been treated in school

Employment and Performance

and cannot sort out the problem informally you have a right to invoke the school's grievance procedures, which all schools are now obliged to have. The statutory grievance procedures have been repealed and replaced by a Code of Practice devised by ACAS. Procedures in maintained schools should not unreasonably depart from the minimum standards in the Code of Practice. A failure by either the school or the aggrieved person to follow the procedure may result in a 25% adjustment to any award at employment tribunal. If you believe you have grounds for a grievance consult your union representative.

Schedule 2 of the Employment Act 2002. School Staffing (England) Regulations 2009. www.acas.org.uk/dgcode2009. *For Welsh Regulations refer to Regulations Section in B5. Quick Guides Grievances (G) Section.*

B31 TRADE DISPUTES

School staff can take industrial action (a strike, or industrial action short of a strike) with 'immunity' from a civil action for damages, if it follows from a majority result in a secret ballot held at the school, and relates wholly or mainly to:

- conditions of employment;
- engagement or suspension of employment;
- allocation of duties;
- discipline imposed by the employer;
- membership of a trade union;
- facilities for trade unions; or
- consultation machinery.

A recognised trade union can hold the ballot on school premises on request, so long as it is reasonably practicable to do so.

A period of strike action is not considered as qualifying service for the pension purposes and may affect the date when you can retire.

A ballot is only valid for a relatively short period of time (depending upon discussion between the union and employer) and action taken after the ballot has expired without a subsequent ballot is not protected.

An employer may refuse to accept the imperfect fulfilment of a contract (e.g. by a work to rule) and deduct pay for the day on which it takes place.

In 2003 the House of Lords decided that the refusal of school staff to teach a pupil reinstated after a permanent exclusion amounted to a trade dispute concerning conditions of employment, which could properly lead to a secret ballot. In a more recent case it has been decided that the head may act as if a ballot has taken place if he is genuinely sure that a ballot, if taken, will lead to industrial action. He does not have to wait until there has been a complete breakdown in relationships before acting.

Contact details of my union representatives:

Employment and Performance

The Advisory, Conciliation and Arbitration Service (ACAS) offers assistance and advice in resolving disputes. Its advice on resolving disputes between individuals and groups can be found on the ACAS website at: www.acas.org.uk.
Quick Guides G3 Grievances: Trade Disputes.

B32 PERSONAL PROPERTY

LA's/schools do not usually insure teachers' personal property, but may make ex gratia payments if personal property is damaged. You should ensure that your domestic insurance covers you for any loss or damage to your property that occurs at school.

If you do sustain loss or damage to your property and wish to make a claim you must give a detailed report to your employer specifying:
* the nature of the loss or damage;
* amount of loss/damage (with any available receipts);
* the circumstances; and
* reasons for believing that a claim is justified.

B33 RESIGNATION DATES

When you obtain a post at another school, or decide to retire, or to leave the profession for some other reason you have to resign formally. You are obliged to give the notice required in your contract of employment. This is 2 months in the autumn and spring terms and 3 months in the summer term. (For headteachers it is 3 and 4 months respectively). If you teach in an independent

school, you will need to ascertain what this is. In maintained schools in England and Wales there are three resignation dates which apply regardless of the actual end of term:
* 31 December (notice to be given by the end of October);
* 30 April (notice to be given by the end of February); and
* 31 August (notice to be given by the end of May).

B34 REDUNDANCY

Redundancy occurs when the need for a particular kind of work ceases or diminishes. In the first instance it is a post which becomes redundant, not a particular person. Any subsequent dismissal of a teacher on the grounds of redundancy must be caused wholly or mainly by the diminution of the work to be done. Once the need to cut down the work has been established, a rigorous process begins in which the union representatives play a major role. If you find yourself threatened by redundancy you should seek early union advice.
Quick Guides Redundancy (R) Section.

B35 CHARTERED LONDON TEACHER STATUS (CLTS)

Teachers serving in inner or outer London areas, who wish to apply for CLTS, must register their intention to do so with the Secretary of State. If the teacher meets the required standards during the relevant period he/she will be awarded CLTS and paid an additional £1000 one-off sum in the year in which he/she receives the award. *The standards may be*

Employment and Performance

found in Annex 1 Section 2 of the STPCD 2009.
Quick Guides PAY22 Chartered London Teacher Status.

B36 EMPLOYMENT TRIBUNALS

There are 25 regional tribunal offices in England, Wales and Scotland. If you have an employment dispute that you have not been able to resolve you can make an employment tribunal claim to your local tribunal office. Contact you union. There are deadlines for submitting claims. Your claim can be sent electronically or in a paper copy. Once the tribunal has accepted your claim a copy is sent to the employer, the respondent, who must reply within 28 days or their response will not be accepted and a default judgement issued unless the tribunal has granted an extension. The tribunal also sends a copy of your claim to ACAS, the independent conciliation service, and they will help you reach an agreed settlement if both parties wish to do this.

Employment tribunal hearings are in public before a panel of three, one of whom is a qualified lawyer, the tribunal judge. Some cases are before the tribunal judge alone. The tribunal can award compensation and can also make re-instatement or re-engagement orders but the employer does not have to action these orders if it is not reasonable practicable to do so. It is unusual for costs to be awarded. You can claim some travel expenses and subsistence for tribunal hearings.

An appeal against a tribunal decision is made to the Employment Appeal Tribunal based in London and Edinburgh. ***Employment tribunal booklets: Making a Claim to an Employment Tribunal, Your Claim: What Happens Next, The Hearing, The Judgment.*** www.employmenttribunals.gov.uk.

B37 HIGHER LEVEL TEACHING ASSISTANTS (HLTAs)
Background

Higher level teaching assistants (HLTAs) came into being as a result of the National Agreement in 2003. A key focus of the Agreement was the use of HLTAs to undertake an enhanced role in the classroom, particularly, but not exclusively, in primary schools, where they would be able to take whole classes, especially when teachers were having their PPA time. It was, however, envisaged from the outset that HLTAs, besides taking whole classes, would undertake a wide variety of different roles, for example, working across the curriculum, acting as special assistants assigned to a specific subject or department or working with individuals or small groups in a range of settings depending on the needs, type and age-phase of the school.

In order to achieve status (it is not a qualification), aspirants must be assessed successfully against 33 professional standards, covering the requisite professional knowledge, understanding, skills and attributes. The **HLTA Candidate Handbook** provides an overview of the essential steps a candidate needs to follow:

Equal Opportunities

- gaining support from the school;
- securing funding;
- identifying any training needs;
- preparing for assessment;
- completing the assessment process; and
- receiving the outcome and deciding the next steps.

Helpful details are provided on each of the standards relating to:
- its scope (what the standard is about);
- things to consider; and
- examples of appropriate evidence as well as some illustrative case studies.

See Guidance for Schools on Higher Level Teaching Assistant Roles for School Support Staff. http://www.teachernet. gov.uk/ doc/7172/HLTA%20 Guidance.pdf. This states that schools should ensure that HLTA deployment is based on sustained roles which reflect the HLTA standards.

C EQUAL OPPORTUNITIES

Note: The Equality Bill 2009 will become law in 2010. It is principally a consolidation act which pulls together previous legislation. Until it takes effect all other legislation remains in effect and legal actions will be under the previous legislation (which means that cases will continue for at least a year under the old legislation). This section continues to refer to the previous legislation but where the new Act will alter the legal position this is made clear.

C1 DISCRIMINATION

Direct discrimination occurs when someone treats you less favourably than someone else because of a 'protected characteristic' you have. The 'protected characteristics' are:
- age;
- disability;
- gender reassignment;
- marriage or civil partnership;
- race;
- religion or belief;
- sex; and
- sexual orientation.

Indirect discrimination occurs when someone applies to you a provision, criterion or practice which puts you at a particular disadvantage in comparison with people who do not share your protected characteristic and which is not a proportionate means of achieving a legitimate aim. (There is an addition duty in regard to people who are disabled - **see below**). Schools have a legal obligation not to discriminate either directly or indirectly against staff or pupils.

Equality duty
The equality duty goes beyond not discriminating. As a result of the *Equality Acts 2006 and 2004* all public authorities (which includes maintained schools, LAs and, probably, academies and CTCs) must promote equality by devising an equality plan in conjunction with those sharing a protected characteristic and by analysing the consequences of their present and future policies and implementing it. This applies only to race, disability and sex until the new Equality Act becomes law. The new *Equality*

Equal Opportunities

Act 2010 also will impose a duty on local authorities to have regard to the 'desirability of reducing inequalities of outcome that result from socio-economic disadvantage' and in doing so take into account any guidance from ministers.

The Equality and Human Rights Commission (EHRC), which replaced separate bodies for different kinds of discrimination in 2007, oversees the promotion of rights and the elimination of discrimination. *Equality and Human Rights Commission (EHRC)*www.equalityhumanrights.com.

Code of Practice on Employment and Occupation 2004.

C2 HARASSMENT OF STAFF

In general **bullying** at work is defined as 'offensive, intimidating, malicious or insulting behaviour'. **Criminal harassment** is a 'course of conduct' (at least twice) causing alarm or distress. **Discriminatory harassment** is 'unwanted conduct related to a protected characteristic' that violates a person's dignity by that intimidating, hostile, humiliating, degrading or offensive conduct. This conduct can be verbal, non-verbal or physical.

It is unlawful for an employer to bully or otherwise harass an employee. It is also unlawful for an employer to connive at any bullying by employees of another employee e.g. by sending a colleague 'to Coventry'. If you believe that you have been bullied or harassed so that your health has been affected or you are driven out of your job you can seek a remedy in the courts. If it is discriminatory you can also seek legal redress for feelings and a punitive award against your employer. Members of staff whose health has not been affected might also obtain compensation for alleged bullying.

Persistent harassment could amount to a criminal offence, but it is more likely that a school would be sued for damages, which could include an amount for anxiety and any financial loss. Your employer must also protect you from sexual harassment by third parties.

In a landmark case in 2006, an NHS employee was awarded compensation for the employer's breach of statutory duty under the **Protection from Harassment Act** in failing to protect him from harassment by his supervisor. Under this act there is no defence of having taken reasonable steps to prevent harassment. This was confirmed by the House of Lords. A subsequent case has established that to engage the **Protection from Harassment Act** harassment must be at a criminal level but further legal consideration has diluted this ruling. **Protection from Harassment Act 1997.**

If you believe you are being bullied or harassed, consult your union.
ACAS has published guidance on bullying and harassment at work – one for employers and one for employees, with examples of behaviour that employees should find unacceptable. Schools

Equal Opportunities

should have policies to deal with bullying and harassment. **Booklets available from ACAS. Tel: 0870 242 9090.** *Quick Guides Equal opportunities (EO) Section; ST15 Tackling Workplace Bullying.*

C3 RACE RELATIONS

Under Race Relations legislation schools are legally required to make efforts to eliminate unlawful racial discrimination or harassment, promote equality of opportunity and foster good relations between persons of different racial groups. Under the **Education and Inspections Act 2006** schools are required to promote community cohesion. Schools must now have policies for achieving this (inspected by Ofsted) and you must work within the policy. The policy must cover all activities in the school during school hours and authorised school activities outside school hours. The government suggests that one important way of fostering racial equality is to involve parents from all ethnic groups in the school community. *Quick Guides GOV23 Promoting Community Cohesion.*

Burden of proof

The burden of proof in race discrimination cases in tribunals or courts now requires the complainant to prove facts from which discrimination could be inferred and for the tribunal to conclude, if there is no adequate explanation from the employer, that race discrimination has occurred.

Genuine occupational requirements

The regulations specify that there may be a 'genuine occupational requirement'. A tribunal will have to determine whether, in the context of the employment, the race, ethnic or national origin is a genuine occupational requirement and that it is proportionate to apply that requirement in the particular case being considered.

In a case in 2009 a charitable organisation was found to have discriminated by refusing to send a Sudanese national to investigate problems in the Sudan even though they concluded that to do so would limit the value of her work and put her at personal risk. Race as a genuine occupational requirement should be used with extreme care.

A statutory **Code of Practice on Racial Equality in Employment** came into play in Autumn 2004. It gives detailed guidance with examples from actual tribunal cases. *Race Relations Act 1975. Race Relations (Amendment) Act 2000. Race Relations Act 1976 (Amendment) Regulations 2003.*
Equality and Human Rights Commission (EHRC) www.equalityhumanrights.com. *The Runnymede Trust - experts on diversity* www.runnymedetrust.org.
Quick Guides EO3 Equal Opportunities: Promotion of Racial Equality.

Equal Opportunities

C4 SEX, SEXUAL ORIENTATION, AND GENDER REASSIGNMENT DISCRIMINATION

If you can present facts that suggest that you have been discriminated against in any aspect of your employment e.g. pay, promotion, access to training, because of your sex, sexual orientation, marriage, civil partnership or pregnancy it will be up to the school to prove that this is not the case. You will need to identify a 'comparator' of another gender whose treatment is, or would be if he/she existed, better than yours. Similarly, if you are discriminated against because you are undergoing a process of gender reassignment you may have a case.

Protection for pregnancy runs throughout the pregnancy itself and for 26 weeks after delivery or still-birth of a child after 24 weeks of pregnancy.

Sexual harassment

Employers are liable if they allow harassment or fail to take reasonable steps to protect an employee from harassment by a third party on at least two other known occasions.

The Appeal Court has ruled that it is possible to claim harassment on grounds of sexual orientation even if the perception of your sexual orientation is incorrect.

A court has held that an employee who worked in a department where other staff downloaded pornography could claim sexual harassment. This was an extreme case but it is possible that it might apply to milder offensive material e.g. sexually-provoking calendars.

Sex Discrimination Act 1975. Sex Discrimination Act 1986. Employment (Sex Discrimination) Regulations 2005. Protection from Harassment Act 1997.

The Equal Opportunities Commission (EOC) was subsumed into the Equality and Human Rights Commission (EHRC) in 2007. **Website at:** www.equalityhumanrights.com.

Quick Guides Equal Opportunities for Staff (EO; Equal Opportunities for Pupils (EOP) Sections.

In 2005 an Employment Tribunal awarded £34000 compensation to a business manager who was forced to resign because his colleagues repeatedly taunted him about his sexuality. Despite numerous complaints, the employer did nothing about it.

C5 RELIGION OR BELIEF

An employee or prospective employee cannot be treated less favourably on the grounds of religion or belief. The regulations up to 2009 cover an extensive set of circumstances from recruitment and selection to promotion and training.

A school will 'indirectly discriminate' against a teacher if it insists that only a teacher with a particular religion or belief is to be employed. The only defence would be that there was a 'genuine occupational requirement' in that particular job. For example, a Church

Equal Opportunities

school can legitimately insist on some of their teachers belonging to a particular religion, so long as that is the genuine reason. It must be a 'requirement', and not just something that would be preferred. (It will be unlawful for a school, for example, to refuse to appoint a suitably qualified gay teacher just to preserve a particular ethos or belief of the school.

In March 2006 the House of Lords supported a school's refusal to allow a pupil to attend the school unless she wore the prescribed uniform. She had insisted on wearing a jilbab rather than the shalwar kameeze that the governing body, after extensive consultation, had agreed. The girl alleged that the decision breached her right to manifest her religion or belief under article 9 of the European Convention on Human Rights. The House of Lords said that the school was justified in its approach. It had gone to great trouble in devising a uniform policy, which respected Muslim beliefs, but had done so in an inclusive way, which had been acceptable to mainstream Muslim opinion. The policy had played a part in helping the school reach a measure of harmony and success. The rules still appeared to be acceptable to mainstream Muslim opinion. This judgement was extended by a further case in 2007.

A girl demanded to wear the niqab (veil) in school. The school resisted this on the grounds of disunity, interference with teaching and learning and security considerations. The judge ruled in favour of the school. He ruled that a change of uniform regulations since her two sisters had been allowed to wear the veil in the sixth form was legitimate. Also in 2006 an employment tribunal supported a school's no veil policy. A young Muslim teaching assistant was suspended because she would not remove her veil while teaching in the presence of men. Her work was with children from predominantly minority ethnic backgrounds learning English as a second language. The tribunal rejected her claim under the **Human Rights Act** as the school's actions, though preventing the manifestation of her beliefs, were held to be a proportionate way of achieving the legitimate aim of providing unhindered language teaching to young children.

(The DCSF issued updated guidance on school uniform in autumn 2007).
www.teachernet.gov.uk/management/atoz/u/uniform.
Guidance for Governing Bodies on School Uniform and Appearance Policies. January 2008.

In 2007 the Scottish EAT considered the genuine occupational requirement provisions of the religion or belief regulations in a case brought by an atheist teacher working in a local authority maintained Roman Catholic school. He made an internal application for the post of acting principal teacher of pastoral care. He was not offered an interview on the basis that being of the Roman

Equal Opportunities

Catholic faith was a requirement for that post. The EAT looked closely at the job of a pastoral care teacher and decided that it did not require its holder to be a Roman Catholic. In a non-denominational school the post could be held by a person who is not a Roman Catholic and the responsibilities of a pastoral care teacher involved giving advice on a large number of issues on which the doctrine of the Roman Catholic Church was not relevant. The teacher was awarded £2000 compensation for injury to feelings caused by religious discrimination.

Victimisation

The law also offers protection against victimisation related to discrimination. Victimisation occurs when someone is treated less favourably because they have exercised a right to use procedures or give information about discrimination. For example, in the second 'veil' case referred to above the tribunal did uphold a victimisation claim. There was a change of attitude to the claimant after she complained of discrimination. She submitted a grievance but got no response. She was awarded £1000 for injury to feelings, increased by 10% because the LA failed to complete the grievance procedure. Allegations made in bad faith or that are false are not protected however, though allegations made by a parent as a result of an allegation by a child are protected even though the child may have acted in bad faith.
Employment Equality (Sexual Orientation) Regulations 2003. Employment Equality (Religion or Belief) Regulations 2003.

See the following websites for more details at: www.cesew.org.uk/standard.asp?id=166www.cofe.anglican.org.
Quick Guides EO11 Religious Discrimination: Points of Law; EO12 Sexual Orientation: The Law and Guidance.

C6 AGE DISCRIMINATION

It is unlawful to directly or indirectly discriminate against teachers on grounds of age unless objectively justified. Harassment and victimisation on grounds of age are also unlawful. This applies to discrimination on grounds of youth as well as age. The guidance suggests 10 year bands of age.

Default retirement age
A retirement age below 65 is unlawful unless the employer can show objective justification. This is likely to affect independent schools rather than maintained schools. In a case brought against the UK government the European Court of Justice ruled that it was capable of justification and within the 'margin of appreciation' allowed to national governments. In a follow-up case in the English courts the judge ruled that it was lawful but that he might have held otherwise if the government had not already undertaken to review it.

Employers must follow a statutory retirement procedure under which the employee can request to continue working after retirement.

Equal Opportunities

In 2008 an employment tribunal decided that a 61-year-old teacher was the victim of indirect age discrimination. She had not been short listed for a vacancy at her school which was advertised as a post that 'would suit candidates in the first five years of their career'. The successful candidate was paid almost £8000 less than the salary that the claimant would have received had she been appointed. The school's decision to appoint a person with five years' experience or less was a provision, criterion or practice which disadvantaged people of her age when compared to other persons because they were likely to have far more than five years' experience. The school failed to show that the decision to appoint a cheaper, less experienced teacher was objectively justified by considerations of cost. For this defence to succeed, the school had to show that it was 'more or less compelled' by cost considerations.

Employment Equality (Age) Regulations 2006. ACAS Booklet: Age and the Workplace: Putting the Employment Equality (Age) Regulations 2006 into practice. Quick Guides EO1 Equal Opportunities: Points of Law.

C7 DISABILITY DISCRIMINATION AGAINST TEACHERS

It is unlawful for a school/college/LA to discriminate against any disabled teacher, or applicant for a post. A person has a disability if he/she has a physical or mental impairment that has a substantial and long-term effect (a year or longer) on his/her ability to carry out normal day-to-day activities. Past disabilities are also covered. Your union would be able to help if you are not sure whether your condition amounts to a disability in law. Since 2005 the definition of disability has included progressive diseases such as HIV, multiple sclerosis and cancer. It also includes mental illnesses and impairments.

The 'reasonable adjustment duty'

This duty applies only in relation to disability. Schools must make reasonable adjustments for disabled employees. In particular schools should do all that is reasonable to make access to premises and facilities accessible to disabled teachers. Disabled teachers should expect heads to discuss issues with them in order to arrive at mutually acceptable solutions.

Disability questionnaire

If you consider that you may have been discriminated against by your employer on the grounds of disability and cannot obtain answers to your questions, you can use the *Disability Questionnaire* which schools/LAs have to respond to. Your union would help you, if you are in such a position.

Disability Discrimination (Questions and Replies) Order 2004.

Equal Opportunities

A fabrics teacher who was suffering from failing eyesight won a case against a school for failing to make reasonable adjustments to enable her to continue working. Among the adjustments that the court considered reasonable were: changing the timetable so that she would take most of her classes in the morning when the light was better and altering the rooming of the subject so that she was in one place and that place was well lit. In 2006 the court awarded £196000 compensation.

In another case, a technology teacher won his case against a college. He was beginning to lose his voice and the college refused to recognise that a loss of voice was a disability. The court disagreed and also said that a reasonable adjustment would have been to have found him, or seriously to have attempted to find him, another job within the organisation.
In 2008 the House of Lords ruled that the comparator to a disabled person who had done, or failed to do, something was a person who was not disabled who had done, or not done, the same act. This reversed the previous understanding which was that the comparator was someone who had not done or omitted to do the act because they were not disabled. This does not mean, though, that the school does not have to make reasonable adjustments.

In 2008 the European Court of Justice ruled that an employee who was badly treated because of her son's disability could claim discrimination by association although she was not herself disabled. This can be applied across all kinds of discrimination.

Quick Guides Equal Opportunities (EO) Section.

The **Disability Discrimination Act 1995** applies to England, Scotland and Wales. The Dept for Health has issued guidance to help with the question of determining disability. Schools/teachers can contact the **Disability Employment Adviser** at the local Jobcentre to get help and information. ***See also:*** the **Disabled Living Foundation** website: www.dlf.org.uk.
Quick Guides EO6 Disability Discrimination: Points of Law.

C8 EQUAL PAY

Men and women teachers, like any other employees, must receive equal pay for work, which is: **like work or work rated as equivalent or work of equal value.**

In a Scottish case, a primary school teacher was allowed to bring a claim by comparing herself to a male secondary teacher employed by a different authority. Although it was conceded that the two local authorities were associated employers, nevertheless, there was a 'sufficient connection in a loose and non-technical sense between the two employers', since, at the time, the salaries of both primary and secondary teachers were set by the same Joint Negotiating Committee.

Equal Opportunities

The argument prevailed that this might be sufficient for the claim to succeed.

It is not clear that the same applies to England and Wales because of the greater degree of delegation, particularly in foundation and voluntary aided schools.

Equal pay claims are very difficult legal cases. In an English case it was held that employees in a voluntary aided school could not compare themselves to LA employees. *(See Dolphin v Hartlepool Borough Council above at B5).*

In another case decided by the EAT in 2007, it was ruled that employees whose jobs are rated as equivalent under a job evaluation scheme cannot backdate their claims for six years as happens in cases involving like work or work of equal value.

A person is in **like work** if he/she does work of a broadly similar nature with no real difference. A person is regarded as on **work rated as equivalent** if his/her job is given equal value in terms of the demands made under various headings, such as effort, skill, decision-making etc, on a job evaluation study.

A person is regarded as doing **work of equal value** if his/her work, in terms of the demands made, is of equal value to a comparator.

Equal Pay Questionnaires
In 2003 Equal Pay Questionnaires were introduced. School staff are able to request information about pay scales and the implementation of pay policies. The questionnaire consists of a number of questions which require the school to state whether the complainant has received less than his/her comparator(s), and, if so, why. The school will also be asked whether the people being compared are doing equal work or work of equal value. The school has eight weeks in which to reply. The school does not have to answer the questions, but if it does not do so an employment tribunal may draw an adverse conclusion. They are intended to promote transparency in pay schemes. Schools should undertake 'pay audits' of their existing practices and policies, both in terms of what is paid and how the decisions are taken. While it is, of course, better for all concerned to settle equal pay issues by discussion and negotiation, schools should be aware that an Equal Pay Questionnaire can be served on them before the employee decides to go to an employment tribunal. In a case brought against a union, however, it was ruled that the questionnaire was not a tick-box exercise. If the information was not held for a genuine reason then that could not be held against the organisation. This justification will not hold now that all employers must have an equality statement which includes monitoring for discrimination and an action plan to remove it.

Equal Pay Act 1970. Equal Pay (Amendment) Regulations 2003. Copies of the questionnaire can be downloaded from the

Teachers' Pay

government's Women and Equality Unit website at:www.equalities.gov.uk.

D TEACHERS' PAY

D1 PAY POLICIES

School teachers' pay and conditions of service in England and Wales are determined by the Secretary of State after formal consultation on the recommendations of the **School Teachers' Review Body (STRB)** and are covered in the **School Teachers' Pay and Conditions Document (STPCD)**, which is published annually. **The STRB Reports are available at:** www.ome.uk.com.

Governing bodies are required to have a pay policy in place, which covers all aspects of pay matters, including the exercise of the permissible discretions, and to update it annually. *The DCSF has produced a model pay policy, which is available on the Teachernet website.*

D2 MAIN SCALE

Classroom teachers are paid on a main scale comprising six points (M1– M6). Newly qualified teachers (NQTs) will normally start on point M1 (unless the relevant body, usually the governing body of the school, decides to award one or more discretionary points on the scale for experience other than teaching, that is deemed

relevant to the performance of the teacher's duties).

Governing bodies are required to award a point for each year of service as a qualified teacher:
- in an MOD school; or
- by an Education Action Forum; or
- in state sector schools in the EEA or Switzerland; and
- for each year of service in the EEA outside England and Wales on the teacher's return to England or Wales. Governing bodies shall also award one point for the completion of satisfactory service in the previous school year.

Governing bodies may also award one point for each year of service in:
- an academy;
- a city technology college;
- a city college for the technology of the arts;
- an overseas maintained school outside the EEA or Switzerland;
- FE, including sixth form colleges;
- higher education; or
- an independent school.

You may be awarded an additional point (double-jumping) if your performance in the previous school year was excellent with regard to all aspects of your professional duties, in particular classroom teaching.
Quick Guides Pay (PAY) Section.

D3 THRESHOLD

A classroom teacher may apply for assessment against the national post-threshold standards when he/she is placed on point M6. Heads are required to satisfy themselves (through the outcomes of performance management/appraisal) that the applicant has continued to meet the core standards before proceeding to assess whether a teacher meets the post-threshold standards (in Wales, heads must satisfy themselves that the applicant has continued to meet the end of induction standards (the equivalent of the core standards), before going on to make an assessment against the post-threshold standards). If the head is not satisfied that this is the case, he/she must reject the application and provide the teacher with a written explanation for the decision within 20 days of informing the governing body of the outcome. In such cases no assessment will be carried out. If the head is satisfied that the applicant has continued to meet the core/end of induction standards, he/she must go on and assess the teacher against the post-threshold standards. Having carried out the assessments, heads are required to inform the governing body of the outcomes. The governing body in turn is obliged to move successful teachers to the first point on the upper pay spine forthwith.

You are eligible to apply for assessment against the national post-threshold standards in the academic year 2009/10 (Round 10), if you:

- have been placed on point M6 of the main scale on the basis of qualifications and experience as from 1 September 2009 or earlier;
- are suitably qualified (QTS), employed by an LA or the governing body of an LA-maintained school in England and Wales and are legally covered by the provisions of the **STPCD 2009**; and
- apply in the school year 2009/10 (by 31 October in England).

Evidence should be as recent as possible (usually from the most recent two-year period up to the date of the application) and may be drawn from any educational setting where the applicant has taught pupils of school age (up to the age of 19).

The statutory requirements cover:

- the application;
- the relevant period;
- eligibility;
- heads' responsibilities in relation to assessment, including advice on areas for development;
- the assessment of unattached teachers;
- heads' feedback to applicants (oral for all applicants and written in the case of those who have been adjudged as not yet meeting the national standards, giving the reasons for the outcome of the application on each standard within 20 days of informing the governing body of their decision);
- the review process; and
- complaints to the employer on grounds of discrimination.

Teachers are only able to apply once in any school year. The deadline for applications in England is 31 October 2010 and in Wales 31 August 2010.

Teachers' Pay

Application forms (which are not mandatory in England, but must be used in Wales) are available electronically on Teachernet.

Teachers who have worked abroad or away from a post covered by the STPCD, whether the break was in-service or not, but who have worked for an aggregate period of at least two years in the five years leading up to the date of their application, may rely on aggregate evidence taken from at least 2 and not more than 3 years in the 5-year period up to the date of the application.

Teachers, who have been absent from their school on maternity leave or on adoption or parental leave, are entitled to count their period of absence towards the 2-year qualifying period. In the case of such absences, teachers (in England) are only required to submit performance reviews covering their 'working' period. This may mean that they have only one review to submit. Where they do not have any reviews to draw on, they may cite evidence from the shorter timeframe to enable them to be assessed fairly. Similar provisions apply in Wales, but teachers have more flexibility in that they still have to use the official application form and provide a summary of the evidence on which they wish to rely for assessment.

Teachers (Round 10 Cohort 17) who were:
a) paid on the leadership spine on or before 31 August 2009; or
b teaching outside the maintained sector in the academic year 2008/09 and had taught for 6 years as a qualified teacher will, if successful in Round 10, be moved to U1 with effect from 1 September 2009 (backdated if necessary).

Teachers (Round 10 Cohort 18), who were already on M6 or who were first placed on M6 on or after 1 September 2009 but before 31 August 2010, will, if successful, be moved to U1 with effect from 1 September 2010.

Teachers are advised by the guidance issued by the DCSF to:
- check their eligibility;
- use Word or black pen in manuscript;
- use bullet points, not prose;
- use not more than 250 words per standard;
- summarise the evidence – with concrete examples to show that he/she has worked at the threshold standards for the 2- 3 year period up to the date of the application;
- avoid unsupported assertions – but to indicate the source/ location of the evidence cited;
- cross-reference the evidence where it relates to more than one standard; and
- sign the form and keep a copy.

Teachers (Round 9 Cohort 15) who first became eligible
- in Round 8 (those placed on M6 on or after 1 September 2007, but on or before 31 August 2008) and chose not to apply; or
- in Round 7 or before (those placed on M6 on or before 31 August 2007) will, if successful in Round 9, be moved to U1 with effect from 1 September 2008.

Teachers' Pay

Teachers (Round 9 Cohort 16) who first became eligible

- in Round 8 (those placed on point M6 on or after 1 September 2007, but on or before 31 August 2008) and applied, but were deemed not to have met the national standards; or
- in Round 9 (those placed on point M6 on or after 1 September 2008, but before 31 August 2009), will, if successful, be moved to U1 with effect from 1 September 2009.

Heads are required to:

- check the applicant's eligibility;
- carry out an assessment of each standard, signifying whether it has been met or not;
- make an overall judgement as to whether the standards have been met or not;
- note any areas for further development;
- indicate whether the evidence supplied is true (in cases where the applicant has not been employed by the school for the whole of the relevant period, verification should be sought from the applicant's previous school); and representative/ typical (some sample checks should be carried out);
- complete the head's declaration section, and
- sign and date the form and take a copy.

After the assessment heads are statutorily under a duty to:

- inform the relevant body of the outcome of their assessments;
- inform all applicants of the outcome of their assessment within 20 days of the relevant body's decisions;

- return all assessed application forms to the teachers concerned;
- give oral feedback to all applicants on each standard and the reasons for the outcome of their applications; and
- give in addition to all unsuccessful applicants written feedback on the reasons for the outcome of the application on each standard, including those that have been met, within 20 working days of informing the governing body of their decision.

Review

Teachers who feel that they have been wrongly assessed may appeal to the governing body on the grounds that they would have met the threshold standards if the head in making his/her decision had:

- taken proper account of the relevant evidence;
- not taken account of irrelevant or inaccurate evidence;
- not been biased; or
- not discriminated unlawfully against them.

Teachers in England
a) Those subject to the 2006 PM Regulations

From 1 September 2009 for teachers in England subject to the 2006 PM Regulations, assessment against the post-threshold standards will be determined solely on the basis of the evidence contained in their PM review statements from the relevant period. For most teachers this will mean the evidence from their last two PM reviews, but some (those who work in more than one school, for example, or supply

Teachers' Pay

teachers) may have more than two reviews covering the two-year period – and some may have fewer (cf. above under 'absence').

Though heads will continue to be responsible for threshold assessment, PM reviewers will have an increasingly important role to play in the process in that they will need to work closely with their reviewees in the two years prior to an application to check that the evidence collected (via objectives, classroom observation and other evidence) will prove sufficient for a successful application against the threshold standards. Reviewers should, however, restrict their observations to those aspects of a reviewee's performance that are specifically covered in the review and the progress made against his/her objectives, rather than comment on whether he/she has met the threshold standards or not.

You, however, will still be required to make an application to indicate your wish to be assessed against the post-threshold standards. The application must contain the results of the PM reviews carried out under the 2006 Regulations and a statement that you wish to be assessed against the post-threshold standards.

b) Those not subject to the 2006 PM Regulations

Eligible teachers should provide a summary of the evidence on which they wish to rely with concrete examples from their day-to-day work from the most recent two-year period (as under the previous arrangements). They may draw on evidence from their PM/appraisal reviews. In all other respects, the process is the same for such teachers as for those subject to the 2006 PM Regulations.

Teachers in Wales

Eligible teachers must apply between 1 September 2009 and 31 August 2010. They must submit a summary of the evidence on which they wish to rely for assessment on the official form (which is available on Teachernet). Any reference to a PM review means any review of performance undertaken in accordance with the **School Teacher Appraisal (Wales) Regulations 2002** and the **School Teacher Appraisal (Amendment) (Wales) Regulations 2009**. When assessing an application, heads must have regard to the results of the most recent appraisal carried out in accordance with these regulations.

In Wales, the end of induction standards are the equivalent of the core standards in England for threshold assessment purposes. In all other respects, the process is the same for teachers in Wales as for their counterparts in England subject to the 2006 PM Regulations.

Teachers not statutorily covered by the STPCD

i) Teachers employed in schools or services similar to the maintained sector

Teachers in settings similar to those in the maintained sector will continue to be eligible to apply for threshold assessment and their status if successful will

Teachers' Pay

be transferable to the maintained sector. These include teachers employed:

- at an MOD school;
- by an Education Action Forum;
- in an academy;
- in a city technology college;
- in a city college for the technology of the arts;
- non-maintained special schools;
- by LAs to work in children's homes maintained by an authority.

The same eligibility rules apply, except for the requirement to be statutorily covered by the STPCD, in cases where such teachers have contracts of employment that tie their pay and conditions to those in the STPCD. Teachers whose pay and conditions differ from those in the STPCD will also continue to be eligible to apply if they:

- have QTS;
- have acquired at least 5 years' post-QTS teaching experience between 1 September 2008 and 31 August 2009;
- were in one of the above categories during that period;
- are in one of the above categories on the date of their application; and
- apply within the school year 2009/10 or by 31 October 2010 if they are teaching in England and they mirror the 2006 PM Regulations for their PM arrangements.

ii) Teachers in independent schools

Teachers who taught in an independent school in 2008/09 and who have moved to the maintained sector as from 1 September 2009 are eligible to apply for threshold assessment provided that they:

- have QTS;
- are paid on point M6; and
- have completed 6 years' employment as a qualified teacher.

They may use any evidence from their experience in such a setting to support their application as long as it entailed teaching children up to 19 years of age.

If successful they will be paid on point U1 from 1 September 2009 (backdated if necessary) and will not be worse off in pay terms than those serving throughout in the maintained sector or if the previous arrangements had continued.

Model application forms continue to be available on the DCSF website for teachers in Wales who are required to use the form for their application and for those in England who have only had one review under the 2006 regulations. *Quick Guides PAY10 Managing Threshold 2009/10: The Performance Threshold (Round 10).*

D4 UPPER PAY SPINE (UPS)

On crossing the threshold, teachers are placed on the first point of the 3-point upper pay spine (U1 to U3). Progress up the spine is usually biennial, but can only be effected if:

- the achievements and contribution of the post-threshold teacher to the school or schools in which he/she has previously worked have been sustained and substantial; and

Teachers' Pay

- he/she has had two successful reviews of overall performance.

A 'successful performance review' is one that involves a performance management process of:
- performance objectives;
- classroom observation; and
- other evidence.

In order for the teacher to meet the criterion of 'sustained and substantial performance and contribution to the school', the review will need to assess that he/she has continued to meet the post-threshold standards and grown professionally by developing his/her teaching expertise post-threshold.

The following expectation of the role of UPS3 teachers is included in the STPCD: *'UPS3 teachers play a critical role in the life of the school. They provide a role model for teaching and learning, making a distinctive contribution to the raising of standards and contribute effectively to the work of the wider team. They take advantage of appropriate opportunities for professional development and use outcomes effectively to improve pupils' learning.'*

Your school should have determined what 'grown professionally' means in its context and to have incorporated that definition into their pay and performance management policies. Post-threshold points are portable – i.e., once awarded, they stay with the teacher even when he/she moves to another school (teachers paid on one of the London scales, however, will move to the equivalent point on

the national scale if they transfer to a new post outside the area). Decisions about UPS progression (in England, under the 2006 PM regulations) are made by the governing body on the basis of pay recommendations in teachers' most recent planning and review statements, which heads are required to pass on unaltered to the governing body.

In Wales, governing bodies must have regard to the outcomes of the two most recent appraisals carried out in accordance with the 2002 regulations.
Quick Guides PAY6 The Management of the Upper Pay Spine (UPS).

D5 PAYMENT OF PART-TIME TEACHERS

Significant changes in the way in which the pay and working time of part-time teachers, including members of the leadership group, is calculated, have been introduced from 1 September 2008. These are covered below:

Calculation of a pro rata salary

Part-time teachers must be paid a pro rata percentage/proportion of the appropriate full-time equivalent salary. This is determined by the proportion of the school's timetabled teaching week (STTW – the school's session hours that are timetabled for teaching, excluding break time, assemblies and registration) that he/she works in comparison with what he/she would have worked if employed in the same post on a full-time basis in the same school. The percentage remains the same whether a school operates a weekly, fortnightly or any other timetable cycle. Thus, if the school's timetabled teaching week is 25 hours and a part-timer is employed to 'teach' for 15 hours of the STTW, he/she works 60% of the time that he/she would have worked as a full-time teacher. He/she is, therefore, entitled to be paid 60% of what his/her full-time equivalent salary would have been.

It is important to note that this mechanism is only used to determine pay, not actual hours worked.

This mechanism must also be used to determine payment for any additional hours that a part-time teacher may agree to work from time to time at the request of the head (e.g., two extra hours of teaching on a Monday afternoon or attendance at an INSET day on a day that he/she does not normally work).

Determination of pro rata directed time

The percentage that is used to determine the salary of a part-time teacher must also be used to calculate the number of hours of directed time as a proportion of 1265 that a part-time teacher may be required to be available for work in any school year. Thus if a part-time teacher is paid a salary of 60% of his/her full-time equivalent salary, then he/she can be required to be available for work for 759 hours (60% of 1265 hours) during the school year.

The requirements that a school has of a part-time teacher in his/her allocation of directed time and how he/she will be deployed

within this should relate pro rata to what would have been expected of that individual if he/she were employed full time. These requirements/expectations should be clearly communicated in writing when the part-time teacher is appointed. The school will need to ensure that its requirements of the part-time teacher with regard to, for example:

- teaching;
- PPA time;
- management and leadership time, if relevant;
- other timetabled non-contact time;
- registration;
- attendance at assemblies;
- pastoral duties/responsibilities;
- attendance at meetings both during and outside school session times;
- attendance at parental consultation evenings; and
- attendance at a proportion of INSET days

can all be accommodated within the amount of directed time that has been determined for him/her.

Part-time teachers (cf. paragraph 74.13) must, besides, work such reasonable additional hours as may be necessary to enable them to discharge their professional responsibilities effectively.

Whilst it is appropriate to use the same mechanism that has been outlined above for classroom teachers for calculating the pro rata salary of part-time members of the leadership group and ASTs, it cannot be used to determine their pro rata allocation of directed time as heads, deputies, assistant heads and ASTs do not

Teachers' Pay

operate on a time-bound contract (cf. paragraph 74.1 (a) of the **STPCD 2009**). The relevant body is, nonetheless, duty bound to ensure that the workload of part-time members of the leadership group and ASTs is reasonable and that such staff are treated fairly in comparison with their full-time equivalents (or with what would have been expected of them if they had been full-time). The relevant body must also have due regard to their work/life balance.

Safeguarding

In cases where, as a result of the new arrangements for calculating their remuneration, part-time teachers, in post before 1 September 2008 suffered a reduction in salary, safeguarding applied. In order to ensure that teachers subject to safeguarding received their September uplift in full, schools should have carried out the following sequence of calculations as from 1 September 2008:

a) calculate the pay that the teacher would have received on 1 September, had no changes to the part-time arrangements occurred, but without taking account of any progression ('the original salary');

b) calculate the percentage of the school's timetabled teaching week applicable to the teacher;

c) recalculate the teacher's pay on this basis, without taking account of any progression ('the new salary');

d) calculate the safeguarded sum – the difference, if any, between the original salary and the new salary;

e) i) where there is no progression, if the new salary is less than the original salary, pay the safeguarded sum in addition to the new salary; or
ii) where there is progression, take the new full-time salary following progression and calculate the part-time salary specified in b) above.

This is the 'revised new salary'. If this exceeds the original salary, then safeguarding is lost; if it does not, then the safeguarded sum is paid in addition to the revised new salary.

As with other instances of safeguarding, the relevant body must notify a teacher in writing within one month of any determination which results in safeguarding of:

- that determination;
- the reason for the determination;
- the teacher's 'original salary';
- the safeguarded sum; and
- the date on which safeguarding will cease (31 August 2011 or sooner if the cessation principles apply – e.g., if he/she ceases to be a part-time teacher, his/her employment at the school ends or his/her salary increase owing to movement up the scale/spine equals or exceeds the safeguarded sum).

In the case of teachers, whose hours changed on 1 September, the 'original salary' should have been determined as set out in (a), but using the new hours' percentage. The remaining stages, b – f, should then be carried out in the same sequence. Any previous safeguarded sums to which a part-time teacher is entitled would be increased if his/

her salary percentage increases, but would not be decreased if the salary percentage decreases following a recalculation under the new arrangements, as under normal arrangements that would in any event trigger safeguarding.

Allowances

Part-time teachers' allowances (e.g., TLRs, SEN allowances or recruitment and retention incentives) are paid pro rata (i.e. at the same percentage as the appropriate percentage of their full-time equivalent salary).

All allowances held by existing part-time teachers must be reviewed and re-calculated in accordance with the new mechanism for determining pro rata payment.

Where the re-calculation produces a figure which exceeds the original allowance, the allowance must be increased by the difference as from 1 September 2008. Where the re-calculation produces a lower figure, the teacher must be paid the cash value of the original allowance (i.e. it is safeguarded) until 31 August 2011 or the cessation principles apply.

Working time

The working time provisions relating to part-time teachers are covered in paragraph 74 of the **STPCD 2009**. In addition to the points made above with regard to directed time, the following should be noted:

- no teacher employed on a part-time basis may be required to be available for work on any day of the week or part of any day that he/she is not normally required to be available for

work under his/her contract of employment (thus a teacher who does not normally work on a Monday could not be required to attend any of the school's INSET days if all of these have been arranged for a Monday or a parental consultation evening arranged on a Monday);

- part-time teachers may, however, be required to undertake duties other than teaching pupils outside school sessions on any day or part of a day that they are normally required to be available for work (i.e. they can be required to attend a parental consultation evening or a meeting after the school day has finished on such days).

TLR holders

TLRs may be job-shared between two part-time teachers, but a TLR may not be shared between two full-time teachers or between a full-time teacher and a part-timer.

Short-notice teachers

Teachers employed on a short-term or daily basis should be paid 1/195th of a full year's salary. Periods of less than one day should be calculated pro rata. In such cases, the teacher must not be paid more than he/she would have been paid if he/she had worked full-time throughout.

D6 SPECIAL EDUCATIONAL NEEDS ALLOWANCES (SEN)

A teacher in a special school or in an ordinary school who is engaged wholly or mainly in:

Teachers' Pay

- teaching pupils with statements of SEN in specially designated classes; or
- taking charge of special classes consisting wholly or mainly of pupils who are hearing impaired or visually impaired, shall be awarded the first SEN allowance.

A teacher in an ordinary school may also be awarded the first SEN allowance if he/she makes a significantly greater contribution to the teaching of pupils with SEN than that which is normally expected of a classroom teacher.

The second SEN allowance may be awarded to a teacher who would otherwise be entitled to a SEN 1 allowance and has the experience and/or qualifications which is considered to be particular to the teacher's work. **The cash values of the SEN allowances are set out in D16.** A SEN allowance may be held in conjunction with a TLR payment.

D7 TEACHING AND LEARNING RESPONSIBILITIES

The previous system of awarding any of management allowances to a teacher who undertakes a specific responsibility beyond that common to the majority of classroom teachers has been replaced by a new teaching and learning responsibility(TLR) framework. Any responsibility post in the new structure must meet the criterion and the factors listed below.

Criterion
'A teaching and learning responsibility payment may only be made to a teacher who is accountable for a significant, specified responsibility focused on teaching and learning, that is not required of all classroom teachers, clearly defined in the job description of the TLR payment holder, and requiring teachers' professional skills and judgement. The TLR payment should be for a sustained responsibility in the context of the school's staffing structure needed to ensure continued delivery of high quality teaching and learning.'

Factors
The 'significant, specified responsibility' should:
- be focused on teaching and learning;
- have an impact on educational progress of pupils other than the teacher's assigned pupils;
- involve leading, developing and enhancing the teaching practice of other staff; and
- require the teacher to lead, manage and develop a subject or curriculum area or to lead and manage pupil development across the curriculum.

In addition, for the award of a TLR1 payment, the significant responsibility must include the line management of a significant number of people. 'Line management' has been clarified as meaning 'the direction, management and professional responsibility for staff on a daily basis'. 'People' includes teachers and support staff. An individual member of staff may, therefore,

Teachers' Pay

have more than one line manager. It is for schools to determine what 'a significant number of people' means in their particular context.

The new structure should include an outline of the responsibilities attaching to each post within it and the cash value of each post.

Payments (reflecting the weight of responsibility attaching to each post) will be spot salaries at the cash values determined by the school within the following maxima and minima:

September 2009
TLR1: £7158 - £12114
TLR2: £2478 - £6057

There must be a minimum differential of at least £1500 between levels or tiers of responsibility within the TLR1 and TLR2 ranges. Responsibilities of equal or similar weight must carry the same cash value.

A teacher may only be awarded one TLR payment and it is not permissible for schools to aggregate TLRs as they may have done with management allowances. A single TLR job description may, however, include a number of different responsibilities which together comprise the relative weight of the post.

TLRs may be job-shared between two part-time teachers, but not between two full-time teachers or between a full-time teacher and a part-time teacher. Part-time teachers who hold TLRs should be paid pro rata at the same proportion as their part-time contract.

Unqualified teachers may not be awarded a TLR payment, but they may be paid an allowance as determined by the governing body for responsibilities undertaken or any qualifications or experience that are deemed relevant to their specialised form of teaching.

TLR payments should cease if a teacher declines to carry out the responsibilities attached to the payment. The payment may also be taken away as a result of poor performance as determined through the application of the school's capability procedures. *Quick Guides PAY9 Teaching and Learning Responsibility (TLR) Payments.*

D8 SAFEGUARDING

Teachers in receipt of a permanent management allowance as at 31 December 2005 were entitled to have the cash value of that allowance safeguarded for the three-year transitional period to 31 December 2008 (or earlier if the cessation principles applied) in accordance with the principles set out below.

If a school restructures again in the transitional period or does so at any stage subsequently and a teacher is set to lose money as a result of the change, he/she will be safeguarded for another 3 years (or less if the cessation principles apply) from that point.

The principles of safeguarding are that:
• teachers at all levels should be protected from sudden drops in total salary which would

otherwise occur through no fault of their own;

- safeguarding principles should be applied on a mandatory basis;
- safeguarding will operate on a fixed-period basis and the period will be three years (subject to the provisions cited below);
- safeguarding will be on a cash basis; and
- the teacher must know at the start of the safeguarding period what safeguarding arrangements are applicable to any particular salary element and this must be set out in the teacher's salary statement at the start of the period.

Safeguarding will apply in circumstances where:

- the item concerned has been removed from the pay system;
- the item concerned has been replaced, directly or indirectly, by another form or forms of payment, which the teacher concerned is not receiving;
- any Individual School Range has been reduced;
- an LA reorganisation, school closure, or redefinition of boundaries, means that a teacher continuing to work in the school or LA as applicable would otherwise receive a reduced rate of pay; or
- internal school reorganisations take place.

Safeguarding will not apply or will cease to apply where any of the following circumstances occur:

- after 3 years;
- the teacher moves to another school voluntarily;
- the teacher unreasonably refuses to carry out duties commensurate with the salary

being received (provided that the sum being safeguarded is more than £500 in toto);

- cumulative movement up the pay scale overtakes the teacher's safeguarded salary;
- the teacher ceases to be a classroom teacher; or
- the teacher is awarded a TLR payment which exceeds or equals the safeguarded sum.

Safeguarding is paid in full or it ceases to be paid – there is no partial erosion. The starting point/ comparator of any safeguarding is a teacher's salary as at the day before the 'loss' takes effect (i.e., as at 31 August 2009 if the safeguarding began on 1 September 2010). The provisions set out above apply equally to all teachers, including members of the leadership group.

A time-limited AST post will only be safeguarded for its fixed-term period. In cases where a full-time teacher becomes part-time, the cash value being safeguarded is paid pro rata; where a part-time teacher becomes a full-timer, the amount safeguarded increases to the full rate. In all cases where safeguarding applies the teacher affected must be notified in writing within one month of the following:

- the reason for the determination;
- the date on which the determination is to be implemented (if known);
- the date on which safeguarding will cease;
- the original (old) salary;
- the value of the safeguarded sum or in the case of a determination that takes effect from a later date (and the effect

Teachers' Pay

on the teacher is unknown) the maximum amount by which his/her salary may be reduced; and

- where a copy of the school's revised staffing structure may be viewed.

In cases where a teacher is awarded a temporary TLR or serves as a member of the leadership group, an ET or an AST in the temporary absence of the substantive postholder, TLR/MA safeguarding is reduced or discontinued, but is restored at the end of the temporary period unless it would have ceased in the interim in accordance with the cessation principles. The governing body must review the responsibilities of teachers in receipt of safeguarding that exceeds £500 in toto and allocate appropriate additional responsibilities focused on teaching and learning that are commensurate with the safeguarded sum for the duration of the safeguarding. If teachers unreasonably refuse to carry out such additional responsibilities, the payment of the safeguarded sum should cease upon written notification (within one month of the determination). Such a determination is subject to appeal.

In the case of a safeguarded TLR payment and of safeguarding for members of the leadership group, ASTs and ETs, the safeguarding period ends on the third anniversary of the relevant date (or earlier if the cessation principles apply). The 'relevant date' (cf. paragraph 5 of the **STPCD 2009**) is:

- 1 January, in the case of a determination made between the preceding 1 September and 31 December;
- 1 April, if a determination is made between 1 January and 31 March; and
- 1 September, if a determination is made between 1 April and 31 August.

General safeguarding

General safeguarding occurs when a teacher loses his/her post, but remains employed in the same LA, as a result of:
- school closure;
- a prescribed alteration to a school or the reorganisation of a school, where the teacher's new post is in a different school; or
- the closure or reorganisation of any other educational establishment or service.

General safeguarding starts on the date that a teacher took/takes up his/her post within the service of the same LA. The principles set out above apply to all cases of safeguarding that have arisen since 1 January 2006 (there will be no 'permanent' general safeguarding in the future). All teachers, including heads, deputies and assistant heads and ASTs, however, who started a post where general safeguarding applied by 31 December 2005, will continue to receive it in the future, except if they refuse an alternative post in the same authority or move post voluntarily. The key issue here is the starting date of a post, not when a re-organisation occurred.

Teachers in receipt of general safeguarding should have any

Teachers' Pay

management allowance reduced by the cash value of any TLR post that is awarded to them. If the value of the TLR is less than the value of the safeguarded MA, it is only the difference that continues to be safeguarded when the teacher begins to be paid the TLR. The DCSF has produced model pay statements that incorporate the safeguarded elements *(cf. Quick Guides PAY16 Salary Statements; PAY14 Safeguarding).*

D9 MULTI-YEAR PAY AWARD

The current three-year multi-year pay deal started on 1 September 2008. *All the relevant figures are provided in D16.* Pay increases from 1 September 2009 and 2010 have been confirmed at 2.3%, following a full-scale review by the STRB.

D10 HEADTEACHERS

Heads are paid on a 7-point range, the individual salary range (ISR), on the leadership pay spine. The ISR is usually within the school group range (as determined by a school's unit total) that is appropriate for the school. In mainstream schools the unit total is calculated by multiplying the number of pupils at a key stage (KS) by the appropriate weighting (e.g. for each pre- KS1, KS1 and KS2 pupil 7 units; for each KS3 pupil 9 units; for each KS4 pupil 11 units and for each KS5 pupil 13 units). Pupils with statements of SEN will attract an additional 3 units. In special schools the unit total is determined by a more complicated formula, involving a

staff:pupil ratio, a staff:pupil ratio modifier and the unit total, as set out in paragraphs 10.1 to 10.6 of the *STPCD 2009.*

Total unit score school group:

Up to 1000	1
1001 to 2200	2
2201 to 3500	3
3501 to 5000	4
5001 to 7500	5
7501 to 11000	6
11001 to 17000	7
17001 and over	8

Once an ISR has been set progress up the range can only be made on performance grounds – at the rate of no more than two points per single performance review. The following expectations have been placed on the leadership group in the *STPCD 2009*: *'Those on the leadership spine play a critical role in the life of the school. They inspire confidence in those around them and work with others to create a shared strategic vision, which motivates pupils and staff. They take the lead in enhancing standards of teaching and value enthusiasm and innovation in others. They have the confidence and ability to make management and organisational decisions and ensure equity, access and entitlement to learning.'*

To merit the award of a performance point(s), leadership group members need to demonstrate sustained high quality of performance and to have had a successful performance review. A 'successful' review involves a performance management process of:
- performance objectives;
- classroom observation (if relevant); and

- other evidence.

In order to meet the criterion of 'sustained high quality of performance', the review will need to assess that leadership group members have grown professionally by developing their leadership and (if relevant) their teaching expertise.

Newly appointed heads may be placed on any of the bottom four points of the ISR.

There must be a minimum gap of at least one point on the pay spine between the lowest point of the ISR and the top of a deputy/assistant head's range. The ISR (and the ranges of a deputy or assistant head) may be changed as at 1 September 2009 to reflect the school's size and circumstances and any significant change in responsibility year on year. The ISR may be set by up to two school groups higher than the school group in which the school has been placed by virtue of its unit total either when a new head is appointed to attract a suitable candidate or at any time to retain the services of an existing head. In such cases, where the school group is 7 or 8, the maximum of the ISR may exceed the maximum on the leadership spine. The relevant body of a school which has been turned round by a seconded head (or a teacher) may award the head (or teacher) a performance point (or two) for one year as a lump sum, if he/she would otherwise be prevented from receiving such an award as a result of returning to his/her substantive post. Such payments are not pensionable and the head (teacher) on his/

her return would be on the same point on the ISR (salary point) as when he/she left to take up the secondment.

In cases where the ISR is re-set from 1 September, any performance point(s) for the previous year must be assigned on the lower (old) ISR before assimilation to the higher (new) ISR.

Heads of more than one school

Where a head is appointed as the head of more than one school, the governing body of his/her original school (or where collaborative arrangements apply, the collaborating body) must determine the head's ISR on the following basis:

a) cases where a head is appointed as an acting (temporary) head of more than one school (in school groups 1 – 6) the ISR must be determined within:
  ◊ the school group of the total pupil unit score of all the schools; or
  ◊ the school group that is up to two groups higher than the school group of any of the schools concerned, whichever produces the higher salary.

b) where a head is appointed as an acting (temporary) head of more than one school and the school group of any of the schools is 7 or 8, the ISR must be determined:
  ◊ within the school group of the total pupil unit score of all the schools; or
  ◊ by the application of an uplift of between 5% and 20% to the maximum of the school group range of the largest school (in such cases

Teachers' Pay

the maximum of the ISR may exceed the maximum of the leadership spine).

The guidance stresses that increases approaching the maximum of 20% should only be given in exceptional circumstances. In such temporary cases, a fixed-term variation of contract must be issued by the contracting employer, which should set out that the head, in addition to his/her substantive post, is for a fixed period employed additionally as head of the additional school(s). At the end of the fixed-term period the head will revert to his/her substantive post. There is a clear expectation that such temporary arrangements should be time-limited, subject to regular review and endure no more than two years. Governing bodies should consider whether any temporary payments should be made to teachers other than the head to reflect any additional duties/responsibilities that might accrue in the light of the head's absence. As such arrangements are temporary, adjustments to pay are also temporary, and safeguarding provisions do not apply when the arrangements cease. Where such an appointment is permanent, the ISR will be determined within the school group of the total unit score or, in cases where the schools are causing concern or on recruitment or retention grounds, by the application of the 'normal rules' (i.e. up to two school groups higher or, if the unit total puts the school(s) into group 7 or 8, whatever the governing body determines – and the maximum of the ISR may exceed the maximum of the leadership spine).

Extended services

In cases where a local authority as part of its local area plan has asked a school to take on the responsibility and accountability for the provision of a range of extended services on its site for children and young people from the area and the head and governing body agree, the governing body has the discretion to take such significant additional responsibility into account when setting the head's ISR. Any salary uplift should be proportionate to the level of responsibility and accountability undertaken. Consideration should be given to remuneration of other teachers who assume additional responsibilities as a result of the head's role. In cases where a head merely has an interest in the quality of a service that is co-located on the school's site (e.g., a speech therapy centre that helps the development of pupils in the school), but is not responsible or accountable for the delivery of that service, it is not permissible to award a salary uplift. Paragraphs 163 ff. cover the extra payments that may be made to a head for the provision of a service (e.g., as a consultant leader or a SIP) to another school, when the head is only accountable for the quality of the service being provided, not for outcomes in that school. In such cases the governing body should determine and enshrine in a formal memorandum of agreement the level of additional payment due to the head and other staff from the income due to the school for the provision of the service in accordance with the considerations and principles set out on p 191 of section 3.

Stepping down

Serving heads, deputies, assistant heads and advanced skills teachers (ASTs), who have stepped down and reverted to classroom teaching, may be placed on any of the points on the upper pay spine (with the proviso that those appointed to the leadership group on or after 1 September 2000, must have served for a minimum of at least one year in that capacity).

D11 DEPUTIES AND ASSISTANT HEADS

Deputies and assistant heads are paid on a 5-point range on the leadership pay spine. The range should reflect the job weight and challenge, the circumstances of the school and any recruitment difficulties. The job weight of a deputy must be more substantial than that of an assistant head. The range chosen should be between the lowest point of the ISR on the pay spine and the salary of the highest paid classroom teacher, as determined by U1 plus any TLR awards and any SEN allowances.

The lowest point of a deputy's range must exceed the bottom of an assistant head's range by at least one point. Newly appointed deputies/assistant heads may be placed on any of the bottom 3 points on their range. Once a range has been set, progress up the range will depend exclusively on performance – as outlined above in D10. No more than 2 points may be awarded at any single performance review. As with heads above, any performance point(s) must be awarded on the lower (old) range

if the range is re-set as from 1 September before the deputy/assistant head is transferred to the higher (new) range. A deputy's or assistant head's range may be re-set as at 1 September when there has been a significant change in responsibility (or when a new deputy/assistant head is appointed) or at any time for retention purposes.

When a teacher undertakes the duties/responsibilities of a head or deputy/assistant head on an acting basis, he/she must not be paid less than the minimum of the ISR/range payable in the school for the post in which he/she is acting.

D12 ADVANCED SKILLS TEACHERS (ASTs)

ASTs are teachers who have been recognised through external assessment as having excellent classroom practice. Teachers must apply for such assessment. The STPCD specifies that ASTs will normally be required to spend 20% of their time on outreach work. Schools may create any number of AST posts. A new assessment procedure has been applicable since 1 September 2007. Heads must first be satisfied, by reference to performance management or appraisal reviews, that an applicant meets the standards applicable to his/her current level before he/she can be assessed against the AST standards. In the case of ASTs, heads must be satisfied that applicants have continued to meet:
a) for teachers on the main scale
   – the core standards;

Teachers' Pay

b) for teachers on the upper pay spine – the core and post-threshold standards;
c) for ETs – the core, post-threshold and ET standards.

If the head is not satisfied that a teacher has continued to meet the standards, which apply at his/her career stage, he/she must reject the application and provide the teacher with a written explanation for that rejection within 20 working days of receiving the application. In such cases no external assessment will be undertaken. If the head is satisfied that the teacher has continued to meet the relevant standards, he/she should complete the application within 20 working days together with an evaluation of the extent to which the teacher meets the AST standards and give a copy to the teacher.

Where a teacher applies for an AST post at the school in which he/she is employed, the head should pass the completed application form to the assessor if the teacher:
i) is selected to be interviewed for the post; or
ii) is selected or recommended by the governing body for appointment without an interview. Where a teacher applies for an AST post at another school, the completed application should be submitted to the head of that school, who should then pass it on to the assessor. When carrying out an assessment against the AST standards, an assessor is required to:
• consider the completed application, any additional evidence supplied by the applicant in support of his/her application and any additional evidence submitted by the applicant's headteacher (or LA line manager);
• interview the applicant;
• observe the applicant teaching (except in cases where the applicant is absent from work on maternity, paternity, parental or adoption leave); and
• interview the applicant's headteacher (or LA line manager).

The assessor may ask for any other additional evidence that he/she deems necessary. Having carried out the assessment, the assessor must inform the applicant of his/her decision, stating the reasons where the applicant has failed to meet the relevant standards. Where the assessor determines that the applicant has met the relevant standards, he/she will issue a certificate to that effect.

Applicants who have been assessed as not meeting the relevant standards have the right to apply for an independent review on the following grounds (only):
• proper account has not been taken of relevant evidence;
• account has been taken of irrelevant or inaccurate evidence;
• the assessment was biased; or
• the assessment was conducted in a way that discriminated unlawfully against the applicant.

Applications for such a review, setting out the grounds on which a review is sought, should be submitted to the review co-ordinator appointed by the Secretary of State within 40 working days of receipt of the decision.

ASTs are paid on a 5-point range on the 18-point AST pay spine.

As with heads, deputies and assistant heads, progress up the range will depend exclusively on performance. The governing body may award up to two points on the scale for performance at any one review. All newly appointed ASTs must be placed on the first point of their range. ASTs are expected to make a significant impact on teaching and learning in the school(s) in which they work, as is outlined in the **STPCD 2009**:

'ASTs play a critical role in the life of the school. Through their own excellent teaching and their work with other teachers or on whole school projects, they play a leading role in enhancing the quality of teaching and learning throughout the school. Their outreach work opens the school to wider relationships, which enrich the experiences and raise the performance of colleagues and pupils. Their outreach work also benefits and is of great value to the wider teaching community.'

To merit the award of a performance point, ASTs need to demonstrate sustained high quality of performance and to have had a successful performance review. As with post-threshold teachers above, a 'successful' review involves a performance management process of:

- performance objectives;
- classroom observation; and
- other evidence.

In order to meet the criterion of 'sustained high quality of performance', the review will need to assess that the AST has grown professionally by developing his/her teaching expertise and performance of AST professional duties.

Schools in England may have access to grant funding for AST posts towards salary and outreach costs.

AST posts can be taken up in Welsh schools, but so far there are no known examples.

Quick Guides PAY7 Advanced Skills Teachers (ASTs).

D13 EXCELLENT TEACHER SCHEME (ETS)

The ETS has been operative since 1 September 2006. Applications for an excellent teacher post should be made in writing. The ETS can be used to reward exemplary classroom teachers with an established record of sustained high quality teaching and of supporting colleagues within the school. There is no outreach function unlike ASTs. An excellent teacher (ET) is not able to hold a teaching and learning responsibility (TLR) award.

A teacher who is placed on point U3 of the upper pay spine and who is employed by a governing body that has a vacant excellent teacher post in its structure may apply for assessment against the standards which are set out in **Annex 1 of the STPCD 2009**. A teacher may be appointed to an ET post if he/she has been on point U3 for two years and has been assessed as meeting the ET standards. A new assessment

Teachers' Pay

procedure has been applicable since 1 September 2007. Heads must first be satisfied by reference to performance management or appraisal reviews that an applicant has continued to meet the core and post-threshold standards before he/she can be assessed against the ET standards. If the head is not satisfied that a teacher has continued to meet the core and post-threshold standards, he/she must reject the application and provide the teacher with a written explanation for that rejection within 20 working days of receiving the application. In such cases no external assessment will be undertaken.

If the head is satisfied that the teacher has continued to meet the relevant standards, he/she should complete the application within 20 working days together with an evaluation of the extent to which the teacher meets the ET standards and give a copy to the teacher. Where a teacher applies for an ET post at the school in which he/she is employed, the head should pass the completed application form to the assessor.

When carrying out an assessment against the standards, an assessor is required to:

- consider the completed application, any evidence supplied by the applicant in support of his/her application and any evidence submitted by the applicant's head (or LA line manager);
- interview the applicant;
- observe the applicant teaching; and
- interview the applicant's head (or LA line manager).

The assessor may ask for any other additional evidence that he/she deems necessary.

The appeal provisions for ETs are the same as those outlined in D12 for ASTs.

Excellent teachers are expected to:

- continue to maintain high standards;
- demonstrate a commitment to develop themselves professionally;
- provide an exemplary role model for staff through their professional expertise; and
- have a distinctive role in achieving improvements in teaching across the school.

In addition the specific duties of an ET should include:

- the induction of newly-qualified teachers;
- the professional mentoring of other teachers;
- sharing good practice through demonstration lessons;
- helping teachers to develop their expertise in planning, preparation and assessment;
- helping other teachers to evaluate the impact of their teaching on pupils;
- undertaking classroom observations to assist and support the performance management process; and
- helping teachers improve their teaching practice including those on capability procedures.

Salary

The salary of an ET is a spot salary within the permissible ranges, *as set out in D1*. The salaries of existing ETs must be re-determined as from 1 September 2008 in line with the criteria listed below. Because ETs are not subject to an annual review of salary, relevant bodies may only re-set the salary of an ET when there are significant changes in the criteria set out below.

Criteria

The criteria for determining the job weight and appropriate spot salary from within the permissible ranges are:

- the degree of challenge of the role; and
- the nature of the work undertaken.

Safeguarding

In view of the requirement to re-set the salaries of existing ETs as from 1 September 2008, new safeguarding provisions were introduced to cover the possibility of a reduction in salary as a result of re-determination. When the salary of an ET is reduced following

a) a re-determination as at 1 September 2008; or
b) subsequently on the grounds that there have been significant changes in the nature of the work undertaken or the degree of challenge in the role safeguarding will apply.

The safeguarding period will end in the case of a) on 31 August 2011 and of b) on the third anniversary of the relevant date in accordance with the principles outlined in paragraph 5.3. Safeguarding, however, will cease to be payable before the end date if:

- the teacher's salary is subsequently increased so that the increase exceeds the safeguarded sum; or
- he/she ceases to be an ET; or

- his/her employment at the school terminates in circumstances other than those specified in paragraphs 42 or 43 of the Document.

ETs must, within one month of any determination to reduce their salary, be notified in writing of that fact and of:

- the reason for the determination;
- the ET's original salary;
- the safeguarded sum; and
- the date on which the safeguarding will end.

The Excellent Teacher scheme is available in Wales, but there is no known example at the moment. *Quick Guides PAY8 Excellent Teacher Scheme.*

D14 UNQUALIFIED TEACHERS

In order to comply with the anti-age discrimination regulations and because of the widely varying cash values of increments at different points on the scale, the previous 10-point scale was reduced to a new 6-point scale as from 1 September 2008.

Assimilation to the new scale in the case of teachers, who were previously employed, but have not been assimilated to the new scale, should be carried out in accordance with the following table:

Previous 10-point scale	Assimilation point on new six point scale
1	1
2	2
3	2
4	3

Teachers' Pay

5	3
6	3
7	4
8	5
9	6
10	6

Unqualified teachers who first take up a post on or after 1 September 2009 must be placed on point 1 of the new scale, unless the relevant body awards a discretionary point or points for other relevant experience. Any scale points awarded to an unqualified teacher are permanent whether he/she remains in the same post or takes up a new one. Schools are legally only permitted to employ the following categories of unqualified teachers:

- trainees working towards QTS;
- overseas trained teachers who have not exceeded the four years they are allowed to 'teach' without having QTS; and
- instructors (people with particular skills and/or expertise), who may only be employed for as long as a qualified teacher cannot be recruited (they should not, therefore be given permanent contracts).

Unqualified teachers may be awarded an allowance if, in the context of the school's staffing structure, they have:

- a sustained responsibility which is focused on teaching and learning and requires the exercise of a teacher's professional skills and judgment; or
- qualifications and experience, which bring added value to their role.

Where an unqualified teacher suffers a loss in salary because the allowance he/she holds is reduced in value or removed from the school's staffing structure, he/she must be paid a safeguarded sum in accordance with the normal principles and be informed of the relevant details. The usual cessation principles will also apply.

D15 RECRUITMENT AND RETENTION BENEFITS

Governing bodies may make such payments or provide other financial assistance, support or benefits to a teacher as they think necessary for the recruitment of new teachers or to retain the services of existing teachers under the provisions of paragraph 50 of the *STPCD 2009*. Any recruitment incentives or benefits, however, may only be awarded for a fixed period not exceeding three years. A similar proviso applies to retention incentives, but these may be renewed up to a maximum of three years in exceptional circumstances.

Governing bodies are obliged to state in their pay policies whether any recruitment or retention incentives will be offered to new or existing teachers and, if so, their nature, value, duration and the basis on which they will be paid. You should be notified in writing of the following at the time when you are awarded any such incentive or benefit:

- whether the incentive is for recruitment or retention;
- whether it is to be a cash payment or, e.g., assistance

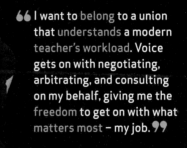

Teachers' Pay

with housing or travel expenses;
- when and how it will be paid; and
- the start date and the duration of the incentive.

Quick Guides PAY11 Recruitment and Retention Incentives (R & Rs).

D16 ANNUAL SALARY STATEMENT

On 1 September each year, or when you cross the threshold, or change jobs, you should receive a salary statement that includes:
- qualification points;
- experience points;
- any additional point awarded to a Fast Track teacher; and
- any additional performance point (double-jumping on the main scale);

or

points on the upper pay spine (U1, 2 or 3);

and

any TLR payments; any SEN allowances; any safeguarding elements; or any recruitment or retention incentives or benefits.

If you are a member of the leadership group or an AST, the salary statement should cover the following instead:
- your ISR/range;
- the salary point on the ISR/range;
- the basis on which remuneration has been determined (e.g., the award of a performance point(s));
- any safeguarded elements; and
- the criteria, including performance objectives

on which your salary will be reviewed in future.

Quick Guides PAY16 Salary Statements.

D17 PAY LEVELS

Pay Levels for the period 1 September 2009 to 31 August 2011 (£s per annum)

Scales for qualified teachers

Main scale
National (England and Wales)

Scale point	1 Sept 2009	1 Sept 2010
M1	21102	21588
M2	22771	23295
M3	24602	25168
M4	26494	27104
M5	28582	29240
M6	30842	31552
Fringe		
M1	22117	22626
M2	23783	24331
M3	25613	26203
M4	27513	28146
M5	29597	30278
M6	31855	32588
Outer London		
M1	24552	25117
M2	26074	26674
M3	27688	28325
M4	29403	30080
M5	31896	32630
M6	34326	35116
Inner London		
M	26000	27000
M2	27493	28408
M3	29071	29889

M4	30739	31446
M5	33103	33865
M6	35568	36387

Upper Pay Spine
National (England and Wales)

Scale point		1 Sept 2009	1 Sept 2010
1.	U1	33412	34181
2.	U2	34650	35447
3.	U3	35929	36756

Fringe

1.	U1	34426	35218
2.	U2	35662	36483
3.	U3	36945	37795

Outer London

1.	U1	36753	37599
2.	U2	38114	38991
3.	U3	39523	40433

Inner London

1.	U1	40288	41497
2.	U2	42267	43536
3.	U3	43692	45000

Allowances

Special educational needs (SEN) Allowances (£s)

	1 Sept 2009	1 Sept 2010
SEN 1	1956	2001
SEN 2	3865	3954

Teaching and learning responsibility (TLR) payments (£s)
The maximum and minimum payments from 1 September 2009 and September 2010 are:

	1 September 2009		1 September 2010	
	Minimum	Maximum	Minimum	Maximum
TLR1	7158	12114	7323	12393
TLR2	2478	6057	2535	6197

The up-rating of 2.3% also applies to the cash value of an individual teacher's TLR that is in the school's staffing structure, even if the post has not been taken up – e.g., because of later implementation.

Excellent teacher scheme (ETS) payments (£s p.a.)
ET salaries are spot salaries payable within the ranges set out below:

The ranges for the four pay bands are as follows:

	1 September 2009		1 September 2010	
	Minimum	Maximum	Minimum	Maximum
National (England and Wales)	38804	50918	39697	52090
Fringe	39901	52015	40819	53212
Outer London	42685	54799	43668	56061
Inner London	47188	59302	48600	60993

Teachers' Pay

Advanced Skills Teachers (ASTs)

National (England and Wales)

	1 Sept 2009	1 Sept 2010
AST1	36618	37461
AST2	37536	38400
AST3	38473	39358
AST4	39432	40339
AST5	40413	41343
AST6	41426	42379
AST7	42542	43521
AST8	43523	44525
AST9	44610	45637
AST10	45755	46808
AST11	46944	48024
AST12	48025	49130
AST13	49226	50359
AST14	50453	51614
AST15	51710	52900
AST16	53084	54305
AST17	54304	55553
AST18	55669	56950

Fringe

AST1	37627	38493
AST2	38546	39433
AST3	39482	40391
AST4	40445	41376
AST5	41429	42382
AST6	42439	43416
AST7	43558	44560
AST8	44532	45557
AST9	45623	46673
AST10	46768	47844
AST11	47953	49056
AST12	49041	50169
AST13	50242	51398
AST14	51466	52650
AST15	52717	53930
AST16	54097	55342
AST17	55323	56596
AST18	56681	57985

Outer London

AST1	39523	40433
AST2	40442	41373
AST3	41376	42328
AST4	42340	43314
AST5	43321	44318
AST6	44331	45351
AST7	45450	46496
AST8	46431	47499
AST9	47516	48609
AST10	48664	49784
AST11	49846	50993
AST12	50934	52106
AST13	52135	53335
AST14	53355	54583
AST15	54612	55869
AST16	55989	57277
AST17	57210	58526
AST18	58577	59925

Inner London

AST1	43538	44540
AST2	44460	45483
AST3	45400	46445
AST4	46356	47423
AST5	47343	48432
AST6	48353	49466
AST7	49472	50610
AST8	50450	51611
AST9	51534	52720
AST10	52682	53894
AST11	53865	55104
AST12	54952	56216
AST13	56153	57445
AST14	57380	58700
AST15	58631	59980
AST16	60011	61392
AST17	61231	62640
AST18	62596	64036

Leadership spine (heads, deputies and assistant heads)

National (England and Wales)

Spine Point	1 Sept 2009	1 Sept 2010
L1	36618	37461
L2	37536	38400
L3	38473	39358
L4	39432	40339
L5	40413	41343
L6	41426	42379
L7	42542	43521
L8	43523	44525

Teachers' Pay

L9	44610	45637	L14	51466	52650
L10	45755	46808	L15	52717	53930
L11	46944	48024	L16	54097	55342
L12	48025	49130	L17	55323	56596
L13	49226	50359	L18	56681	57985
L14	50453	51614	L19	58062	59398
L15	51710	52900	L20	59480	60849
L16	53084	54305	L21	60929	62331
L17	54304	55553	L22	62413	63849
L18	55669	56950	L23	63929	65400
L19	57049	58362	L24	65495	67002
L20	58464	59809	L25	67092	68636
L21	59910	61288	L26	68733	70314
L22	61398	62811	L27	70405	72025
L23	62919	64367	L28	72126	73785
L24	64479	65963	L29	73893	75593
L25	66082	67602	L30	75700	77442
L26	67717	69275	L31	77552	79336
L27	69394	70991	L32	79455	81283
L28	71116	72752	L33	81404	83277
L29	72877	74554	L34	83391	85309
L30	74691	76409	L35	85438	87404
L31	76537	78298	L36	87526	89540
L32	78439	80244	L37	89677	91740
L33	80389	82238	L38	91871	93985
L34	82376	84271	L39	94082	96246
L35	84423	86365	L40	96411	98629
L36	86514	88504	L41	98792	101065
L37	88664	90704	L42	101244	103573
L38	90858	92948	L43	103750	106137
L39	93072	95213			
L40	95395	97590	**Outer London**		
L41	97779	100028	L1	39523	40433
L42	100228	102534	L2	40442	41373
L43	102734	105097	L3	41376	42328
			L4	42340	43314
Fringe			L5	43321	44318
L1	37627	38493	L6	44331	45351
L2	38546	39433	L7	45450	46496
L3	39482	40391	L8	46431	47499
L4	40445	41376	L9	47516	48609
L5	41429	42382	L10	48664	49784
L6	42439	43416	L11	49846	50993
L7	43558	44560	L12	50934	52106
L8	44532	45557	L13	52135	53335
L9	45623	46673	L14	53355	54583
L10	46768	47844	L15	54612	55869
L11	47953	49056	L16	55989	57277
L12	49041	50169	L17	57210	58526
L13	50242	51398	L18	58577	59925

Teachers' Pay

L19	59958	61338	L24	71406	73049
L20	61372	62784	L25	73006	74686
L21	62819	64264	L26	74641	76358
L22	64303	65782	L27	76316	78072
L23	65824	67338	L28	78040	79835
L24	67384	68934	L29	79804	81640
L25	68988	70575	L30	81617	83495
L26	70622	72247	L31	83464	85384
L27	72299	73962	L32	85363	87327
L28	74022	75725	L33	87313	89322
L29	75782	77525	L34	89302	91356
L30	77596	79381	L35	91349	93451
L31	79446	81274	L36	93437	95587
L32	81344	83215	L37	95594	97793
L33	83297	85213	L38	97782	100031
L34	85284	87246	L39	99996	102296
L35	87328	89337	L40	102325	104679
L36	89416	91473	L41	104709	107118
L37	91572	93679	L42	107152	109617
L38	93764	95921	L43	109658	112181
L39	95977	98185			
L40	98304	100565			
L41	100687	103003			
L42	103130	105502			
L43	105640	108070			

Inner London

L1	43538	44540
L2	44460	45483
L3	45400	46445
L4	46356	47423
L5	47343	48432
L6	48353	49466
L7	49472	50610
L8	50450	51611
L9	51534	52720
L10	52682	53894
L11	53865	55104
L12	54952	56216
L13	56153	57445
L14	57380	58700
L15	58631	59980
L16	60011	61392
L17	61231	62640
L18	62596	64036
L19	63976	65448
L20	65391	66895
L21	66837	68375
L22	68325	69897
L23	69840	71447

Teachers' Pay

School groups
National (England and Wales)

Group	Range of Spinal points	Salary range 1 September 2009	Salary range 1 September 2010
1	L6 – L18	41426 – 55669	42379 – 56950
2	L8 – L21	43523 – 59910	44525 – 61288
3	L11 – L24	46944 – 64479	48024 – 65063
4	L14 – L27	50453 – 69394	51614 – 70991
5	L18 – L31	55669 – 76537	56950 – 78298
6	L21 – L35	59910 – 84423	61288 – 86365
7	L24 – L39	64479 – 93072	65963 – 95213
8	L28 – L43	71116 – 102734	72752 – 105097

Fringe

1	L6 – L18	39501 – 52761	40491 – 54081
2	L8 – L21	41451 – 56715	42489 – 58134
3	L11 – L24	44637 – 60963	45753 – 62490
4	L14 – L27	47904 – 65535	49104 – 67176
5	L18 – L31	52761 – 72189	54081 – 73995
6	L21 – L35	56715 – 79530	58134 – 81519
7	L24 – L39	60963 – 87576	62490 – 89766
8	L28 – L43	67137 – 96576	68817 – 98991

Outer London

1	L6 – L18	41265 - 54525	42297 – 55890
2	L8 – L21	43218 - 58473	44301 – 59937
3	L11 – L24	46398 - 62724	47559 – 64293
4	L14 – L27	49665 - 67299	50907 – 68982
5	L18 – L31	54525 - 73950	55890 – 75801
6	L21 – L35	58473 - 81288	59937 – 83322
7	L24 – L39	62724 - 89340	64293 – 91575
8	L28 – L43	68901 - 98334	70626 – 100794

Inner London

1	L6 – L18	45006 - 58266	46134 – 59724
2	L8 – L21	46959 - 62214	48135 – 63771
3	L11 – L24	50139 - 66468	51393 – 68130
4	L14 – L27	53409 - 71040	54/47 – 72816
5	L18 – L31	58266 - 77691	59724 – 79635
6	L21 – L35	62214 - 85032	63771 – 87159
7	L24 – L39	66468 - 93081	68130 – 95409
8	L28 – L43	72642 - 102075	74460 – 104628

Teachers' Pay

Unqualified teacher scale
National (England and Wales)

Scale Point	1 Sept 2009	1 Sept 2010
1	15461	15817
2	17260	17657
3	19058	19497
4	20856	21336
5	22655	23177
6	24453	25016

Fringe

1	16477	16856
2	18274	18695
3	20072	20534
4	21870	22374
5	23668	24213
6	25466	26052

Outer London

1	18366	18789
2	20165	20629
3	21964	22470
4	23764	24311
5	25562	26150
6	27362	27992

Inner London

1	19445	19893
2	21242	21731
3	23041	23571
4	24838	25410
5	26636	27249
6	28434	29088

D18 TEACHERS' PENSIONS

The Teachers' Pension Scheme is the responsibility of the Secretary of State for Children, Schools and Families. The scheme is governed by *Teachers' Pensions Regulations 1997*. It is administered by Teachers' Pensions (TP) and run by *Capita plc, Mowden Hall, Darlington, Co. Durham DL3 9EE. Tel: 0845 6066166, Fax: 01325 745789*

and *Minicom: 0845 6099899.* Both employees and employers make regular contributions related to the gross annual earnings of the teacher. Teachers currently contribute 6.4% and employers 14.1%.

Part-time teachers who want to join the scheme no longer have to elect to have their part-time employment treated as pensionable. Calculations of pension and lump sum benefits are the same as for full-time teachers.
More information at: www.teachernet.gov.uk/ educationoverview/briefing/ currentstrategy/Pensions.

Benefits
Existing scheme members
Benefits on retirement relate to the total pensionable service of the teacher (i.e. the period for which contributions have been made). On retirement you can expect to receive as pension one eightieth of your final average earnings for every year of pensionable service and three eightieths of your final average earnings as a lump sum. While the lump sum is not subject to income tax deductions, the pension is subject to the normal income tax arrangements. The calculation is based on the final year's salary or the average of the best three consecutive years' salary (indexed linked) in the last ten years, whichever is the higher. Final average earnings are taken as the best 365 consecutive days' earnings over the final 1095 days of service.

You can get an exact calculation of your potential benefits at www.

teacherspensions.co.uk if you are between the ages of 50 and 59 and in pensionable service. You are automatically entitled to access benefits at the age of 60, or to a proportion before the age of 60. You may remain in service after the age of 60 but the maximum service that may be allowed for pension purposes is 45 years. While service beyond the 45 years does not count, the final benefits are still calculated on the final average earnings. The maximum service you can have at 60 is 40 years and between 65 and 70 is 45 years.

New entrants

Changes for new entrants into the profession have applied from 1 January 2007. A new entrant means a person who joins the scheme with no previous pensionable service or returns to teaching after a gap of more than five years.

Benefits are calculated on one-sixtieth **NOT** one-eightieth of salary. Normal pension age will be 65 **NOT** 60. There is no automatic right to a lump sum but some of the pension may be transferred to a lump sum. The normal retirement age is 65, not 60, and the minimum retirement age (except for illness) is 55.

Added years

You can increase your benefits by buying in past-added years of service, back to age 20, by paying additional voluntary contributions (AVCs) or by paying freestanding additional voluntary contributions (FSAVCs). Inland Revenue rules allow a further 9% (making 15% in total) of salary to be used to enhance retirement benefits. Provision is made for teachers who wish to step down from their existing posts to posts of less responsibility to protect their accrued pension benefits. If you consider this seek advice from your professional associations.

Phased retirement

All scheme members can draw some of their pension early while continuing to work as teachers in a reduced capacity which involves at least a 25% reduction in salary. The draw down pension is actuarially reduced.

Ill-health

If you have to stop work through ill health you can apply for ill-health benefits.

There are two different levels of benefit depending upon how serious the illness is. Total incapacity benefit (TIB) applies if you are assessed as being permanently unable to teach or to undertake any other gainful employment. Partial incapacity benefit (PIB) is awarded if you are assessed as being permanently unable to teach but able to do other work. An award of TIB includes enhancement, but there is no enhancement with PIB.

Note: Under the Age Discrimination Regulations there is a default retirement age of 65. A compulsory retirement age below 65 is unlawful unless the employer can show objective justification.

A Guide to the Teachers' Pension Scheme at: www. teacherspensions.co.uk. Government Green Paper: Simplicity, Security and Choice: Working and Saving for Retirement. More information

Teachers' Pay

at www.teacherspensions.co.uk.
Tel: 01325 745746.
Or: www.teachernet.gov.uk/
pensions.
*Quick Guides TP1 The Teachers'
Pension Scheme.*

D19 THE SINGLE STATUS AGREEMENT

Pay for your support staff colleagues is subject to a single status agreement negotiated by the National Joint Council (NJC) in 1997. The agreement covers:

- a standard working week of 37 hours for all employees; and
- a pay and grading review (job evaluation) based on principles of equal pay for work of equal value.

LAs are required to introduce a fair and non-discriminatory pay and grading structure for all workers below chief executive officer level. This job evaluation should:

- create a rank order of jobs;
- provide a fair, transparent and equal pay structure; and
- define job families and create pathways.

Job evaluation schemes are either analytical schemes or non-analytical schemes. In analytical schemes the jobs are broken down into their core components to be assessed and points allocated according to the level identified as being needed for the job. Non-analytical schemes look at jobs as a whole and include job ranking, putting jobs in order of importance to a particular service. Job rankings are then put into grades and the grades allocated a pay spine.

D20 THE SCHOOL SUPPORT STAFF NEGOTIATING BODY (SSSNB)

A new body, the School Support Staff Negotiating Body (SSSNB), responsible for the pay and conditions of service of school support staff in England was set up under statutory provisions in the *Apprenticeships, Skills, Children and Learning Act 2009.* The SSSNB is a negotiating body and comprises representatives (there are 30 voting members, 15 representing the employers and 15 the support staff unions, under an independent chair) from the:
a) employers:

- the Local Government Association;
- the Foundation and Aided Schools National Association;
- the Church of England Education Division; and
- the Catholic Education Service for England and Wales;

b) trade unions:
- UNISON;
- GMB; and
- Unite

The SSSNB covers support staff employed under a contract of employment in England:
a) by the local authority to work wholly or mainly in a maintained school or schools – excluding academies, but including short stay schools (PRUs); and
b) by the governing body of a maintained school.

The Secretary of State's remit letter tasks the SSSNB to:
- produce a core contract of employment to cover remuneration, duties and working time;

- design national job profiles;
- develop a method for converting those job role profiles into a salary structure; and
- develop a strategy to implement the national pay and conditions' framework in all maintained schools in England.

The SSSNB has been asked to submit any agreements it has reached by 28 May 2010. In the longer-term, the establishment of the SSSNB is likely to spell the end of single status in that there will be a separation of those employed by the local authority from support staff working in schools. The existence of a national statutory scale for support staff in maintained schools will also end the freedom of foundation and voluntary aided schools to set their own scale, though this does not affect their status as single employers for other purposes and they will remain free to use the national scales as they see fit.

E PUPILS

E1 ADMISSIONS OF PUPILS TO MAINTAINED SCHOOLS

Parents are entitled to express a preference for a school. Under the *Education and Skills Act 2008* pupils seeking post-16 education may apply to school sixth forms in their own right. The admission authority for community and voluntary controlled schools is the LA, which determines how many children the school will admit (subject to its capacity) and criteria for dealing with over-subscription. These functions are performed by the governing body for voluntary aided and foundation schools.

Objections to admissions policies go to the schools adjudicator who has the final word. The admissions forum for an area has the duty to try to encourage cooperation and fairness in admissions policies. Schools may object to the admissions policies of another admissions authority than the one for their own school. The forum may also examine the effect of admissions policies on 'fair admissions' by which is meant the equal chance of children from deprived backgrounds to get into the best schools. An admissions forum may refer unfair admissions to the adjudicator. The LA has a duty to refer to the adjudicator any apparently unfair admissions policy. The adjudicator also has a duty to investigate if it seems to him that unfair policies are being pursued. The LA has to make a report on the effect of admissions policies and the schools commissioner is under a duty to make a biennial report.

All maintained school admissions must be part of co-ordinated local schemes, although governing bodies of aided and foundation schools still control admissions to their schools. The aim is to make the admission arrangements clearer and more parent-friendly. All admission authorities must act 'in accordance with' the two codes published by the DCSF: one on admissions and the other on admissions appeals. The current codes are the 2009 codes. *Education and Inspections Act 2006 - EIA 2006.* Admissions

Pupils

Code of Practice for Schools published by Stationery Office customer.services@tso.co.uk. *Further information can be found at:*
www.dcsf.gov.uk/sacode/

The School Admissions Code and the School Admission Appeals Code (Wales) July 2009 impose requirements in respect of the discharge by local education authorities, governing bodies of maintained schools, admission appeals panels and admission forums of their school admissions and school admission appeals functions under the *School Standards and Framework Act 1998.* The codes include guidelines setting out the aims, objectives and other matters relating to the discharge of admissions and admission appeals functions. Each of the bodies or persons covered **must** "act in accordance with" the codes. The codes replace the Welsh *Office Code of Practice on School Admissions* which was published in April 1999; and the *National Assembly for Wales Code of Practice on School Admission Appeals* which was published in September 1999.

Parents may appeal against decisions not to admit to the school's or LA's independent appeals panel.

School information
Information in LA prospectuses must now detail each school's admission arrangements separately and all prospectuses must contain details of the new co-ordinated admissions. *More information at* www.teachernet. gov.uk/ *and then search for admissions.*

Quick Guides Admissions (AD) Section.

E2 SCHOOL ATTENDANCE

Schools should have attendance policies setting out roles and responsibilities, which should link with the school's behaviour and anti-bullying policies. The DCSF expects schools to monitor attendance and deal with unauthorised absence and late arrivals.
A model attendance policy for schools can be viewed at:
www.teachernet.gov.uk/ management/atoz.

Some schools now employ attendance officers. Job descriptions vary from purely administrative roles to much more active roles including monitoring and holding formal meetings with parents and other agencies.
The Department recommends a range of actions to overcome attendance problems, including;
* meetings with parents;
* consideration of timetable and curriculum;
* use of learning mentors;
* use of reports and letters home;
* extra help with work missed;
* in-school counselling;
* a pastoral support programme (PSP); and
* working with the Education Welfare Service.

Education welfare officers would normally assume responsibility for the more difficult cases involving formal meetings with parents, issuing penalty notices and prosecutions. As well as establishing a good relationship with your education welfare officer, there are many other agencies who may be extremely valuable in securing regular attendance, such as the school nurse, social services, the Connexions service and youth and community workers.

A recent case established that only schools can authorise absence and that parents taking their child away on holiday cannot authorise that absence. This can only be authorised at the headteacher's discretion.

The DCSF Guidance on the Legal Measures to Secure Regular School Attendance at www.dcsf.gov.uk/school attendance *explains:*

- the roles and responsibilities of parents, schools and LAs;
- the law relating to school attendance;
- the range of intervention strategies available to LAs;
- the procedure for bringing prosecutions against parents; and
- the procedures in court hearings and the sentencing options available.

Each year schools have to provide the DCSF with information on authorised and unauthorised absence for the preparation of national statistics, which are then published annually in tables. The government sets target for LAs to secure reductions in the levels of unauthorised absence. *The Education (School Attendance Targets) Regulations are at* www.opsi.gov.uk and then type in 'school attendance'.

In Wales the regulations are *The Education (School Performance and Unauthorised Absence Targets) (Wales) (Amendment) Regulations 2006.*

Failure to attend regularly

If a pupil of compulsory school age fails to attend regularly his/her parent commits an offence.

Truancy

The LA and police can exercise their powers to enforce truants caught in a public place to attend school. LAs, authorised school staff and the police have the power to issue a penalty notice. There is no requirement for them to do so. In a school the 'authorised staff' are the headteacher and any member of the staff authorised by the headteacher. The penalty notice will require a parent to pay a fixed sum of money to the LA by a given date, instead of being taken to court on account of their child's truancy. Initially the set sums are:

- £50 if paid within 28 days of the receipt of the notice; or
- £100 if paid within 40 days.

No prosecution will follow if the penalty is paid within 42 days.

A pupil at a secondary school was frequently absent. The LA took her mother to court. The mother claimed that the absence was due to an 'unavoidable' cause, as the girl had been bullied at the school. Her daughter had become almost suicidal, she claimed, hence she had taken her out of the school. She also claimed that the school had interfered with the right to family life under the *European Convention on Human Rights.* Magistrates held that the bullying was no more than commonplace in the majority of schools. The interference had been necessary to ensure

Pupils

school attendance. On appeal the High Court agreed with the magistrates.

In a separate case, a mother claimed 'duress' as the excuse for failing to send her child to school. The court rejected the claim. Although the boy concerned was violent towards his mother, there was no evidence that a person of reasonable fortitude would have felt in danger of serious injury or death, which is the test for duress. Failure to send a child to school is a strict liability offence: if it happens you are guilty; and the child had not attended school, and that was all that was needed for a conviction.

The *Crime and Disorder Act 1998* allows schools to release the names of persistent offenders to the police, along with other information. *DCSF Guidance on the Legal Measures available to Secure Regular School Attendance* : www.dcsf.gov.uk/schoolattendance.

Penalty notices during exclusion

From September 2007 full time education must be provided from and including the sixth day of exclusion, which would normally be at a school or a pupil referral unit. Parents will be responsible for supervising their child during the first five days of any exclusion and will face a penalty notice if their child is found in a public place in school hours without reasonable justification.

Encouraging parents

The government recognises the importance of parents in establishing good attendance

patterns at an early age and has produced a free leaflet for parents. *(School Attendance: Information for Parents)*.

Parenting contracts

A LA or governing body of a maintained school can enforce a parenting contract when they have reason to believe that a pupil's behaviour at school is likely to cause significant disruption to the education of other pupils, or is a significant detriment to the welfare of the child, or of other pupils, or to the health and safety of staff, or forms part of a pattern of behaviour which, if continued, may put the child at risk of exclusion on disciplinary grounds.

Parenting orders

The governing body of a maintained school or LA may now apply to a magistrate's court for a parenting order in respect of a pupil who appears to be engaging in behaviour which would warrant exclusion for a fixed period or permanently. (Previously only a LA could apply). *The Anti-Social Behaviour Act 2003. Education and Inspections Act 2006.*

Parenting orders can be imposed on parents of pupils in Wales whose behaviour has led them to be excluded. *Education (Parenting Orders) (Wales) Regulations 2005.*

Taking a pupil off the register

A child's name can only be taken off the register in circumstances designated in the regulations. *(Pupil Registration Regulations 2006).*

School attendance orders

Parents who fail to ensure that their child is admitted onto a school roll or fail to provide education 'otherwise than at school' to an acceptable standard can face a school attendance order. The process is managed by the LA, which has a choice of which maintained school it can name in the notice to parents – including schools outside its area. If the LA chooses to serve a school attendance order on a child who has a statement of special educational needs, the order must specify the name of the school in the statement, if one is named. If the statement does not name a school, the LA must amend it by naming a school. Parents do not have to accept the named school. They have 15 days to negotiate another.

Quick Guides Registration and Attendance (RA) Section.

E3 REGISTERING PUPILS' ATTENDANCE

Governing bodies, or proprietors, of every school must ensure that an attendance register is kept (except where the pupils are boarders). They can be kept manually or electronically. If on a computer, there must be a printout at least once per month. At the end of the year the printouts must be bound into annual volumes. The responsibility for monitoring school attendance rests with the school at which a pupil is registered. If a pupil is attending other institutions, arrangements must be made to monitor attendance. Regular checks should be made during the school day in order to avoid post-registration truancy

Taking the register

The register must be updated twice daily at the start of the morning session and once during the afternoon. Your school should have a policy on how long registers remain open. You should not allow children to take the register. This creates a risk that a legal action for non-attendance may fail. The register must record the following:

- whether the pupil is present, absent, or attending an approved educational activity.

An 'approved educational activity' is defined as:
- one taking place off the school premises;
- approved by a person authorised by the governing body or the head;
- supervised by a person approved by the governing body or head;
- of an educational nature, including work experience, field trips and educational visits, interviews with prospective employers, or for a place in higher or further education; or
- link courses where pupils attend an FE college for part of their time, or franchised pupils receiving part of their education off-site at another location while remaining on roll and under school supervision (e.g. sick children being taught at home), or attending an approved sporting activity.

- the nature of the approved educational activity (for a pupil of compulsory school age);
- whether the absence of a pupil of compulsory school age is an

Pupils

'authorised' or 'unauthorised' absence.

NB. The DCSF have ruled that absence because of a school target-setting day or study leave must be recorded as an absence. Only activities off-site that are supervised may be recorded as approved educational activity. As of January 1010 this is under review.

Authorised absence is when the school has given approval in advance or has accepted an explanation after the absence. All other absences are 'unauthorised'. Schools, not parents, authorise absence and must be consistent in applying DCSF guidelines. Schools should ensure that parents know their responsibility for their children's regular attendance at school.

Inspection

School admission and attendance registers must be available for inspection by HMIs, registered inspectors and for LA maintained schools, by an LA officer.

Failure to attend regularly

If a pupil of compulsory school age fails to attend regularly his/her parent commits an offence. Schools should have a policy on how long registers remain open.

Taking a pupil off the register

A child's name can only be taken off the register in circumstances designated in the regulations. Essentially these cover situations where the destination is known; or the transfer is agreed with the knowledge of the local authority; or where a pupil 'disappears' and reasonable efforts by both the school and local authority have failed to discover the pupil's whereabouts.

Ensuring attendance

The LA and police can exercise their powers to enforce truants caught in a public place to attend school.

Prosecution of parents

Parents who fail to educate their children suitably can face a school attendance order. The process is managed by the LA, which has a choice of which maintained school it can name in the notice to parents - including schools outside its area. If the LA chooses to serve an attendance order on a statemented child, the order must specify the name of the school in the statement, if one is named. If the statement does not name a school, the LA must amend it by naming a school. Parents do not have to accept the named school. They have 15 days to negotiate another.

On-the-spot fines

Heads as well as education officers of an LA and the police now have the power to penalise parents if a pupil's absence is not authorised by the head - a possible £50 for the first offence, rising to a maximum of £100 with more offences. *Details from* www.dcsf.gov.uk *or Tel: 0870 0002288.*

Encouraging parents

The government recognises the importance of parents in establishing good attendance patterns at an early age and has produced a free leaflet for parents. *School Attendance: Information for Parents. Call 0845 6022260, quoting reference PPY 181 (REV 2002).*

The Crime and Disorder Act 1998 allows schools to release the names of persistent offenders to the police, along with other information. *DCSF Guidance on the Legal Measures available to Secure Regular School Attendance at* www.dcsf.gov.uk/schoolattendance. *Anti-social Behaviour Act 2004. A Model Attendance Policy can be viewed on:* www.teachernet.gov.uk/management/atoz. *Quick Guides Registration and Attendance (RA) Section* contains a model policy.

E4 LEAVE OF ABSENCE FOR PUPILS

Leave can be granted by a person authorised by the governing body - usually the head. It is normally granted for family holidays, but it can be granted to allow a pupil to undertake paid or unpaid employment - except for taking part in a performance for which a licence has been granted, or employment abroad where a licence has been granted. (**NB** work experience is not employment).

Holiday leave
Each parental request must be judged on a case-by-case basis. The head should not give leave automatically, but should take into account:
- the age and attainment of the child;
- ability to catch up with work;
- the time of the year and nature of the proposed holiday; and
- parental wishes.

If the pupil still goes on a holiday without permission, it counts as unauthorised absence. Parents could be fined.

Short-term leave
Schools can grant short-term leave for family reasons. It is up to the school to determine the reasonableness.

Medical
Where a pupil becomes pregnant, leave should be given for no more than 18 weeks after which the absence would be unauthorised. The school should do all it can to support the pupil remaining in school as long as possible. Dental and medical appointments are valid reasons for missing registration and constitute authorised absence. Schools can authorise absence for other unavoidable causes, so long as the unavoidability refers to the pupil and not someone else in the family. Schools, however, may sanction limited absence for young carers until other arrangements can be made. Heads should set a time limit for such absences. If the pupil leaves for an appointment after registering no absence needs to be recorded.

Religious observance
There is no legislation or regulation or DCSF guidance on this matter. Schools must review each application sensitively and reasonably. It would be reasonable to insist on advance notice, as religious festivals are likely to be fixed well ahead. Sometimes schools have to consider the question of what action to take if the child asks for time off for a different religious

Pupils

festival than the religion followed by his/her parents.

'Precautionary leave of absence'
The DCSF guidance on exclusions states that where a pupil needs to be removed from the school for an investigation to be carried out, whether by the police or by the school, it is permissible to grant leave of absence, with the parent's consent. It must not be proposed by the parent as the result of a threat by the school.

Distance from school
A pupil will not have failed to attend regularly if the parent can prove that the school is not within walking distance (defined as two miles for children under 8 and three miles for children over 8), in each case measured by the nearest available route and where the LA has not made other suitable arrangements, such as to provide transport. Sometimes the LA will be obliged to provide free transport if the parents apply, even if the pupil is within the limit, depending on the child's age and nature of the route. *Circular 10/99 and Annex A: Reasons for Absence.*
Quick Guides Registration and Attendance (RA) Section.

E5 CONSULTING PUPILS

Maintained schools in England have a duty under the *Education Act 2002* to take notice of the DCSF guidance on consulting with pupils on decisions that affect them. An advisory group has been set up at the DCSF. This was further reinforced by *The Children Act 2004*, which changed LAs to Children's Services Authorities (CSAs), with

a brief to co-ordinate all the agencies which deal with children and young people. The title has now been withdrawn but the responsibility remains the same. A national Children's Commissioner in England, is Professor Al Aynsley-Green. He will be replaced by Dr Maggie Atkinson from April 2010. www.11million. org.uk/commissioner.

Wales
The Commissioner for Wales is Keith Towler.

The Schools Councils (Wales) Regulations 2005 require maintained schools in Wales to set up school councils providing pupils opportunities to discuss and make representations about matters relating to the school or other issues of concern to them.

E6 COMPLAINTS

All maintained and independent schools must have procedures to deal with complaints from pupils, parents and members of the public. The school should ensure that you know its procedures and should train you in how they are used in the school. *Education Act 2002.*

In Wales guidance about handling complaints is contained in *School Governing Bodies Complaints Procedures 03/2004*. There is also *Guidance for School Governing Bodies on Procedures for Complaints involving Pupils 39/2006.*
Quick Guides PC1 Parental and Other Complaints: Guidance for Schools; PC1A Independent Schools: Parental Complaints; PC2 Complaints Policy:

Maintained Schools; PC2A Independent Schools: Parental Complaints Policy.

E7 ANTI-BULLYING

In a court case in 2000, bullying was defined as 'conduct intended to cause hurt, either physical or psychological, which is unprovoked and which continues over a long time'. All schools should now have anti-bullying policies, which should be communicated to staff, pupils and parents. Procedures should be in place to ensure that the policies are properly put into practice. If you come across any sign of bullying you can try to prevent its escalation on the spot, but whatever immediate action you take, you must report the incident to the person named in the school's procedures.

Bullies are making increasing use of computers and mobile phones to harass their victims. This cyberbullying can include posting offensive or defamatory comments or messages online, or harassment using mobile phones. The type of bullying may be sexist, racist, homophobic or attacking the victim's disability, their cultural or religious background or other kinds of difference. In some cases cyber bullying may be a criminal offence.

Two bullying cases

Two cases where parents have claimed damages from schools for alleged negligence in combating bullying have emphasised the need for schools to have clear policies and procedures in place. In one case, the parents of a young teenage girl alleged that the girl had been bullied out-of-school by pupils belonging to the school. The Court held that the school's duty did not extend to bullying outside the school. But the school did have a duty to prevent any bullying from spilling over into the school.

In the second case the school was criticised for its institutional attitude to bullying and its lack of positive procedures. A boy claimed that he had been bullied throughout his secondary school career, in the school and on a school visit. The school had been negligent in dealing with his problems. The judge said that the evidence showed that for most of the time, the school did not have a policy; there seemed to be a breakdown in communication between the responsible teacher and at least one member of staff had shown manifest indifference to the boy's plight. He held that the school had been negligent and awarded damages to the pupil.

Compensation for bullying

Torfaen County Borough Council made an out-of-court settlement of £20000 to a 23-year-old woman in compensation for bullying. The claim was that bullying at her primary school had led to depression and attempted suicide. The conclusion was reached twelve years after the date of the bullying.

What schools should do:

- ensure that anti-bullying policies and procedures are in place;

Pupils

- ensure that all meetings where bullying is alleged are recorded. (The records should be kept until the pupil is at least 24, although some LAs recommend an even longer time limit); and
- ensure that all teachers and other school staff are trained in the school's policies and procedures and, in particular, in the procedures for passing on confidential information and monitoring any strategies put into place. **The School Standards and Framework Act 1998** requires schools to have anti-bullying procedures.

Under the ASCLA 09 parents will be able to take a complaint to the Local Government Ombudsman.

Guidance

In December 2000 the government issued non-statutory guidance, *(64/2000) Bullying – Don't Suffer in Silence – An Anti-Bullying Pack for Schools.* The pack gives guidance on whole-school policies, pupils' experiences, finding out about bullying in school, strategies to combat bullying, working with parents, beyond the classroom and advice for pupils, parents and families, along with case studies and advice on materials.

The National Assembly for Wales has published similar guidance, *Respecting Others: Anti-Bullying Guidance (23/2003). The Welsh guidance on bullying can be found at: www.learning. wales.gov.uk.*
Inclusion and Pupil Support Circular 47/2006. Exclusions Circulars 1/2004 and 1A/2004.

Ofsted has also published a report on bullying in schools, *Bullying: Effective Action in Secondary Schools HMI 465. The Anti-Bullying Alliance* is based at the National Children's Bureau and brings together 65 organisations to combat bullying. It provides resources and ideas for schools and has run an annual anti-bullying week for the last three years. *More information at: www.anti-bullyingalliance.org.*

The DCSF has an anti-bullying charter for schools. The charter commits the school community to discuss, monitor and review the school anti-bullying policy on a regular basis and to report back quickly to any parents/carers who have concerns about bullying.

See the anti-bullying website on: www.teachernet.gov.uk/wholeschool/behaviour/tacklingbullying.
DCSF website at www.dcsf.gov.uk/bullying.
Access the Ofsted report at www.ofsted.gov.uk.
Government advice and model policy on: www.teachernet.gov.uk/wholeschool/behaviour/tacklingbullying.
See also: www.anti-bullyingalliance.org.uk and www.childline.org.uk/Explore/Bullying/Pages/Bullyinginfo.aspx
Safe to Learn: Embedding Anti-Bullying Work in Schools, DCSF 2007. This includes specialist advice on cyberbullying and homophobic bullying.
Another website dealing with bullying is www.parentscentre.gov.uk.

Quick Guides CP6 Child Protection: Anti-Bullying Advice; CP6A Model Anti-Bullying Policy; CP6B Safe to Learn: New Anti-Bullying Guidance.

E8 PUPILS' PROPERTY

Looking after pupils' property

It is unlikely that your LA or school will accept liability for the loss or damage to a pupil's property. Pupils, like teachers, can make a claim if they think the loss/damage was caused by the school's negligence. Schools usually make it clear in their prospectuses that they refuse to look after pupils' personal property brought into the school. But there may be times when it is unavoidable. The school must have a clear procedure for such occasions. You should not normally be expected to look after pupils' property, but, if you do, you must take reasonable care of it and should normally aim to return it by the end of the school day.

Confiscated property

The *Education and Inspections Act 2006* puts confiscation on a statutory basis. There is a statutory defence for school staff who have reasonably confiscated pupils' property. A staff member has a defence to all proceedings against him or her and is not liable for any damage or loss arising. Your school should have informed parents (usually via the prospectus) that staff have the right to confiscate pupils' property for disciplinary reasons. It should also state the time within which parents must collect confiscated property which the

school is not willing to return to the pupil (e.g. cigarette lighters) or the LA or governors (on behalf of maintained schools) reserve the right to sell it. It should also be made clear that illegal items may be handed over to the police or destroyed by the school.

Heads and authorised teachers also have a statutory right to search pupils for offensive weapons. *(See Section H10).*

You are obliged to take reasonable care of confiscated property. If it is damaged or lost through your negligence you could be held personally liable. Some confiscated items, e.g. mobile phones, are high-value items. Therefore, the school should ensure that confiscated property can be locked away and a record taken of the owner, who confiscated it, when and how long the confiscation is to last, and who returned the property to the pupil and when.

If the property is illegal (e.g. drugs), or even against the school's rules, you should inform the head as soon as possible and hand the property to the head. The head will have to determine whether to hand the property to the police. ***Education and Inspections Act 2006.***

Lost property

Schools will have their procedures for dealing with staff and pupils' lost property. Reasonable attempts should be made to find the property, but you should not search pupils' clothing or bags without their consent unless you have involved senior staff.

Pupils

Cigarettes and alcohol

It is an offence to sell cigarettes and alcohol to children under 18, but it is not illegal for a child under 18 to possess them. Teachers can confiscate cigarettes and alcohol and any other unacceptable items found on pupils, but must not destroy or consume them, as this would amount to criminal damage or theft. It is usual to invite the pupil's parents to collect the items from the school.

Education and Inspections Act 2006. DCSF School Discipline and Pupil Behaviour Policies 2007.
Quick Guides PD8 Confiscating Pupils' Property: Points of Law.

E9 PHOTOGRAPHING PUPILS

Schools should have their own policies on photographing pupils. The policy should cover parents photographing and videoing school events and the school using photographs and video images for their own publicity purposes. Photographs and video images of pupils are personal data under the **Data Protection Act 1988** and parental consent is required. Parents should be told what the photographs will be used for and whether copies will be kept. Pupils' names should not be published along with their photographs. It is reasonable for schools to monitor parental use of photography and video during school activities and to tell parents that any images (photographic or video) must not be used inappropriately.

In 2007 the GTC ruled that a supply teacher who secretly filmed disruptive pupils for TV was guilty of unacceptable professional conduct. Also in 2007, the Press Complaints Commission (PCC) upheld a complaint against a newspaper for publishing photographs taken from a video of an unruly maths class taken by a 16-year-old pupil. She wanted to explain poor results to her parents. The pupils could be identified from the pictures. The paper also published the moving images on its website. This was in breach of the PCC code of practice which says that young people should be free to complete their time at school without unnecessary intrusion. Although the story was a matter of public interest, the paper should have taken steps to obscure the pupils' identities.

The Information Commissioner's Office has issued guidance on taking photographs in school. This can be found at the Information Commissioner's website: www.ico.gov.uk .The basic principle is that where the photographs are for personal use or incidental use (e.g. in a school prospectus) they are unlikely to infringe the **Data Protection Act**. Schools also have to take into account issues of safeguarding. You should seek advice before photographing children or allowing them to be photographed.

E10 PUPILS' FINGERPRINTS

The government's school technology agency, BECTA (British Education & Communication

Technology Agency) has issued guidance about biometric technology in schools. Biometric technology is used to confirm identity and schools can use biometric systems based on fingerprint recognition for:

- cashless catering;
- automated attendance and registration; and
- school library automation.

Schools must comply with the **Data Protection Act 1998**. Biometric data must be handled in the same way as other personal data. Schools wishing to use biometric technology should explain to pupils and parents:

- what biometric technology they intend to use;
- what this will involve;
- what data will be held and stored.

Biometric data can only be used for the express purpose for which it was collected;

- how it will be secured. There should be appropriate security measures. Schools cannot pass biometric information to any outside organisation; and
- how long it will be retained. Pupils' biometric data should be destroyed when they have left the school. **BECTA Guidance on Biometric Technologies in Schools.** www.becta.org.uk.

Quick Guides DA13 Biometric Technology in Schools.

E11 DISABILITY DISCRIMINATION AND PUPILS

It is illegal to discriminate against pupils with disabilities as well as against staff. Schools must also make reasonable adjustments to enable such pupils to have access to buildings, facilities and the curriculum. Disability includes mental impairments e.g. ADHD and Tourette's syndrome. All primary, secondary and special schools should have a disability equality scheme.

All public bodies, including schools, have a duty to promote equality of opportunity for disabled persons, including pupils. This includes extended school activities. To enable this to happen, all schools must have accessibility plans in place. In disciplining a child with a disability you (and the school) should take the disability into account. If you suspect a child you teach has a disability you should inform the school's SENCO. **More information at:**

www.teachernet.gov.uk/ management/sen/schools/ accessibility.

Quick Guides has extensive guidance, points of law, model disability equality statements, policies and schemes in its **Equal Opportunities for Staff (EO)** and **Equal Opportunities for Pupils (EOP)** sections.

In 2007 a disabled student won a claim against a university for denying him wheelchair access at his graduation ceremony. The county court ruled that the university had failed to make reasonable adjustments by providing temporary ramps onto the stage for graduation day. The student who was in a wheelchair was given his graduation certificate at the bottom of the steps up to the stage.

Pupils

E12 SAFEGUARDING CHILDREN

All schools must have arrangements in place to safeguard and promote the welfare of pupils. Protecting from harm and neglect has a wide application. It includes practices such as female circumcision (female genital mutilation) and forced marriage. Schools have a duty to act on these matters and where they suspect that a child in at risk. If you suspect a child is at risk you must report it to a senior designated member of staff immediately. The DCSF has issued guidance. The Department of Health has also issued guidance on what you should do if you think a child is being abused. The phrase 'safeguarding children' has taken over from 'child protection'. *What to do if you're worried a child is being abused 2006. Safeguarding Children in Education 2004. Guidance for Safe Working Practice for the Protection of Children and Staff in Education Settings (IRSC2005). Safeguarding Children and Safer Recruitment in Education 2007* – updated in 2010. More information at: www. teachernet.gov.uk.
Quick Guides Child Protection (CP) Section.

Safeguarding Children in Education Circular 005/2008

Guidance is issued by Welsh ministers in the exercise of the powers conferred on the National Assembly by Section 175 of the **Education Act 2002** and now vested in the Welsh ministers in accordance with Schedule 11 of the **Government of Wales Act 2006**. This supplements guidance in **Safeguarding Children: Working Together** under the **Childcare Act 2004** published in March 2007 and should be read in conjunction with **All Wales Child Protection Procedures** published in April 2008. **The Education (Miscellaneous Amendments relating to Safeguarding Children) (Wales) Regulations 2009.**

Local Safeguarding Children Boards (LSCB)

These replaced Area Child Protection Committees (ACPC) on 1 April 2006.
Each local authority will have an LSCB, although it will be possible for LAs to join together to run a joint board. Each board must develop policies and procedures to safeguard and promote the welfare of children in the LA area, including:

- action to be taken where there are concerns about a child's safety or welfare, including thresholds for intervention;
- training of persons working with children or in services affecting the safety and welfare of children;
- recruitment and supervision of persons who work with children;
- investigation of allegations concerning persons who work with children;
- safety and welfare of children who are privately fostered;
- co-operation with neighbouring children's services authorities and their board partners;
- communicating to persons and bodies in the area of the authority the need to safeguard and promote the welfare of children. Raising

their awareness of how this can best be done, and encouraging them to do so;

- monitoring and evaluating the effectiveness of what is done by the authority and their board partners individually and collectively to safeguard and promote the welfare of children and advising them of ways to improve;
- participating in the planning of services for children in the area; and
- undertaking reviews of serious cases and advising the authority and their board partners on lessons to be learned.

In 2009 the parents of a boy who had been subject to a violent gang attack were given the right to force an LSCB to undertake a Serious Case Review into the matter even though a civil case for compensation was being taken.

Local Safeguarding Children Boards Regulations 2006.

The education of 'looked after children'

New regulations require admission authorities in England to give priority to children who are looked after by any LA under s22 of the **Children Act 1989** (so long as the LA expects the child to remain looked after at the time of the proposed admission). However, there are provisos. The priority does not prevent schools giving priority on the grounds of ability or aptitude or religious faith. If an LA or school prioritises admissions in ability bands in order to spread ability evenly, the looked after children will have

priority within their own band, but not over children in any other band. *Education (Admission of Looked After Children) (England) Regulations 2006.* *The Education (Admission of Looked After Children) (Wales) Regulations 2009* prescribe the actions to be taken and the circumstances in which an admission authority for a maintained school must give priority in their admission arrangements to a 'relevant looked after child' (a child who is looked after by a Welsh local authority within the meaning of section 22 of the **Children Act 1989** at the time of their application and who will still be so looked after at the time when he/she is admitted to school).

Quick Guides CP11 Example of a Policy for Looked After Children (LAC).

Designated teacher

Guidance in **Safeguarding Children and Safer Recruitment in Education** advises that each school must have policies and must train staff and appoint a 'designated teacher' with responsibility for safeguarding children and liaison with the governing body's 'nominated governor'. There must also be a designated deputy. The teacher should be trained to the standard required by the LSCB, particularly in relation to inter-agency working and the training should be refreshed every two years.

Designated teacher and deputy

Designated teachers must know:

- how to identify abuses;

Pupils

- the local LSCB/LA procedures;
- roles of investigating organisations and how to liaise with them;
- what records to keep;
- how to contribute to a case conference; and
- who the 'nominated governor' is and how to contact him/her.

You must know:
- who the designated and deputy designated teacher are;
- the common categories of abuse and how to recognise the main characteristics:

neglect; physical injury; sexual abuse; emotional abuse; and
- what the school's safeguarding children procedures are.

Confidentiality

You should be aware of the need for confidentiality about a pupil. But you cannot guarantee to a pupil that you will keep confidential anything they want to tell you. You can tell them that you will only tell the designated teacher. Such reports can be kept on computer and are exempt from the data protection provisions.

In October 2008 HM Government issued extensive guidance on information sharing, including a pocket guide which can be accessed at: www.everychildmatters. gov.uk/deliveringservices/ informationsharing .

You should also be aware of the school's *Sex and Relationships: Confidentiality Policy.*

Role of statutory agencies

The government's child protection guidance **Working Together to Safeguard Children** outlines the roles and responsibilities of statutory agencies, professionals, the voluntary sector and the wider community. It provides advice on what should happen if somebody has concerns about the welfare of a child. **Children's Commissioner** www.childrenscommissioner.org.
Working Together to Safeguard Children Department of Health; Home Office and DfEE 2006.
Quick Guides CP3 Sex and Relationships: Framework for a Confidentiality Policy.

Name of designated teacher:

Name of deputy designated teacher:

E13 ADVICE ON SEX AND RELATIONSHIPS

Teachers (and support staff e.g. school nurses) can give confidential advice to pupils about sexual issues in certain circumstances.

A court has ruled that a doctor could provide contraception services and advice to a young person, including, in this case to a girl of 16, in confidence, if the doctor considers that the young person is competent to understand the consequences of the advice/treatment. There is a presumption that a young person may be 'competent' to make decisions on their own behalf at 11, though there is no legal warrant for this particular age and you will have to decide case by case.

There is no direct ruling that this also covers teachers. What we

have is advice in the Department's **Sex and Relationship Education Guidance 2000**.
(In Wales the **Rights of the Child** as espoused in the United Nations Convention).

In paragraph 7.11 of the DCSF guidance teachers are advised that when they believe that a person under the age of 16 is engaging or about to engage in sexual intercourse they should attempt 'wherever possible to persuade' the young person to talk to their parent or carer.

Teachers are further advised to ensure that the pupil is aware of contraception and where to access such advice and service. However, the guidance also states that 'trained staff' must be available in all secondary schools to give young people 'full information' about contraception, including emergency contraception and where such services can be obtained. Where a pregnant pupil asks for advice but insists that her parents should not be told, you should not promise absolute confidentiality. Confidences can be over-ridden by public good e.g. where an offence has been committed against a child.

Parents of secondary pupils in the maintained sector have the absolute right in England and Wales to withdraw their children from sex education that is not part of the national curriculum.

Sex education in science is compulsory for all pupils, but sex education in sex and relationship/citizenship/PSHE classes is compulsory only for those pupils whose parents have

not withdrawn them from it. There is no clear official advice on how schools should handle this. The issue has been further complicated by a judge's ruling in January 2006 that it was legal for a girl aged under 16 to be given an abortion without her parents being notified. This had nothing to do with the actions of a school but it makes it more rather than less difficult to decide where a teacher's duty ultimately lies.

Schools should have a sex and relationship education policy, which should be a governing body policy drawn up after consultation with staff, parents and, we suggest, the pupils. All secondary schools should also ensure that there is a trained person on the staff to give confidential advice to pupils.

Schools will now have to decide whether they tell girls under 16 that they can probably have an abortion without parents being informed, or whether they recommend the child to ask the medical services for their advice. We believe that schools are likely to choose the latter course **Gillick v West Norfolk and Wisbech Area Health Authority 1985. R v Secretary of State for Health and Family Planning Association 2006.**
Quick Guides CP2 Sex and Relationships Education: Guidance; CP3 Sex and Relationships: Framework for a Confidentiality Policy.

E14 LISTENING TO CHILDREN

Children who report an abuse to a teacher (or to any other member

Pupils

of staff on the school site) must be listened to and heard, whatever form their attempts to communicate their worries take. The following points give guidance on how to deal with a child who makes an allegation:

- the child should be listened to but not interviewed or asked to repeat the account;
- avoid questions, particularly leading questions;
- the child should not be interrupted when recalling a significant event;
- all information should be noted carefully, including details such as timing, setting, who was present and what was said, in the child's own words. The account should be obtained verbatim or as near as possible;
- care should be taken not to make assumptions about what the child is saying or to make interpretations;
- listened to means just that; on no account should suggestions be made to children as to alternative explanations for their worries;
- the written record of the allegations should be signed and dated by the person who received them as soon as practicable; and
- all actions subsequently taken should be recorded.

E15 ALLEGATIONS AGAINST TEACHERS

If an allegation is made against you, you must contact your union immediately.

Abuse of trust
All education staff need to know that inappropriate behaviour

with or towards children is unacceptable. It is an offence for anyone over 18 to have any sexual activity with someone under 18 if they are in a position of trust to that person, even if the relationship is consensual. Clearly school staff are in a position of trust.

A school may also take disciplinary action against you if you behave inappropriately with pupils over 18. This includes conduct that might bring the school into disrepute or cause parents to lose confidence in the school.

Your role
All school staff are expected to play a part in the prevention of abuse and in maintaining a safe environment. From early school days teachers must help children understand what is unacceptable behaviour and to speak out if they are worried. Once they do, they must be listened to, and their concerns passed on to the school's 'designated teacher'. Given their daily contact with children in a variety of situations, including the wider caring role, all staff are vulnerable to accusations of abuse. Their relationships with pupils may lead to allegations against them being made by pupils or parents. Only in rare instances have teachers been found to be responsible for child abuse, but the consequences of false, malicious or misplaced allegations can be severe. Sometimes allegations may be well founded.

Teacher unions counsel that teachers should:
- never speak to a child alone;

- never give a pupil a lift in a car; or
- never administer medicines, unless you are trained and are contracted to do so.

Teachers sometimes feel they want to comfort a child who is upset. There is nothing intrinsically wrong with this; indeed it might be the best thing that could happen to the child. But you must ensure that other staff are around and can see you and that such a reaction is within the policies of the school and that you report your actions at the earliest opportunity.

Allegations

If allegations are made against you, you must co-operate immediately with your union and head. At the moment it is almost impossible to keep such allegations out of the media and heads, LAs and unions need to act as speedily as possible. All allegations which are considered to be a potential criminal act will be reported to the LA designated officer (LADO). The LADO will have established contacts with police, social services and other external agencies and will be able to advise the school on whether a potential criminal act has occurred. Where the allegation relates to the reasonable use of force, the head will deal with the matter at school level.

Action to be taken by staff who hear an allegation

If you receive an allegation of abuse against another member of staff you should report this immediately to the head, unless the head is the person against whom the allegation is made. An allegation against the head

should be reported immediately to the designated teacher or the nominated governor where the head is the designated teacher. The LA/school must have procedures for dealing with the allegations and may require you to provide more details. You should keep a written note of what the allegations were, who made them, when and where.

Considering whether suspension is appropriate

Decisions on suspensions are taken by the head or the governing body (action by the chair in relation to the head must be notified to the full governing body). In the case of unfounded allegations suspension is unlikely. The head should consult with the LA lead officer and consider any recommendation, which may be made by the child protection agency before a decision to suspend is taken.

> **Circumstances in which suspension properly occurs include:**
> - where a child or children is/ are at risk;
> - where the allegations are so serious that dismissal for gross misconduct is possible; or
> - where a suspension is necessary to allow the conduct of the investigation to proceed unimpeded.

In all cases where suspension is being considered, the head or nominated governor should advise the individual to seek assistance from his or her trade union and provide support. Suspension is a neutral act, not a disciplinary sanction, and will be

Pupils

on full pay. You should be kept in touch with school life during the suspension.

Alternatives to suspension

Paid leave of absence, mutual agreement to stay away from work, alternative duties/locations, or removal from contact with the pupil may also be used as an alternative to suspension.

Action by schools

All teachers should have relevant training in child protection procedures and the part that all staff, including support staff, can play in improving protection. Training should be regular and the programme should ensure that you are trained and that your training is reviewed. If you become involved in interviewing then your training should be more detailed and cover deterring and identifying potentially abusive candidates.

If an allegation is false

The guidance distinguishes between allegations that are **unproven**, where there is insufficient evidence; **mistaken or unfounded**, where a mistake has been made; **false**, where the allegation is deliberately untrue and made for some purpose (e.g. attention seeking); and **malicious**, where the intention is to damage a blameless teacher. If the allegation can be proved to be malicious the school may consider disciplinary action against the child.

Working Together to Safeguard Children 2009 at www.everychildmatters.gov.uk
Protection of Children Act 1999. Sexual Offences

(Amendment) Act 2000 (created the offence of 'abuse of trust'). *More information at:* www.teachernet.gov.uk/wholeschool/familyandcommunity/childprotection.
Safeguarding Children and Safer Recruitment in Education, Chapter 5 DCSF 2007 www.everychildmatters.gov.uk.
Physical and Mental Fitness to teach of Teachers and of Entrants to Initial Teacher Training; Circular 4/99. Joint NEOST and Teacher Union Guidance on Staff Facing an Allegation of Abuse, September 2002 at: www.teachernet.gov.uk/management/childprotection.
Guidance for Education Staff Facing Allegations of Abuse. Published by the National Network of Investigation and Referral Support Co-ordinators; December 2003: http://www.teachernet.gov.uk/wholeschool/familyandcommunity/childprotection.
Keeping your child safe on the Internet http://bit.ly/5v7a1X or *available in hard copy from 0800 77 1234.*
Quick Guides CP4 Staff Facing an Allegation of Abuse: New Guidance; CP5 Dealings with Allegations of Abuse give summaries of the guidance.

In Wales the *Staffing of Maintained Schools (Wales) Regulations 2006* require a governing body's staff disciplinary committee to appoint an independent person to carry out investigation in the case of allegations relating to child protection against a member of staff. In addition the governors must appoint an independent non-governor with voting rights to the Staff Disciplinary Committee and the Staff Disciplinary Appeals Committee.

Local contacts:

Designated teacher:

Deputy designated teacher:

Nominated governor:

LA Officer responsible for child protection:

E16 RESTRAINING PUPILS

Corporal punishment is banned in schools. This includes slapping, prodding, shaking, chalk-flicking, board-duster throwing and ruler-flicking! However, under the **Education and Inspections Act 2006**, teachers, if authorised by the head, may use 'reasonable force' to prevent a pupil from:

- committing an offence;
- causing personal injury or damage (including to themselves); or
- engaging in any activity prejudicial to the maintenance of good order, whether during a lesson or at any other time.

Your school should have a policy on the use of reasonable force, which should make clear to staff and parents the context in which reasonable restraint is allowed. The degree of force used should be the minimum needed. Staff should not give the impression of being angry, frustrated or wanting to punish the pupil. The intention of the legislation is to prevent teachers from being prosecuted for using normal physical interventions. It is not intended to extend the scope of teachers' powers of duties. You should note that if you are dealing with pupils with known severe behavioural difficulties, certain authorised restraint techniques can be used. However, you should not attempt to restrain such pupils without having been trained in the appropriate technique and in any case, should not do so on your own. For any pupil with known behaviour problems, the school should carry out a risk assessment and organise a behaviour plan. The DCSF has issued guidance on the use of physical interventions for pupils with severe behavioural difficulties.

DCSF Guidance (2007) The use of force to control or restrain pupils – gives examples of when physical intervention might be appropriate, and factors that teachers should consider before deciding to intervene. This guidance is being revised in 2010. *DCSF Guidance on the Use of Restrictive Physical Interventions for Pupils with Severe Behavioural Difficulties (Ref: LEA/0264/2003).* A risk assessment proforma can be downloaded from the *DCSF Special Needs website* www.dcsf.gov.uk/sen. *Education and Inspections Act 2006.*
The equivalent Welsh circular is (37/98) – *The Use of Reasonable Force to Control or Restrain Pupils.* Additional guidance, *Respecting Others: Anti bullying Guidance Circular*

Pupils

23/2003. Inclusion and Pupil Support 47/2006.
Quick Guides PD4 Corporal Punishment and Justifiable Restraint.

E17 PUPILS' DRESS AND APPEARANCE

Governing bodies of maintained schools have the legal duty, as part of their responsibility for 'the conduct of the school', to decide whether school uniform should be worn or not. As a result of the case **SB v Denbigh High School** it has been established that a school can legally compel pupils to wear a school uniform or any other standard dress.

The DCSF has issued guidance recommending schools to be sensitive to cost and equality issues and this is part of the statutory **Code of Practice on School Admissions.** The DCSF confirms that schools can exclude pupils for persistent and defiant non-compliance with school uniform but exclusion is not normally appropriate.

In a court case specifically on the issue of school uniform, in 1954, a parent was charged with failing to send his daughter to school, because the head sent her home every day when she turned up in trousers against the school rules. Father claimed that this was for medical reasons but refused to provide a medical certificate. The Court of Appeal said that the school had not only the right to enforce this kind of discipline but a duty to do so. The parent had committed an offence. The question of exclusion did not arise, said the judge, because the head was always ready to accept the child but required her to be properly dressed. Because of the changes in society since then the particular details of the case have been viewed with caution, but the judge made clear that:

- school rules must be reasonable;
- schools have both a right and a duty to enforce reasonable rules; and
- courts will always be prepared to test any rule for its reasonableness. **(Spiers v Warrington Corporation).**

Implications

The recent House of Lords case (**see below**) suggests that the principles still apply.

In 2006 the House of Lords decided that a school had acted properly in refusing to admit a Muslim girl who insisted on wearing a jilbab rather than the official shalwar kameeze. The Lords said that 'this is a case about a particular pupil, in a particular school, in a particular place at a particular time.' A school with a head from a Muslim background, with Muslim governors had consulted parents and a range of local Islamic scholars to arrive at a uniform which, in their view, met the religious requirements of Islam. It should not be assumed that the same decision would be arrived at in other circumstances.

Subsequent cases in 2007 have reinforced this judgement and made it more generally applicable, ruling in favour of schools banning the niqab and a silver chastity ring. The general principle is that sending a pupil home to change was not an exclusion on disciplinary grounds and hence not subject to the exclusion rules.

In contrast to these cases in a further case in 2008 a judge ruled that sending home a Sikh girl for wearing a kara bracelet was a breach of race relations legislation and because it was unlawful, the sending home became unlawful exclusion. The Sikh community is unique in Britain in that by a previous ruling of the House of Lords, Sikhs are an ethnic group defined by religion. The school's action was deemed not to be proportionate. This leaves the situation in some confusion but in general schools may still act on uniform provided that they have good reason to do so.

Quick Guides PD11 School Uniform Policies; EO11 Religious Discrimination: Points of Law; EO12 Sexual Orientation: The Law and Guidance.

Appearance

School rules about hairstyles will pass the reasonableness test if governing bodies have:

- taken professional advice from the head;
- consulted staff and parents and where relevant the LA;
- discussed the issue with pupil representatives; or
- it is explained in the school prospectus what the purpose of the rule is.

Schools with numbers of pupils from different ethnic backgrounds should consider religious and traditional reasons for particular dress and appearance. The Equal Opportunities Commission (now the EHRC) has also asked schools to observe the spirit of the sex discrimination legislation in relation to girls wearing trousers and boys wearing earrings in order to ensure that neither is treated 'less favourably'. The nature of the punishment for any transgression is ultimately at the discretion of the head.

In Spring 2003 a 14-year-old boy was excluded for wearing a 'Beckhamesque' hairstyle. As usual the decision was welcomed by some and denounced by others. There is no unanimity on the approach to extremes of dress and appearance, but the law on this issue has remained consistent.

Improving School Behaviour and Attendance: Guidance on Exclusions from Schools and PRUs 2003. School Uniform Guidance – DCSF 2007.
Welsh Assembly Circular Exclusions from Schools and PRUs (1/2004) and (1A/2004).
Guidance for Governing Bodies on School Uniform and Appearance Policies revised February 2010.
Quick Guides Pupil Discipline Documents PD1-PD13 give summaries of the law and guidance on pupil discipline and a model discipline policy.

Pupils

E18 PUPIL BEHAVIOUR

All maintained schools are expected to have strategies in place to identify and meet the needs of pupils who require help, in order to avoid truancy and disaffection. One strategy recommended by the DCSF is to have a system of home/school agreements. They do not have the force of law, but parents, pupils and schools would be expected to honour them. Under the **Education and Inspections Act 2006** a school has the right to regulate conduct when pupils are under the lawful control of staff and may impose disciplinary penalties on pupils for conduct out of school or when pupils are not under lawful control in certain circumstances (the DCSF has issued guidance on these circumstances which essentially are those in which a school's reputation or the authority of staff will be damaged by acts outside school).

Your school should also have a behaviour policy, which you should know, and act within. This policy should promote self-discipline amongst pupils, encourage good behaviour and respect for others and secure acceptable standards of behaviour. For pupils whose behaviour becomes too difficult a 'pastoral support programme' (PSP) should be put in place. Teachers and others authorised by the head now have a statutory right to impose 'disciplinary penalties', where a pupil's behaviour falls below the standard which could be reasonably expected of him/her, whether because he/she fails to follow a school rule, or an instruction given by a member of staff (whether in school or on a school activity off-site).

In determining whether a disciplinary penalty was 'reasonable' the following must be taken into account:
- whether the penalty was a proportionate punishment in the circumstances; and
- any special circumstances which are known to the person imposing the penalty, including:
  ◊ the pupil's age;
  ◊ any special educational needs;
  ◊ any disability; or
  ◊ any religious requirement affecting him/her.

Schools should have procedures for handling pupils whose behaviour is threatening. If you are not satisfied with the action taken, you should approach your union.

The power to discipline

Teachers and other staff in charge of pupils have the power to discipline them for unacceptable behaviour, breaking school rules or failure to follow a reasonable instruction. This power is set out in the **Education and Inspections Act 2006** and **DCSF Guidance School Discipline and Pupil Behaviour Policies** gives detailed advice. Disciplinary penalties must be reasonable and proportionate and corporal punishment remains unlawful.

All Wales Travel Behaviour Code

In Wales there is a statutory *All Wales Travel Behaviour Code* effective from 4 January 2010 that LAs, schools and FE institutions must have regard to when dealing with incidents of unacceptable behaviour. Advice on sanctions will follow in the WAG guidance document *Safe and Effective Intervention*.

Violent pupils

In a landmark judgement in February 2003 the House of Lords supported teachers who refused to teach violent and disruptive pupils. The five law lords held unanimously that industrial action in such cases was lawful. In a second case they decided by a majority of three to two that it was allowable for a Year 11 pupil reinstated by an appeal panel to be taught in isolation, when teachers backed by their union refused to teach him in class. Two of the Lords considered that the pupil must be substantially reintegrated into the social and educational life of the school. The other three held that the possible effects on the victim if an assailant was allowed unfettered social contact had to be taken into account. Isolating the boy while ensuring that the examination course was completed was a permissible response.

The Anti-Social Behaviour Act 2003. Education and Inspections Act 2006. The Behaviour Improvement Programme (BIP) is being rolled out across a number of LAs. *DCSF website on pupil behaviour at* www.teachernet.gov.uk/behaviour. Children with emotional difficulties - *see website of SEBDA (social emotional and behavioural difficulties) Association on* www.sebda.org *The Education of Pupils with Emotional and Behavioural Difficulties 9/94 (England)* and *47/06 Pupil Support and Social Inclusion (Wales). Quick Guides PD1C Bad Behaviour Measures.*

E19 EXCLUSION FROM SCHOOL

Government policy is to prevent exclusions where possible. All schools are required under ASCLA to be members of a Behaviour and Attendance Partnership with at least one other school which can use funds from any school in the partnership to fund work to prevent exclusion.

Only the headteacher can exclude a pupil (of any age). This power cannot be exercised indiscriminately. The headteacher has to have regard to the government guidelines last updated in 2007. It is important that schools have clear behaviour policies that are understood by staff, pupils and parents. It is equally important that exclusion procedures are followed carefully and consistently. Detailed contemporary records are important in order to demonstrate fairness and consistency. School staff have a statutory power to impose sanctions. Sanctions must be reasonable and proportionate to the circumstances of the case. Schools should monitor the use of sanctions by age, ethnicity, gender, special educational need and disability.

In line with the above, pupils may be excluded for one or more fixed periods not exceeding 45 school days in any one school year. Indefinite exclusions (e.g. until a meeting can be arranged) are not permissible.

A decision to exclude a pupil permanently should only be taken as a last resort when a range of strategies for dealing with disciplinary offences has been employed to no avail or if an exceptional 'one-off' offence has been committed, c.g.:

- serious violence, actual or threatened, against a pupil or member of staff;
- sexual abuse or assault;
- supplying an illegal drug; or
- carrying an offensive weapon.

In such cases in England, the Secretary of State would not expect the pupil to be re-instated either by the governing body or the LA appeal panel. Regulations in both England and Wales provide that the headteacher, governing body or appeal panel must establish facts on a 'balance of probabilities'.

A child was hit by another child with an iron bar, damaging his skull. The governors decided not to uphold a decision to exclude permanently because the aggressor was shy and would have difficulty integrating into a new school. The parent of the victim sought a judicial review, and eventually the decision was sent back to be reheard by the governors. The governors reversed their decision, new evidence having come to light.

Drug-related exclusions

Any decision to exclude for drug-related issues should be based on the criteria set out in the school's drug policy.

Alternatives

Before resorting to exclusion, schools are expected to try alternative solutions.

Examples include:

- a restorative justice process, whereby the harm caused can be redressed;
- internal exclusion (removal from class, not the site);
- a pastoral support programme (PSP);
- an amended curriculum. Flexible solutions in terms of provision particularly exist at KS4;
- a managed move to another school; or
- formal assessment of a pupil's special educational needs to identify additional support or the possibility of a statement of special educational needs.

It is important to carry out risk assessments for pupils with behavioural difficulties, particularly where there are medical issues.

Providing full-time education from the sixth day of exclusion

The law requires full-time education for all excluded pupils from the sixth day of exclusion. For permanently-excluded pupils this responsibility will clearly fall to the LA, but it also is a statutory requirement for schools for any fixed-term exclusion for six days or longer. Work should be sent home during the first five days while the parent is responsible for the child.

Education must be full-time and suitable to the age, ability and aptitude of the pupil, taking account of any special educational needs. The manner of provision may vary, but it must be of the same high standard as what the pupil would receive in a school.

Under the **ASCLA 2009** schools must be in a behaviour and attendance partnership with at least one other school. Schools should work collaboratively in order to meet the 'full time education' requirement. For example a group of schools could invest in and share an off-site facility, or schools could support excluded pupils from other schools in the area. External providers, including FE Colleges, youth workers, e-learning centres etc. could also be contracted to make provision. The LA has a duty to ensure that there is a lead officer who monitors school arrangements to ensure that appropriate provision is made.

Parents are responsible for supervising their child during the first five days of any period of exclusion and face a penalty notice if their child is found in a public place in school hours without reasonable justification. A**pprenticeships, Skills, Learning and Children Act 2009.**

Lunch-time exclusion

A disruptive pupil may be excluded from the site for the duration of the lunch break.

In Wales lunchtime exclusion can be counted as one quarter of a school day, and will appear in the statistics on exclusions.

Parental co-operation

Where a parent refuses to abide by the terms of a fixed-term exclusion (e.g., by collecting the child), schools will continue to be responsible for the pupil's welfare until alternative arrangements can be made (e.g., via the LA's legal remedies or by notifying the EWO).

However, the **Education and Inspections Act 2006** provides that from September 2007 parents are required to take responsibility for excluded pupils in their first five days of exclusion – whether fixed-term or permanent. It also provides for prosecution of parents where excluded pupils are found in a public place during school hours without reasonable excuse. Parents should be warned of this in an exclusion letter.

Governing bodies are required to provide alternative provision from the sixth day of the exclusion. Reintegration interviews are compulsory for pupils who have been excluded (i.e. no longer dependent on the parent requesting such a hearing). However, if a parent refuses to attend, the school will have discharged its duty. **Education and Inspections Act 2006.**

A pupil, with special educational needs, who was in possession of a knife on school premises, was excluded permanently for good reason. The school had made an absolute rule that the possession of a knife on school premises would be punishable by permanent exclusion, regardless of circumstances. When the decision was challenged both the High

Pupils

Court and the Court of Appeal supported the school, since the rule was well known and was reasonable.

Review and appeal procedures

Governing bodies have a responsibility for reviewing promptly all permanent exclusions and all fixed-term exclusions of over 15 days in a school term or if the pupil were to miss a public examination. Arrangements must also be in place to review fixed-term exclusions over 5 days but not more than 15 days if the parent has asked to make representations.

Governors, when considering an appeal, must consider whether to reinstate the pupil immediately, or by a particular date, or whether it would be practicable for the head to comply with a direction to reinstate. The LA is required to arrange a meeting of the Independent Appeals Panel in cases of permanent exclusion, where the pupil has not been reinstated by the Governors' Discipline Committee and the parent and/or pupil indicates, in writing, a desire to appeal against the exclusion.

In Wales, pupils over the age of 11 can decide to appeal against their own exclusion and have a right to access their own school records to aid themselves in doing so. However, a letter from the parent of a pupil stating that there is no desire to appeal shall be regarded as final.

Continuing education

Schools must continue to provide education for an excluded pupil (whilst he/she remains on roll) and in the case of an exclusion of more than 15 days, schools must consider:
- how the pupil's education will continue;
- how his/her problems night be addressed in the interim; and
- reintegration post-exclusion.

Improving Behaviour and Attendance: Guidance on Exclusion from Schools and Pupil Referral Units (PRUs) DfES 2003.

Exclusions from Schools and Pupil Referral Units Exclusions from schools and Pupil Referral Units 1/2004 and 1A/2004.

Education (Pupil Exclusions and Appeals) (Wales) (Miscellaneous Amendments) Regulations 2004. This document provides guidance on exclusions and appeal procedures for both mainstream schools and PRUs. This guidance replaces that currently contained in Chapter 6 and Annex E of Circular 3/99 following the making of two new sets of regulations under Section 52 of the Education Act 2002 which came into force in January, 2004. This document also incorporates the amendments from Circular 1(A)/2004 following the making of the *Education (Pupil Exclusions and Appeals) (Wales) (Miscellaneous Amendments) Regulations 2004* which came into force on 1 September 2004. w w w . d c s f . g o v . u k / behaviourandattendance/ g u i d a n c e / e x c l u s i o n s / introduction.cfm.

Quick Guides PD5 Guidance on Exclusion from Schools and Pupil Referral Units; PD5A Example of a Pupil Exclusion

Policy: Maintained Schools; PD5C Exclusion Cases.

Contact details for LA officers:

EWO contact details:

Social services:

E20 DETENTION

Under the **Education and Inspections Act 2006** schools can put pupils in detention on disciplinary grounds, during the week or at weekends, without parental consent, so long as certain conditions are fulfilled. Heads must ensure that parents, pupils and staff are aware that the school uses detention as a sanction and is a sanction that parents might expect if a pupil misbehaves. The information should normally be given in the school prospectus, but other means could be used.

If you are allowed by the school to keep pupils in formal detention it must be on reasonable grounds and proportionate to the offence. The school must consider:

- the pupil's age;
- whether parents can make alternative arrangements for their child to travel home if they cannot collect him/her; and
- any special educational needs (and disabilities) and any religious requirements.

This means that you must know what the school's policy is and should only act within it. DCSF guidance advises against whole class detentions where the innocent suffer with the guilty. The reasons for keeping a whole class beyond a token ten minutes would have to merit the action.

Timings

Detentions can be imposed at other times than after school or lunchtimes. For example, Saturday morning detentions are allowed, but in these cases the pupil and parents must agree voluntarily.

Whole class detentions

Some years ago blanket detentions were a common way of sharing out punishment for unruly behaviour when the culprits could not be identified. But since a case in 1986 this has become more problematic. A father claimed damages for false imprisonment of his son who had been kept in detention with the rest of the class for a little over ten minutes. The judge decided that it did amount to false imprisonment, but that in the particular circumstances, it was justified. He accepted that at times it may be necessary to hold a whole class responsible for indiscipline.

Notice

The school must give parents at least 24 hours' notice in writing of a detention. The note has to state:

- why the detention is being given;
- when it is to take place;
- where it is to take place; and

Pupils

- for how long the pupil will be required to remain at school.

The parent must have time to raise problems and so a detention imposed on a Monday cannot take place until Wednesday. The notice can be posted or delivered by other means including pupil post. Email or telephone text may only be used if the parent has previously given consent to this procedure. Notifying one parent (or person with parental responsibility and custody) would normally suffice. The head is expected to use common sense in deciding this and if you consider there is a problem with a particular pupil, you should consult the head (or the relevant senior member of staff).

Parental objections

Parents may object to the detention. The head, or other authorised teacher, then has to consider whether to defer it, continue with it or withdraw it. There is no right of appeal to the governing body, but parents can complain under the school's normal complaints procedure. The governing body, however, cannot overturn a decision to continue with the detention.

Failure to attend

If a pupil fails to attend the detention the head has to determine how to deal with the original misbehaviour and the absence. So long as the new punishment is proportionate, a more severe sanction could be imposed.

Education and Inspections Act 2006 (section on Discipline). Quick Guides PD3 Detention: Points of Law.

E21 LEARNING SUPPORT UNITS (LSUs)

Schools may create self-contained units to help keep pupils in school while their behaviour problems are tackled and to help reintegrate them into mainstream classes. www.dcsf.gov.uk/ibis *for guidance on LSUs, behaviour and bullying.*

E22 PUPIL INFORMATION ON REQUEST

Regulations have required all schools, since 12 December 2005, to provide the following information about pupils on request:

- the date pupil left the school;
- the pupil's address;
- the pupil's SEN type ranking (if any);
- whether the pupil is in the 'gifted and talented' cohort;
- the number of authorised and unauthorised absences from the total number of sessions held by the school; and
- whether the pupil is taught in an SEN unit or in other resourced provision.

For certain excluded pupils, the manner of collecting the information about the exclusions has changed. Schools can be required to provide:

- the exclusion start date;
- the type of exclusion;
- the reason for the exclusion; and
- the number of sessions to which the exclusion applies.

(NB, Regulations on exclusion in 2002 provide that any lunchtime exclusion for a fixed period

The Curriculum

counts as half a school day.)
Education (Information about Pupils) (England) (Amendment) Regulations 2005.
Quick Guides Pupil Information (PI) Section; GOV16 Annual Reports and Parents' Meeting.

F THE CURRICULUM

F1 THE SCHOOL CURRICULUM

Each school's curriculum must be balanced and broadly based and promote the spiritual, moral, cultural, mental and physical development of pupils and 'prepare them for the opportunities, responsibilities and experiences of adult life'. Thus the whole school curriculum consists of more than the national curriculum. Each school is likely to provide a variety of experiences outside the national curriculum.

Qualifications and Curriculum Authorities

In England up to 2008, the government's Qualifications and Curriculum Authority (QCA) was charged with the general oversight of qualifications, the curriculum and assessment. The government has replaced it with: QCDA; JACQA; and Ofqual. QCDA, the Qualifications and Curriculum Development Agency, retains the curriculum development functions of QCA.

In Wales, the responsibility for the policy and implementation of the national curriculum and the regulation of qualifications in Wales rests with the Welsh Assembly Government. (Curriculum and Qualifications is one of the four divisions of DCELLS, Department of Children, Education, Lifelong Learning and Skills.)

JACQA

JACQA, the Joint Advisory Committee on Qualifications is the body which decides whether a qualification, after it has been developed and approved by Ofqual as being of a sufficient standard, should be accepted as a qualification that can be publicly funded.

OFQUAL

Ofqual, the Office of the Qualifications and Examinations Regulator, is the regulator of qualifications, exams and tests in England. It oversees the qualifications and examinations system to make sure that it is fair, provides value for money and meets the needs of learners and employers. Ofqual also makes sure that the qualifications available meet the needs of learners and employers.

The national curriculum

The curriculum is divided into subjects. There are core subjects (English, mathematics, science, information and communication technology and religious education) and the remainder are called foundation subjects (geography, history, design and technology, art and design, music and physical education). Not all subjects have to be taught in every key stage.

In England there are three useful publications for parents, which

The Curriculum

give an overview of the curriculum taught in schools. *'The Learning Journey-a parents guide to the curriculum' is a series of three booklets (3-7 ref:0122/2000) (7-11 ref 0123/2000) and (11-16 ref:0124/ 2000).*

The Welsh Assembly Government (WAG) has published *How is your child doing at Primary/ Secondary School?A parent's guide to the National Curriculum 2009. Email :* parentguides2009@ wales.gsi.gov.uk .

Both booklets explain the national curriculum in Wales and how it changes through the four key stages of a child's compulsory school life. They also explain how the assessment and reporting arrangements fit into the framework. Teacher assessments will continue and parents will receive a report on their child's progress in English, Welsh (where taught as a first language) maths and science.

http://curriculum.qca.org.uk *is the website for the National Curriculum On-line (includes England and Wales).* Sources of guidance on organising and teaching the curriculum are listed in: www.qca.org.uk.

The Basic Curriculum for Wales (Amendment) Order 2003 sets out the requirements for the curriculum for maintained schools in Wales as follows: Section 101(1) of the *Education Act 2002 (the Act)* requires the curriculum for every maintained school in Wales to include a basic curriculum comprising religious education, the national curriculum for Wales and sex education. Subsection (3) enables the National Assembly

for Wales to make an order amending subsection (1) by adding further requirements.

This order, which is made under subsection (3), adds two new requirements to the basic curriculum. The first, which applied from 1 September 2003, requires the basic curriculum to include provision for personal and social education for registered pupils of compulsory school age. The second, applied from 1 September 2004, requires the curriculum to include provision for work-related education for pupils who are in key stage 4, 14-16. In teaching personal and social education and work-related education regard must be had to *Circular 13/2003, Personal and Social Education and Work-Related Education in the Basic Curriculum.*

Further amendments have been made by *The School Curriculum in Wales (Miscellaneous Amendments) Order 2008* that came into force on 1 August 2008. The amendments made by this order omit the 'technology' and 'art' subjects and replace them with 'information and communication technology', 'design and technology' and 'art and design'.

The Education (School Day and School Year) (Wales) Amendment Regulation 2008 provides for up to four sessions 2009/10 for training, or preparation and planning, for:
- introduction of the foundation stage;
- implementation and facilitation the transition plans KS1 to KS2 or KS2 to KS3;

The Curriculum

- changes in the national curriculum; and
- extending learning options for 14-19 year olds.

The Education (Disapplication of the National Curriculum for Wales at Key Stage 1) (Wales) Regulations 2008 provides for the disapplication of the requirements of the national curriculum for Wales specified for KS1.

Revised curriculum for Wales

A revised curriculum for 3-19 year-olds in Wales was implemented from September 2008. In revising the curriculum, the challenge was to establish a curriculum for the twenty first century that meets the needs of individual learners whilst taking account of the broader needs of Wales. To help achieve this, the revised school curriculum aims to:

- focus on the learner;
- ensure that appropriate skills development is woven throughout the curriculum;
- offer reduced subject content with an increased focus on skills;
- focus on continuity and progression 3-19, by building on the foundation phase and linking effectively with the 14-19 Learning Pathways Programme;
- be flexible;
- support government policy, including bilingualism, Curriculum Cymreig/Wales, Europe and the World, equal opportunities, food and fitness, sustainable development and global citizenship and the world of work and entrepreneurship; and

- continue to deliver a distinctive curriculum that is appropriate to Wales.

The Revised Curriculum comprises the following six areas:
1. Foundation phase.
2. Skills development.
3. National curriculum.
4. Personal and social education.
5. Careers and the world of work.
6. Religious education.

For RE a model framework has been produced which local authorities, in partnership with their Agreed Syllabus Conferences can adopt as a basis for their locally agreed syllabus. The skills framework describes progression from 3-19 in developing thinking, communication, ICT and number skills.

For careers and the world of work, one framework has replaced two and is now extended to cover 11-19 year-olds. In personal and social education the framework covers 7-19 year-olds and important social and personal issues are covered as diet and health, money management, first aid and personal relationships, sustainable living and citizenship. The revised national curriculum is being implemented as follows:

Sept 2008	Years 3, 4 and 5, Years 7 and 8.
Sept 2009	Year 6, Year 9, Year 10 Welsh second language and PE.
Sept 2010	Year 10 English, Welsh and maths; Year 11 Welsh second language and PE.
Sept 2011	Year 11 English Welsh and maths.

The Education (National Curriculum) (Attainment Targets

The Curriculum

and Programmes of Study) (Wales) (Amendment) Order 2008 came into force on 1 August 2008. The order gives legal effect to the programmes of study which set out what pupils should be taught and attainment targets for them in respect of pupils in KS2 to 4.

The Education (National Curriculum) (Foundation Stage) (Wales) Order 2008 phases the introduction of the foundation stage, the period of the foundation stage and gives legal effect to areas of learning which set out the desirable outcomes and educational programmes.

Key stages
The Early Years Foundation Stage

The Early Years Foundation Stage (EYFS) has legal force through orders made under the Childcare Act 2006. It covers children from birth to five. The overarching aim of the EYFS is to help young children achieve the five Every Child Matters outcomes:

1. staying safe;
2. being healthy;
3. enjoying and achieving;
4. making a positive contribution; and
5. achieving economic well-being.

The EYFS contains legal requirements relating to:
• learning and development; and
• welfare.

The learning and development requirements comprise three elements:
• early learning goals;
• educational programmes; and
• assessment arrangements.

The welfare requirements are the over-riding aim of safeguarding and promoting children's welfare. They cover appointments of suitable persons, suitable premises, environment and equipment, organisation and documentation.

In Wales the new foundation phase combines into a single framework for children's learning (Early Years 3 - 5) and KS1(5 - 7 years). It was introduced to 3-4 year olds in September 2008. It will be statutory for all 3 to 7 year olds from 2010-2011. The phased introduction of the foundation phase is as follows: 4-5 year olds from September 2009; 5-6 year olds from September 2010; 6-7 year olds from September 2011.

The primary strategy

Following The DCSF publication of Excellence and Enjoyment. A strategy for primary schools, schools are likely in the future to have more freedom in delivering the primary curriculum. The vision is for a sector where high standards are obtained through a rich, varied and exciting curriculum. For more information go to: www.standards.dcsf.gov.uk/primary/publications/literacy/63553.

Key stages 1 and 2

Primary education is divided into two phases: KS1 (5 – 7) and KS2 (7 –11); the second part of KS2 can be taught in middle schools.

In Wales the national curriculum at KS1 and KS2 is made up of the following subjects English, Welsh, mathematics, science (core subjects); design and technology, information technology, history,

Creative
Teaching & Learning

Incorporating creativity and critical thinking into your school

The school curriculum is changing! Learning, Personal and Thinking Skills are a key part of the secondary curriculum, and cross-curriculum project based work is now central to teaching in primary schools and Key Stage 3. The government wants the endowment of creativity and critical skills in pupils to be a core mission of schools. *Creative Teaching & Learning* magazine under its old name *Teaching Thinking & Creativity*, has been providing this for schools for the past 10 years. Recognised as the most cutting edge curriculum magazine in the country, it has championed such approaches as Philosophy for Children, Building Learning Power, Intelligent Learning and Mantle of The Expert. The magazine investigates how the curriculum can be remodelled and explores how thinking skills approaches can be embedded within subject and project-based teaching. In every issue it has project resource packs which show how project work can be given much more meaning and pedagogic depth.

Creative Teaching & Learning magazine is dedicated to promoting critical and creative thinking at both primary and secondary level. Packed with practical information, guidance and jargon free advice, it makes education more imaginative and effective and helps to raise the standards of teaching and learning by developing children's thinking skills.

IM IMAGINATIVE MINDS
CT/02/10

Subscriptions hotline:
0121 224 7578

Fax orders:
0121 224 7598

Post:
Imaginative Minds, 215 The Green House,
Gibb Street, Birmingham, B9 4AA

The Curriculum

geography, music, art, PE and religious education

Transition planning for KS2 pupils moving to KS3 is laid out in the **Transition from Primary to Secondary Schools (Wales) Regulations 2006** and guidance is available in **Circular 30/2006 Guidance on the Preparation of Key Stage 3 Transition Plans.**

Key stage 3

Each school has to teach the national curriculum and religious education. A school is expected to customise this basic entitlement to learning and in the context of the KS3 strategy and other relevant government initiatives, create its own distinctive and unique curriculum.

In Wales the national curriculum at KS3 is made up of the following subjects English, Welsh, mathematics, science (core subjects); design and technology, information technology, history, geography, music, art, PE and religious education. At KS3 a modern foreign language is added. Welsh is taught mainly as a first language in Welsh-speaking schools and as a second language in non-Welsh-speaking schools

Key stage 4

The statutory requirements at this key stage are currently: English, ICT, mathematics, science (for which there will be a smaller programme of study), citizenship, PE, RE and work-related learning. There is an entitlement for all students at KS4 to be able to study subjects from: the humanities; arts; technology and at least one modern foreign language.

Assessment remains mostly via GCSEs, but hybrid GCSEs offer students a chance to work for a combination of common and discrete modules that result in an academic or applied GCSE. Fourteen new specialised diplomas are being introduced, available to every 14-19 young person in the country. Some will offer a route to success for pupils who wish to learn through practical experience. Regulations and guidance were introduced in 2006-7. Five diploma courses were introduced in September 2008:

- Construction and the built environment;
- Creative and media;
- Engineering;
- Information technology; and
- Society, health and development.

Five more subjects were added for September 2009:

- Environmental and land-based studies;
- Business, administration and finance;
- Manufacturing and product design;
- Hospitality; and
- Hair and beauty studies.

The diplomas will be available at three levels - level 3 being equivalent to A Level standard. LAs will be given the strategic lead for securing the entitlement, as no single school can be expected to provide them all on its own.

Sex education is a mandatory element of the curriculum in biology but not in its wider aspects of human relationships. School governors carry the responsibility

The Curriculum

for determining provision of teaching on human relationships and parents have the right to withdraw their children from those lessons.

ICT must be included, and is taught across the curriculum. *Go to:* www.teachernet.gov.uk and type in 'ICT'. The ICT Register is a unique database, which captures ICT and e-learning expertise in cutting edge primary, secondary and special schools across the nation. All Register Schools will respond to enquiries free of charge but if you need to engage a school to give you extended help and advice you may be able to use standards fund 'Hands on Support' budget for this. www.ict-register.net.
BECTA also have a very useful site for teachers http://schools.becta.org.uk.

Modern foreign language is not a statutory requirement at KS2 until 2011.

CILT is the national centre for languages and has lots of useful information on its website at www.cilt.org.uk

In Wales at KS4 the national curriculum comprises only five subjects: English, Welsh (either as a second language or in designated Welsh medium schools as part of a bilingual system) mathematics, science and PE. Children must also study RE (according to the syllabus laid down by the local authority) and all schools are required to provide some personal and social education, careers and the world of work and sex education. The limitation of five compulsory subjects allows pupils to choose additional subjects and courses for GCSE and vocational qualifications.

The Welsh Assembly Government passed the *Learning and Skills Measure* in May 2009 which aims to drive the implementation of the Learning Pathways 14 to 19. The aim of the legislation is to give learners aged 14 to 19 the right to follow a course from a local area curriculum. The Measure will ensure wider choice is available to all 14-19 year-olds in schools and colleges. The proposed roll-out programme is: September 2009 Year 10 students (non statutory); September 2010 Year 10 and 11 students; September 2011 Year 10, 11 and 12 students ; September 2012 Year 10, 11, 12 and 13 students.

Personal, social and health education at Stage 3 from 2004. Citizenship may be delivered in many ways, but the most common is through the PSHE curriculum.

Personal and social education (PSE) is part of the basic curriculum in Wales and there is no requirement for citizenship as a separate subject, nor for assessment.

Enterprise education
From September 2005 secondary schools in England have had to provide all KS4 pupils with the equivalent of five days' activity focused on enterprise capability, innovation, creativity, risk management and risk taking and a 'can do attitude'. Schools at the moment are free to develop their own programmes, which dovetail with their existing arrangements,

The Curriculum

activities and partnerships. However, the five days should include activities towards the latter part of the KS4 in Year 11, enabling pupils to draw on their previous enterprise learning in applying their skills, knowledge and understanding, in order to demonstrate their enterprise capability. *Citizenship: A Scheme of Work for Key Stage 3 (2001) from the QCA (QCA/02/944). National Curriculum Citizenship: Citizenship in Secondary Schools: Ofsted 2005:* www. ofsted.gov.uk/Ofsted-home/ Publications-and-research .
http://curriculum.qca.org.uk/ - *is the website for the National Curriculum On-line (includes England and Wales).*
Sources of guidance on organising and teaching the curriculum are listed in www. qca.org.uk.
Work-related learning for all at Key Stage 4: guidance for implementing the statutory requirement. Additional information and guidance on the changes, including statutory entitlement areas, work-related learning for all and pace and progression are on the 14-19 Learning website. *QCA Publications, PO Box 99, Sudbury, Suffolk, CO10 2SN; Tel: 01787 88 4444: Fax: 01878 31 2950.*

Careers education and guidance (CEG)

Careers education is now a requirement from Year 7. Though statutory, it does not have a programme of study, but is supported by a non-statutory framework. The non-statutory framework for careers education: *Careers education*

and guidance in England: A National framework 11-19 (DfES/0163/2003) ISBN: 1 84185 89/9 includes:

- recommended learning outcomes and suggested content for careers education programmes KS3, 4 and post-16;
- advice on helping young people to gain maximum benefit from careers guidance provided by their school or college, the Connexions service and their parents/carers; and
- advice on how to assure the quality of CEG programmes within a process of continuous improvement.

Other relevant guidance includes:

- *First Impressions: career-related learning in the primary school (ref. 0061/20001)* – looking at the foundations for later careers education.

Available as a download from the Connexions website;

- *Work-related learning for all at Key Stage 4: guidance for implementing the statutory requirement form 2004. (ref. QCA/03/1168);*
- *School improvement: how careers work can help (ref.: 0207/2000);*

and

- *Preparing pupils for a successful future in learning and work (ref. 0208/2000):* an outline of the QCA statutory requirement from September 2004.

Careers Wales consists of seven independent careers companies in different areas of Wales, which provide careers information

Office of
Qualifications
and Examinations
Regulation

Ofqual is the independent regulator of general and
vocational qualifications in England and vocational
qualifications in Northern Ireland. Our work ensures that
children, young people and adult learners get the results
their work deserves, that standards are maintained and
that the qualifications people achieve count now and in
the future.

Ofqual has launched a series of free learner guides which
provide useful advice and information on key areas of
interest to you and your students. These include plagiarism
guides for parents, students and teachers and student
guides to A Levels, GCSEs and the Diploma.

For more information on Ofqual, or to receive a copy
of the guides, please visit www.ofqual.gov.uk or contact
our helpdesk on 0300 303 3346 or by e-mailing
info@ofqual.gov.uk

Ofqual/10/4707

The Curriculum

to those who are in education or have left education. **Search under Careers Wales for your relevant area and company at** www.careerswales.com.

Attainment targets

Each programme of study for each subject contains attainment targets against which your pupils are measured. There are eight level descriptions for each attainment target (with an extra level above 8 for exceptional performance). You are required to choose the 'best fit' description for each of your pupils. Pupils are assessed at 14, but some pupils can be accelerated. The statutory tests in English, maths and science were abolished in 2008. Teacher assessments in all areas of the programme of study will continue and 'test when ready' assessments are to be developed for schools. The government provides materials for assessment in ICT. The assessment must be reported to parents. Each school should have the national curriculum key stage training and information documents. (**See** www.qcda.gov.uk.)

Assessment
Key stages 1 and 2

Primary education is divided into two phases: KS1 (5 – 7) and KS2 (7 –11); the second part of KS2 can be taught in middle schools.

Key stage1 assessment in England

The QCA **Assessment and Recording Arrangements 2005** document gives clear guidance on the statutory requirements for assessment in foundation stage and KS1. The National Assessment Agency (NAA) has a range of support materials which have been sent out to schools. A guidance booklet **- Building a picture of what children can do - introducing changes to Key Stage 1 assessment arrangements in 2005** has been released by the NAA. The booklet gives guidance on building assessment into every-day classroom activity, together with some examples of level judgements for reading, writing and mathematics. **Further details on National Assessment Agency website at** www.naa.org.uk. **The QCA Assessment and Reporting arrangements for key stages 1,2,3 and Years 7 and 8 can be found at:** http://testsandexams.qcda.gov.uk/25337.aspx

Assessment in Wales
Baseline assessment

Each child's language, school mathematical, personal and social skills will be assessed in their first term in and reported to parents before the end of the term.

Teacher assessment

Teacher assessment will assess progress in all subjects and activities but especially progress in English, Welsh (where taught as a first language), maths and science when pupils are aged 7 and 11. Teachers look at the component parts of the subject and decide which level on the national curriculum scale a pupil's work best fits their performance

In 2005 a primary school teacher was found guilty by the GTCE of helping pupils with their KS2 tests. He had made inappropriate comments to pupils about erasing and changing answers.

The panel found that he had coached the pupils before the test by reminding them about the internal angles of a triangle. The school dismissed him for gross professional misconduct. The GTCE served him with a conditional registration order not allowing him to invigilate exams again until he had undertaken appropriate training.

Key Stage 3

From 2009 the statutory tests in English, maths and science were replaced by improved classroom assessment by teachers and frequent reporting to parents in Years 7, 8 and 9. There are proposals for the introduction of a new system of report cards showing schools' academic attainment and pupil well-being to be implemented in 2011.

In Wales teachers assess all subjects and activities and record progress in English, Welsh (first or second language), maths, science, design and technology, information technology, geography, history, a modern foreign language, music, art and PE.)

Assessment at key stage 4

Assessment at KS4 remains mostly via GCSEs or GNVQs, but from September 2004 hybrid GCSEs offer students a chance to work for a combination of common and discrete modules that result in an academic or applied GCSE. It is also possible to be assessed in Diplomas in a number of subjects.

In Wales most pupils opt for GCSE courses. Schools can offer GCSE short courses which are equivalent to half a full GCSE. A number of schools offer opportunities to develop key skills. There are 6 key skills qualifications each available at levels 1 to 4 of the NQF (National Qualifications Framework). A wide range of vocational qualifications are also offered and the Welsh Baccalaureate qualification is being rolled out across Wales. It is offered at foundation, intermediate and advanced level and is an over-arching qualification comprising two parts. At KS4 pupils would normally study the first two levels.

Assessment for Learning

Assessment for Learning is the process of seeking and interpreting evidence for use by learners and their teachers to decide where the learners are in their learning, where they need to go and how best to get there. *More information from:* www.qcda.gov.uk/7659.html.
Quick Guides Curriculum (CU) Section;CU9 Assessment for Learning (AFL).

The 14-19 Gateway is a one-stop shop for those engaged in transforming the 14-19 phase of learning. It provides access to up-to-date information, guidance and good practice. *Information about these changes and the implementation can be found on:* www.dcsf.gov.uk/14-19/index.cfm?go.

Literacy, numeracy and computer skills

In addition, young people are entitled to study literacy, numeracy and computer skills until 19 to level 2 standard (GCSE or equivalent). Schools and colleges will be encouraged

The Curriculum

increasingly to enter pupils for exams when they are ready. Modern apprenticeships will be improved and expanded; GCSEs or A Levels will no longer be separately described as 'vocational' or 'academic'.

A unified framework will be designed to provide opportunities for young people of all abilities, by promoting progression from foundation through intermediate to advanced levels. **More information at:** www.teachernet.gov.uk/teachingandlearning and at www.niace.org.uk.

16-19
Students can study for a variety of qualifications - usually A Level and AS Level GCE, or National Vocational Qualifications (NVQ). The government also believes that students need to develop 'key skills' in order to be a member of a flexible, adaptable and competitive workforce. The key skills are:
- communication;
- application of number; and
- information technology.

Plus the wider skills of 'working with others', problem solving, and improving own learning and performance. There is a key skills qualification available.
See details at: www.qcda.gov.uk.

The International Baccalaureate (IB)
The IB is also widely used. It is an international qualification, which is currently (January 2010) taught at 2800 schools in 138 countries around the world under the auspices of The International Baccalaureate Organisation. There are three programmes covering the following year ranges:
- Primary Years Programme (PYP) ages 3-12;
- Middle Years Programme (MYP) ages 11-16; and
- Diploma Programme (DP) ages 16-18. http://www.ibo.org.

A new 'English' (as opposed to International or Welsh) Baccalaureate is offered by the AQA Exam Board. Students studying the AQA baccalaureate must take three A Levels, a paper in critical thinking, citizenship or general studies; a project; and 100 hours of personal-development activity, work-based learning or community work. Candidates will be awarded pass, merit or distinction. This qualification is not officially recognised as a separate qualification but like the Welsh Baccalaureate (see below) is made up of existing elements. This qualification provides an English alternative to the International Baccalaureate and the new diploma courses as an overarching course for 16-19 year-olds.
Education and Inspections Act 2006.

14-19 Learning Pathways and Welsh Baccalaureate
The Welsh Baccalaureate is currently being rolled out to all post-16 learning providers in schools and colleges in Wales and leading to qualifications at intermediate and advanced level. A foundation level Welsh Baccalaureate has been piloted from September 2007. There are six main elements of the programme:

The Curriculum

1. Individual learning pathways to meet the needs of each learner.
2. Wider choice and flexibility of programme and ways of learning.
3. A learning core where there are learners 14-19.
4. The support of a learner coach.
5. Access to personal support.
6. Impartial careers advice and guidance.

Learners have an entitlement to a wide range of courses of study, including general (academic) and applied (vocational) options within all five domains of learning which are:

- maths, science and technology;
- business administration and law;
- services for people;
- arts, media, culture and language; and
- humanities, social services and preparation for life and work.

The Welsh Assembly Government proposes to formalise collaboration among schools and FE colleges with regulatory powers made under Section 166 of the **Education and Inspections Act 2006** through the **Collaboration Arrangements (Maintained Schools and Further Education Bodies) (Wales) Regulations 2008** and the **Learning and Skills (Wales) Measure 2008.** The Measure provides the minister with regulation-making power to define the range of options to be made available to meet learners' entitlement; to provide guidance on the decision by a headteacher or principal to disentitle a learner from specific provision; allow directions to be issued and guidance to be developed to enhance learning coach support to develop key skills. **The Education (Local Curriculum for Pupils in Key Stage 4) (Wales) Regulations 2009. Guidance Circular 37/2004 Learning Pathways Guidance for the 14-19 Curriculum.**

Welsh Baccalaureate

Overall a total of 169 centres including 62 new centres across Wales are delivering the qualification to 30,000 students from the Autumn of 2009. The Welsh Baccalaureate is available at foundation, intermediate and advanced level for students aged 14-19. Amongst other things, it focuses on developing key skills, including problem solving, communication and team work and encourages students to study independently and be active in their local community. The qualification meets the diverse needs of learners of different abilities, providing progression to higher levels and adding breadth to learning via academic and vocational routes.

From September students will have the opportunity to access additional course options within the Welsh Baccalaureate. These will enable students to embark on vocational courses through learning providers such as school and colleges working together. The **Learning and Skills (Wales) Measure 2008** will ensure the delivery of the various 14 -19 choices through the collaboration of various providers, principally schools and FEI's. The new options are called the Principal Learning and Project qualifications.

The Curriculum

F2 POLITICAL EDUCATION

LAs and governing bodies have to forbid 'the pursuit of partisan political activities by any junior pupils'. If the political activities are off-site, this only applies if organised by a member of the school staff. LAs and governors also have to forbid 'the promotion of partisan political views' in the teaching of any subject in any maintained school. You can, however, include political issues in your teaching so long as they are in a balanced presentation of opposing views. The intention is not to stifle political debate, but to prevent indoctrination. You must, therefore, adhere to the policies of your school.
DES Circular 7/87 Education (No2 Act) 1986: Further Guidance (Annex 11) gives advice on how to approach this issue.

In a case in 2008 a judge ruled that the showing of a film on global warming infringed the 'partisan political activities' rule because it made assertions that went beyond mainstream scientific opinion. He said that it would have been sufficient to make this clear to comply with the rule. He also ruled that there was no need to give equal time to patently ridiculous theories (e.g. that the moon was made of green cheese). You should be careful in making sure that material you present is presented in a fair way and that you are aware of different angles on the subject.

F3 SEX EDUCATION

In England governing bodies of maintained primary schools must decide whether sex education should be taught at all in the school. In secondary schools sex education (including education about AIDS and other sexually transmitted diseases) must be provided for all pupils, but parents have a right to withdraw their children from non-national curriculum sex education.
In Wales some form of sex education is recommended for all pupils.

Sex education must be provided in such a way as to encourage young people to take into account moral considerations and the value of family life.
See sections E12 and E13 above for advice on confidentiality in dealing with sex and relationship issues.
Sex and Relationship Education Guidance; Government guidance 0116/2000, July 2000. Welsh Assembly Circular 11/02 Sex and Relationships Education in Schools.
Parentline Plus: a confidential helpline for parents worried about their children's sexual behaviour. Tel: 0808 800 2222.
For guidance on HIV and AIDS see the government booklet:
HIV and AIDS: A Guide for the Education Service (available from DCSF Publications).
Sense Interactive CDs: Sex and Relationships - CD Rom available from www.sensecds.com.
Quick Guides CP2 Sex and Relationships Education: Guidance.

The Curriculum

F4 RELIGIOUS EDUCATION AND COLLECTIVE WORSHIP

The curriculum in every maintained school must include religious education for all pupils in the school, in accordance with locally agreed syllabuses, which must reflect the fact that the religious traditions in the UK are in the main Christian, while taking into account the practices of other religions. In religious schools the governors may determine the syllabus in accordance with any trust deed. There are no nationally prescribed programmes of study, attainment targets, nor national assessment.

Religious education that is different from that provided by the school may be arranged on or off the premises, if a parent requests it. In a voluntary school, which is designated as being of a religious character, the exact nature of the religious education school will depend on the religious character of the school. Non-statutory schemes have been produced by the QCA. *More information at:* www.reonline.org.uk.

The teacher's position

You cannot be directed to participate in RE lessons, nor be discriminated against for holding particular religious views. Religious schools can, however, make it a 'genuine occupational requirement' for specific posts in the school to be filled by persons of their particular faith. The courts have taken a restrictive view of this 'genuine occupational requirement' so far.
Designation of Schools Having a Religious Character (England) Order 1999.

Collective worship

All pupils in maintained schools must take part in a daily act of worship. It can be in large or small groups. The worship must be wholly or mainly of a broadly Christian character but not distinctive of a particular Christian denomination. Parents have a right to withdraw their children from acts of collective worship.

Under the *Education and Inspections Act 2006* sixth formers may opt out of the act of worship of their own accord.
You are not obliged to take part either, although you can be required to attend the non-religious part of a school assembly. *Education Act 1996* – outlines right of parents to withdraw their children from RE lessons.
S 6 School Standards and Framework Act 1998 - daily acts of worship. Circular 1/94 Religious Education and Collective Worship.

F5 THE NATIONAL LITERACY AND NUMERACY STRATEGIES

The national literacy and numeracy strategies are a concerted attempt to drive up standards of literacy and numeracy. There is, however, no legal requirement to organise literacy or numeracy education in any particular way. The KS3 strategy aims to do the same for all the subjects across the curriculum. Each school has training and information documents and videos on the national literacy and numeracy strategies. You are required to conform to the policies of

The Curriculum

your particular school. **More information at** www.standards.dcsf.gov.uk/primary

F6 CHARGING FOR EDUCATION

Education for pupils in maintained schools is, in the main, free if it takes place in school hours. If it is outside school hours, but is part of a prescribed examination course or part of the national curriculum, it is also free. Schools can charge for individual instrumental music tuition where it is not part of the national curriculum and for items made by a pupil which he/she wishes to keep. Charges can also be made in certain circumstances for residential visits, which are mainly outside school hours. Parents can also make voluntary contributions to the school for the cost of these trips or visits.

If you are planning a trip you should check the school's charging policy. Schools must have a charging and remissions policy, which you must have regard to. **More information will be found at:** www.teachernet.gov.uk/management/atoz/c/chargingforactivities.
Circular 2/89 Education Reform Act 1988: Charges for school activities.
Quick Guides GOV13 Charging for Education: Points of Law.

F7 HOMEWORK

There are no statutory requirements, but the government in 1998 recommended the following:

Primary Schools

Years 1 and 2 - 1 hour per week (reading, spelling, and other literacy and numeracy work;

Years 3 and 4 - 1 hour per week (literacy, numeracy, with occasional assignments in other subjects);

Years 5 and 6 - 30 minutes per day (regular weekly schedules with an emphasis on literacy and numeracy, but also other subjects).

Secondary Schools

Years 7 and 8 - 45 to 90 minutes per day;
Year 9 - 1 to 2 hours per day;
Years 10 and 11 - 1 to 2 hours per day;
Years 12 and 13 - depends on the subjects, but guidance should be included in school policies.

F8 CLASS SIZES

The **School Standards and Framework Act 1998** placed a duty on LAs and schools to limit the size of infant classes for five-, six- and seven-year-olds taught by one qualified teacher to 30 or fewer pupils. There are no limitations on classes above this age group but there may be health and safety issues in particular subjects in particular circumstances. If in doubt, discuss this with your union safety representative.

In Wales the regulations are: *Education (Infant Class Size) (Wales) Regulations 1998 and Education (Infant Class Size) (Wales) (Amendment) Regulations 2009.*

The Curriculum

F9 NATIONAL QUALIFICATIONS FRAMEWORK

These include: GCSEs; A/AS; Advanced Extension; NVQs and GNVQs. There is also a european and international dimension. The QCA is reviewing the National Qualifications Framework. **See** www.qca.org.uk/qca_5967.aspx Vocational qualifications (VQs) are being revised, in order to give more flexibility to 14-19 pupils enabling those who want to, to take more practical courses. www.teachernet.gov.uk
Information about BTEC, HNDs and HNCs from: www.qcda.gov.uk/5967.aspx.

F10 PUPIL PERFORMANCE

Achievement and attainment tables (formerly performance tables)
The latest tables published by the DCSF cover KS2 achievement and attainment, secondary school GCSE and equivalent, school and college post-16, and information on the pace and progression pilot at KS. *More information at:* www.dcsf.gov.uk/performancetables.

Setting Targets
KS1 there is no statutory requirement to set targets at this stage.
KS2: the new Primary Strategy places an emphasis on schools setting their own targets, rather than having them imposed by the LA. There is a greater emphasis than ever on schools using data to analyse the performance of pupils and setting themselves challenging targets.

Key Stages 3 and 4 and Post-16
LAs set targets in consultation with the school.

More information at www.qca.org.uk/qca_8839.aspx and www.qca.org.uk/qca_8840.aspx details how schools can use pupil performance data.

F11 CURRICULUM RECORDS

A curriculum record for each pupil must be kept i.e. a formal record of a pupil's academic achievements, skills and abilities and the progress he/she is making. Parents are entitled to receive information about both the school's performance and their child's performance. Pupils are entitled to see any information held on them by the school under the *Data Protection Act 1998.*

Heads must provide available information to governing bodies, who must provide LAs with information about KS1 results. Governing bodies of maintained schools must also provide individual pupil information relating to pupils who are eligible for assessment in KS2 and 3 to the National Data Collection Agency and the external marking agency.

F12 REPORTING TO PARENTS

Headteachers must ensure that parents receive a written report on their child's achievements at least once during the school year. Schools may issue more than one report, provided the minimum information is sent to parents by the end of the summer term. The DCSF have been discussing with

The Curriculum

schools the possibility of 'real-time' reporting by means of email etc. Headteachers may also:

- arrange for a report to be translated;
- include in the progress report additional information beyond the minimum requirements; and
- decide when to issue reports to parents, as long as minimum information legally required is sent to parents by the end of the summer term.

The minimum content of reports is:

For children in Year R:

- brief particulars of achievements in all subjects and other activities. Comments should be included for each of the six areas of learning, where appropriate;
- comments on general progress; and
- arrangements for discussing the report.

For children at the end of Year R:

- a written summary reporting progress against the early learning goals and the assessment scales.

Schools must offer parents a reasonable opportunity to discuss the outcomes of the foundation stage profile with their child's teacher. This meeting should be within the term in which the foundation stage profile has been completed. Teachers may wish to consider making the child's profile available to parents as part of this discussion. If parents ask to see a copy of their child's profile, the school should make this available.

For all pupils in KS1 and above

- brief particulars of achievements in all subjects and activities forming part of the school curriculum;
- comments on general progress;
- arrangements for discussing the report with the pupil's teacher;
- attendance record, except for Year 12 or 13 (no longer of compulsory school age);
- the results of any public examinations taken, by subject and grade;
- details of any vocational qualifications or credits towards any such qualifications gained; and
- the results of any NC tests taken during that year, by level.

For KS1, 2 and 3

- a brief commentary;
- the results of the teacher assessment of NC levels of attainment, excluding English at the first key stage and citizenship;
- particulars of any NC attainment targets or subjects the pupil is exempted from;
- comparative information about the NC levels of attainment of pupils of the same age in the school; and
- comparative information about the NC levels of attainment in the core subjects of pupils of the same age nationally.

Requirements specific to KS1

- a statement that the teacher assessment of NC levels of attainment takes into account the results of any NC tasks and NC tests taken in accordance with the statutory arrangements; and

- if applicable, a statement explaining why any NC tasks or NC tests have not been taken or why the teacher assessment has been disapplied.

Requirements at both KS1 and 2

- the results of the teacher assessment of NC attainment targets in English; and

Requirements at KS2

- the results of the NC tests taken, by level; and
- a statement that the NC levels of attainment have been arrived at in accordance with the statutory arrangements.

Requirements at KS3

- With the key stage 3 national tests no longer being compulsory a statement of level reached as assessed by teachers.

Children with statements of special educational needs

Reports for the annual review of a child's statement of special educational needs may, if schools wish, serve as the annual report to parents. If so, headteachers must ensure that the minimum information required is provided. Schools should always provide contextual information in reports to parents on children who have special educational needs through a detailed account of the child's progress in relation to the curriculum specific to that child.

Reporting religious education

It is a general requirement that schools report children's progress on religious education to their parents, but there is no required format for such reporting nationally. Locally agreed syllabuses or faith community guidelines might contain requirements or guidance on reporting religious education, especially if an eight-level scale is used.

Religious education: the non-statutory national framework is available on the QCA website at: www.qca.org.uk/ qca_7886.aspx *The booklet is also available from the QCA orderline at* http://orderline.qca. org.uk/ *or by calling 08700 60 60 15 and quoting reference QCA/04/1336.*

Information that is exempt from disclosure

At the end of KS1, schools must report a child's teacher assessment levels to the child's parents. However, there is no requirement in education law to report task or test results or to allow parents to see, or have copies of, their child's marked scripts.

Further details are available on the Information Commissioner's Office website at www.ico. gov.uk. Information that is exempt from disclosure includes information recorded by a child during a test.

The Education (Pupil Information) (England) Regulations 2005.
www.qca.org.uk/eara/102.asp.
An HMI Report Transition from the Reception Year to Year 1: An Evaluation by HMI highlights a number of problems in foundations stage profiles. *See:* www.ofsted.gov.uk.

Quick Guides CU4 Information and Reports on Performance.

The Curriculum

F13 RAISEonline

This interactive package was introduced by the DCSF from September 2007. It comes with your pupils' details and results for KS1, 2, 3 and 4 already in the system and gives an overview of each school's performance in relation to other schools using data from Ofsted, the DCSF and the QCA.

It is made available to schools and local authorities, and contains national pupil performance data. this is taken from the results of statutory and optional national curriculum tests taken at key stages:

Key Stage 1: Ages 5-7
Key Stage 2: Ages 7-11
Key Stage 4/GCSE/GNVQ: Ages 14-16

The information in the package can be used to measure the overall performance of a school against a similar school, or to compare with schools nationally, or to track individual pupils' progress.

It includes Contextual Added Value (CVA) information which makes adjustments for gender, social class and ethnicity and is designed for use as a management tool to help schools in the development and implementation of plans to raise standards. It will form part of the discussions the head has with the School Improvement Partner (SIP); and in the completion of the school's Self Evaluation Form (SEF). The data in it form a key part of Ofsted inspection and may be taken into account in performance management. *More*

information at: www.standards.dfes.gov.uk/performance/www.raiseonline.org.uk
www.ofsted.gov.uk (and follow the menu).

F14 CONNEXIONS SERVICE

The Connexions service, which offered differentiated support to all young people aged 13 to 19 in England by providing integrated advice, guidance and access to personal development opportunities for the whole group to help them make a smooth transition to adulthood and working life, ceased to exist as a national service in April 2008 when funding transferred to local authorities. Your LA will have decided how best to provide the service, whether by providing it as part of youth services; sub-contracting to an external provider; or continuing to fund the existing Connexions service.

F15 THE LEARNING AND SKILLS COUNCIL (LSC)

The LSC was responsible for funding and planning education and training for all over 16-year-olds. This function is being replaced by the Young People's Learning Agency for 16-19 year olds and the Skills Funding Council for over 19s. The funding responsibility for post-16 education of young people will transfer to LAs in 2010.

The Curriculum

F16 USEFUL SITES FOR RESOURCES

The most useful website for teachers is the Teacher Resource Exchange: www.tre.ngfl.gov.uk.
Lesson Plans (formerly AskEric) www.eduref.org/virtual/lessons/index.shtml/#search
BBC Web Guides: www.bbc.net.uk/schools/
European Sports Linguistics Academy: www.soccerlingua.net.
Last Minute Lessons: www.lastminutelesson.co.uk.
Lesson Plans Page: www.lessonplanspage.com.
*Prim-Ed Publishing:*www.prim-ed.com.
Schoolsnet Lessons: www.schoolsnet.com.
Schoolzone Teacher Share: www.schoolzone.co.uk.
TagTeacherNet: www.tagteacher.net.
Teachernet useful plans and resources: http://www.teachernet.gov.uk/teachingandlearning/resourcematerials/Resources/
Subjects: Citizenship, PSHE: www.mta-international.com.
Design and Technology: www.howstuffworks.com and www.design-technology.info.
English: www.nate.org.uk.
History: www.activehistory.co.uk. and www.schoolhistory.co.uk.
ICT: www.tre.ngfl.gov.uk.
Languages: www.alienlanguage.co.uk/alienlanguage.
Mathematics: www.math2.org.
*Maths for All:*www.livingworksheets.co.uk.
Multi-cultural/respect for all: http://www.qca.org.uk/qca_6753.aspx.
Music: http://www.teachingideas.co.uk/music/contents.htm.

Physical Education: www.worldofsportexamined.com.
Science: www.scienceweb.org.uk.

F17 EXTENDED SCHOOLS

The government has expressed a wish (though this is not statutory) that all school schools should offer students, parents and the community an **extended schools** offer by 2010. The core offer for mainstream and special schools is:

• high quality 'wraparound' childcare provided on the school site or through other local providers, with supervised transfer arrangements where appropriate, available 8am–6pm all year round;

• a varied menu of activities to be on offer such as homework clubs and study support, sport (at least two hours a week beyond the school day for those who want it), music tuition, dance and drama, arts and crafts, special interest clubs such as chess and first aid courses, visits to museums and galleries, learning a foreign language, volunteering, business and enterprise activities;

• parenting support including information sessions for parents at key transition points, parenting programmes run with the support of other children's services and family learning sessions to allow children to learn with their parents;

• swift and easy referral to a wide range of specialist support services such as speech therapy, child and adolescent mental health services, family

Special Educational Needs and Disabilities

support services, intensive behaviour support, and (for young people) sexual health services. Some may be delivered on school sites;

- providing wider community access to ICT, sports and arts facilities, including adult learning.

A school is not supposed to provide all these activities itself but may do so jointly or by facilitating commercial or voluntary organisations to do so. The motivation is partly to improve involvement of parents; partly to compel schools to offer extra-curricular activities; and partly to provide extended child care to enable lone parents to return to work. Limited resources have been made available but the activities, whether provided by the school or by external providers is supposed to be self-funding. Although it is not statutory, Ofsted enforces it.

G SPECIAL EDUCATIONAL NEEDS AND DISABILITIES

G1 DEFINITIONS

Children have special educational needs if they have a learning difficulty, which calls for special educational provision to be made for them. Children have a learning difficulty if:

- they have a significantly greater difficulty in learning than the majority of the children in the same age group;

- they have a disability which either prevents or hinders them in any way from making use of the educational facilities generally provided for children in the same age group in the same local authority;
- they are under the age of 5 years and are, or would be, if special educational provision was not made, likely to fall within the above categories, when above that age.

Section 312, Education Act 1996.

It is important to note that a child does **not** have a learning difficulty simply because English/Welsh is not their first language.

Special educational provision is additional to or different provision from that normally made available to children of a similar age in schools maintained by the LA. SEN provision should enable a child with SEN to make adequate progress and/or access the curriculum.

The legal definition of disability is different from that for SEN. A disabled child or young person has a physical or mental impairment which has a substantial long-term adverse effect on their ability to carry out normal day-to-day activities. ***Disability Discrimination Act (DDA) 1995.***

It follows that a pupil can have SEN and also be disabled or vice versa. Some pupils with SEN will not be disabled and neither will all disabled pupils have SEN. A medical diagnosis may mean that a child is disabled but that does not automatically imply SEN. It is the child's educational needs rather than a medical diagnosis

Special Educational Needs and Disabilities

or disability that **must** be considered.

DCSF team responsible for special educational needs and disability:
Hardip Begol, Special Educational Needs and Disability Division, Department for Children, Schools and Families, Sanctuary Buildings, Great Smith Street, London SW1P 3BT. Email: hardipbegol@ dcsf.gsi.gov.uk.
Quick Guides SEN1: Special Educational Needs: Points of Law; SEN2: Special Educational Needs: Code of Practice: A Brief Summary.

G2 SEN CODE OF PRACTICE

The ***Special Educational Needs Code of Practice 2001*** and the ***SEN Code of Practice for Wales 2002*** are very similar as they are based on the same legislation. However they also reflect the slightly different education systems and practice of both countries.

Both SEN Codes provide advice to all education professionals, schools, LAs, health and social work professionals on the help to be provided for children with SEN. Schools and LAs **must** take account of the Code in relation to:

- the identification, intervention and management of children with SEN in schools, including children under compulsory school age;
- the assessment/re-assessment/ review of children who may require a statement of SEN; and
- the contents of statements of SEN.

But the legislation still leaves room to exercise professional judgement about how to carry out these duties; and the Codes provide practical advice on how to meet these duties effectively.

In mainstream schools, the Special Educational Needs Co-ordinator (SENCO), should be able to provide information about the Code and the statutory requirements.

The Code promotes a common graduated approach to identifying, assessing and providing for children's SEN. It is a model of action and intervention to help children who have SEN make adequate progress and access the curriculum. It recognises that there is a continuum of SEN and that, where necessary, specialist expertise should increasingly be brought to bear on the difficulties that a child may be experiencing.

School Action: when a class or subject teacher identifies that a pupil has SEN, they should provide interventions that are additional to or different from those provided as part of the school's differentiated curriculum. An Individual Education Plan (IEP) or an alternative form of recording individual strategies and pupil progress should be devised and implemented. Parents **must** be informed.

School Action Plus: when there is little progress or the child cannot access the curriculum successfully, the class or subject teacher and the SENCO are provided with advice or support from outside specialists, so that alternative interventions and additional or different strategies to those

Special Educational Needs and Disabilities

provided through *School Action* can be put in place. The SENCO usually takes the lead but day-to-day provision continues to be the responsibility of the class or subject teacher. A new plan should be devised. Parents **must** be consulted before any referral to outside specialists is made.

Statements of SEN: A statement is a legal document that sets out all the child's special educational needs and the provision to meet those needs.

If, despite the strategies that have been tried at *School Action Plus* a child fails to make adequate progress and/or access the curriculum satisfactorily, schools or parents may ask the LA to carry out a statutory assessment of a child's SEN. If the LA decides that an assessment is necessary, it **must** seek advice from the school, parents, the authority's educational psychology service and health and social care.

The LA is responsible for deciding whether or not to make a statement. If the LA drafts a proposed statement the parents have a right to express a preference for a particular maintained mainstream or special school and the school **must** be consulted before the statement is finalised. A final statement **must** be issued no later than 26 weeks from the initial request. The LA **must** inform parents how to appeal against the contents of the statement if they so wish and explain their rights. The LA is responsible for arranging the educational provision specified in the statement, even where the provision is made by the school, in a cost-effective manner consistent with the child's assessed needs.

Annual review of statements
The purpose of the yearly review of a statement of SEN is to make sure that parents, the pupil, the LA, the school and all the professionals involved monitor and evaluate the continued effectiveness and relevance of the provision set out in the statement. There is a statutory process to be followed and it is likely that responsibility will be delegated to the SENCO to manage.

If the pupil is in Year 9 then a Transition Plan must be drawn up. Even where the Connexions Service helps with the plan it is still the headteacher's responsibility, however a Connexions Personal Adviser (PA)/Careers Wales Advisor should co-ordinate the plan's delivery and advise on all post KS4 options.

Individual Education Plans (IEPs)
Most teachers have used Individual Education Plans (IEPs) as a record of what is planned for the individual child. However, IEPs are **not** statutory; they are **not** a legal requirement. The SEN Code suggests that IEPs are just one way in which individual planning and recording could be carried out. Many schools and LAs have moved to Provision Management or Provision Mapping, whereby all the different interventions are listed and pupil progress recorded and evaluated. Other schools have a policy of individual planning and recording for *all* pupils, then SEN interventions can be recorded as part of class lesson plans with a record of the child's progress,

Special Educational Needs and Disabilities

the outcomes of the intervention being recorded in the same way as for all other pupils. Whatever approach is taken, it is important that there are regular reviews of the plan involving both pupils and their parents.

SEN Code of Practice 2001. www.teachernet.gov.uk/docbank/index.cfm?id=3724.

SEN Code of Practice for Wales 2002. Alongside the Code, a **Handbook of Good Practice for Children with SEN** has been developed.

http://new.wales.gov.uk/dcells/publications/publications/circularsindex/03/handbookofgoodpractice/senhandbook-e.pdf?lang=en .

G3 ROLES AND RESPONSIBILITIES

The governing body, in co-operation with the head, determines the school's SEN policy. The head has day-to-day responsibility for the management of the policy. The SENCO should:

- be closely involved in the strategic development of the policy and provision;
- oversee the day-to-day operation of the school's SEN policy;
- liaise with and advise fellow teachers;
- manage the SEN team of teachers and learning support assistants;
- coordinate provision for pupils with SEN;
- oversee the records on all pupils with SEN;
- liaise with parents of pupils with SEN;
- contribute to the in-service training of staff; and

- liaise with external agencies, including educational psychology services, Connexions, medical and social services and voluntary bodies.

As from September 2009 all SENCOs in maintained mainstream schools in England **must** be qualified teachers. **The Education (Special Educational Needs Co-ordinators) (England) Regulations 2008** sets out all SENCO responsibilities. The TDA for Schools has developed nationally accredited training for all new SENCOs. **Details of providers can be found at:** www.nasen.org.uk/national-award-for-sen-co-ordination.

G4 PUPIL PARTICIPATION

Pupils are expected to give their views and opinions throughout their school life, including in the early years. They have a unique perspective and may be able to say how they can be helped to learn. They should be involved in target setting and when their progress is being reviewed. Where children with SEN find this difficult, teachers should help them to express their views and make sure that they are heard. Pupils with SEN should always be involved in their annual review. Staff should also be aware of advocacy services available for children and young people.

G5 PARTNERSHIP WITH PARENTS

Since the Code was written, the strong message that parents have an integral and pivotal role

Special Educational Needs and Disabilities

to play, 'parent empowerment' has become an evermore central feature of the government agenda. Partnership with parents plays a key role in promoting a culture of co-operation between parents, schools, LAs and others. This is important in enabling children and young people with SEN and disabilities to achieve their potential. The families of these pupils may need more support than most, as they may be anxious about their child's progress. It is particularly important to try to involve them in the life of the school.

G6 FIRST-TIER TRIBUNAL SEN AND DISABILITY

The **Tribunals, Courts and Enforcement Act 2007** means that from 3 November 2008 the Special Educational Needs and Disability Tribunal ceased to exist as a stand-alone body and became part of a new two-tier Tribunal structure; the First-tier Tribunal and the Upper Tribunal.

The SEN Tribunal for Wales is a separate entity - **Special Educational Needs Tribunal for Wales (SENTW)** based in Llandrindod Wells. **Helpline:** 01597 829800. Although the 2007 Act did not change its composition or remit, the Act provides an onward appeal route to be aligned to the Upper Tribunal for both countries (i.e. to prevent there being no onward right of appeal or for the appeal route to be via the courts).

The tribunals consider parental appeals against local authority decisions about their child's SEN.

The Tribunals can hear appeals about:
- refusal to conduct a statutory assessment or reassessment;
- refusal to make or amend a statement of SEN after an assessment;
- the contents of statements of SEN;
- refusal to change the name of a maintained school on a statement; and
- decisions to cease to maintain a statement of SEN.

The Tribunals also consider parents' disability discrimination claims against responsible bodies in relation to:
- admissions to non-maintained and independent schools;
- permanent exclusions from non-maintained and independent schools;
- fixed-term (temporary exclusion) from any school; and
- education and services linked to all schools.

Quick Guides SEN 1: Special Educational Needs Points of Law; EO1: Disability and Special Educational Needs: Points of Law

First-Tier Tribunal (SENDIST) is based in Darlington **SEN helpline: 0870 241 2555 Discrimination helpline: 0870 241 2555.** **SEN Tribunal for Wales (SENTW)** is based in Llandrindod Wells. **Helpline: 01597 829 800.**

G7 THE INCLUSION DEVELOPMENT PROGRAMME (IDP)

The Inclusion Development Programme (IDP is a significant 3-year programme of professional development for all school staff:

Special Educational Needs and Disabilities

- Ist Year - speech, language and communication needs, (SLCN) and dyslexia;
- 2nd Year - autistic spectrum disorders (ASD); and
- 3rd Year - behavioural, emotional and social difficulties (BESD).

The programme can be accessed at: http://nationalstrategies. standards.dcsf.gov.uk/primary/ features/inclusion/sen/idp.

G8 AREAS OF NEED

Pupils in your classes may have a variety of special needs. The SEN Code of Practice gives four broad areas of need:

1. Communication and interaction;
2. Cognition and learning;
3. Behavioural, emotional and social development; and
4. Sensory and/or physical needs.

These are not hard and fast categories. They overlap and inter-relate and some children may have needs that fall into more than one category. These areas can be sub-divided into the categories that are consistent with those used by Ofsted.

Communication and interaction

Children with communication and interaction needs will have -

- speech, language and communication needs (SLCN), or
- autistic spectrum disorder (ASD);
- elective/selective mutism.

All schools will have children with SLCN. Children with SLCN cover the whole ability range. Needs can be diverse, from mild to severe and short or long-term with difficulties in understanding and/or making others understand information conveyed through spoken language, or difficulties with speech sounds, rhythm, organisation and the use of language in social settings. Some will have delayed language development, while others will have a specific language impairment (SLI) and need input from a speech and language therapist (SaLT).

I CAN is a charity that helps children to communicate: www. ican.org.uk.

Afasic is a charity providing information and training for parents and professionals: www. afasic.org.uk .

Autistic spectrum disorders (ASD)

Most schools have pupils with ASD, as it has a reported prevalence of up to one in 100. Children with ASD cover the full range of ability and the severity of their impairment also varies widely. Some children may also have learning disabilities or other difficulties, sometimes making identification more difficult. All children with ASD (including those diagnosed with Asperger's syndrome) will have varying degrees of difficulty with communication, socialisation and imagination.

The Autistic Spectrum Disorders Good Practice Guidance www. teachernet.gov.uk/asd.
A full description of the symptoms and characteristics can be found on the website of the ***National Autistic Society*** www.nas.org.uk. ***Further information is available from the Autism Education Trust*** www.autism.org.uk, and also from the IDP.

Special Educational Needs and Disabilities

Elective/selective mutism

There is some professional debate as to how to categorise elective/selective mutism. It is usually categorised within the broad area of communication and interaction, but separate from SLCN or ASD. Some experts however consider mutism as more of an emotional difficulty. You will need to take the advice of the experts in your area.

Quick Guides SEN 4: Communication and Interaction.

Cognition and learning

Children and young people with difficulties in cognition and learning will be identified as having a:

- moderate learning difficulty (MLD);
- severe learning difficulty (SLD);
- profound and multiple learning difficulty (PMLD);
- specific learning difficulty (SpLD).

Some children who struggle to keep up at school could be considered to have mild learning difficulties, but such pupils are unlikely to be considered to have SEN. Those with more significant problems, depending on the severity and complexity of their needs, will be identified as having moderate learning difficulties (MLD), severe learning difficulties (SLD) or profound and multiple difficulties (PMLD). The greater their needs, the more likely they are to be educated in a specialist setting.

Specific learning difficulties (SpLD) is an umbrella term indicating that pupils display differences across their learning. SpLD include dyslexia, dyspraxia, dyscalculia and dysgraphia.

Dyslexia means difficulty in acquiring literacy skills, particularly learning to read and to spell. Up to 10% of pupils may have some degree of dyslexia. As well as their difficulties in becoming literate, dyslexic pupils are often disorganised and find it hard to sequence.

Dyspraxia is the term used for children who used to be described as 'clumsy', because they have difficulty co-ordinating their movements. The condition is also known as 'developmental co-ordination disorder' or DCD. Although varying in severity, it is likely to affect gross and fine motor skill development and the ability to balance. Some children have 'verbal dyspraxia', where they find it hard to control the muscles to do with speech.

Dyscalculia affects a pupil's ability to acquire mathematical concepts, as well as to sequence, to set sums out correctly and to understand direction, time and space.

Dysgraphia is the least well known of the SpLDs. It affects pupils' ability to form letters and to organise their thoughts in order to put them down on paper. These pupils may have abnormal body posture when writing: lying across the desk or moving the whole body as the writing moves across the page.

Sir Jim Rose's report **Identifying and Teaching Children and Young People with Dyslexia and Literacy Difficulties** was published on 22 June 2009 http://publications.dcsf.gov.uk/eOrderingDownload/00659-2009DOM-EN.pdf.

Special Educational Needs and Disabilities

Dyslexia-SpLD Trust at www.thedyslexia-spldtrust.org.uk.
Dyslexia Action, (formerly Dyslexia Institute) at: www.dyslexiaaction.org.uk.
Dyspraxic Foundation at www.dyspraxiafoundation.org.uk.
The DCSF Standards Site www.standards.dcsf.gov.uk has information on 'mathematics, dyslexia and dyscalculia.' This gives many further sources of information.
Quick Guides SEN5: Cognition and Learning.

Behavioural, emotional and social difficulties (BESD)

Pupils with behavioural, emotional and social difficulties cover the full range of ability and a continuum of severity. Their behaviours present a barrier to learning and persist despite the implementation of an effective school behaviour policy and personal/social curriculum. They may be unusually quiet and withdrawn or isolated, disruptive and disturbing, hyperactive and lack concentration, have immature social skills or present challenging behaviours such as violence and aggression.

A range of difficulties, including emotional disorders such as depression and eating disorders; conduct disorders such as oppositional defiance disorder (ODD); hyperkinetic disorders including attention deficit disorder or attention deficit hyperactivity disorder (ADD/ADHD); and syndromes such as Tourette's may all be considered kinds of BESD.

Whatever behaviours the pupil presents their behaviour is likely to have an adverse effect on their ability to learn and may also affect other pupils learning. If a pupil's condition presents a danger to your health or well-being your employer's duty of care is engaged.

In a case in a Scottish Sheriff Court a teacher in a special school was found to have a case in negligence against her employers who failed to protect her from assaults by an autistic pupil resulting in her developing a stress-related condition or post traumatic stress disorder. The judgement is relevant in England and Wales. **McCarty v Highland Council.**

Education of Children and Young People with Behavioural, Emotional and Social Difficulties as a Special Educational Need DCSF 2008. http://www.teachernet.gov.uk/doc/12604/ACFD633.doc
Intervening Early DfES 2002: http://publications.teachernet.gov.uk/default.aspx?PageFunction=productdetails&PageMode=publications&ProductId=DfES+0131+2002&.
SEBDA (Social, Emotional and Behavioural Difficulties Association) www.sebda.org.
Quick Guides SEN8: Behavioural, Emotional and Social Difficulties.

Sensory needs

There are three categories of need under 'sensory'. These are:

- Hearing Impairment (HI). Ranges from those with a mild or temporary loss of hearing to those who are profoundly deaf and may need to have access to British Sign Language (BSL).

- <u>Visual Impairment (VI).</u> Includes the partially sighted through to those who are registered blind and may need access to Braille.
- <u>Multisensory Impairment (MSI).</u> Pupils have a combination of hearing and sight loss to some degree.

Physical needs

There is a wide range of physical disabilities and pupils cover the whole ability range. Some pupils are able to access the curriculum and learn effectively without additional special educational provision. They have a disability but do not have SEN. For others, the impact on their education may be severe. Similarly a medical diagnosis does not necessarily mean that a pupil has SEN. It depends on the impact the condition has on their educational needs.

There are a number of medical conditions associated with physical disability which may impact on mobility, such as cerebral palsy, spina bifida and muscular dystrophy. Pupils with physical disabilities may also have associated sensory impairments, neurological problems or learning difficulties.

Association for Spina Bifida and Hydrocephalus (ASBAH) www. asbah.org.
Muscular Dystrophy Campaign www.muscular-dystrophy.org.
Royal National Institute for the Deaf (RNID) www.rnid.org.uk.
National Deaf Children's Society (NDCS) www.ndcs.org.uk.

Royal National Institute for the Blind www.rnib.org.uk.
SENSE - for children and adults who are deafblind www.sense. org.uk.
SCOPE (cerebral palsy) www. scope.org.uk.
To advise on software and making ICT more accessible: www.inclusive.co.uk and www. semerc.com.
Quick Guides SEN7: Sensory or Physical Difficulties.

G9 MEDICAL CONDITIONS

Most children with long-term medical conditions are protected from discrimination under the *Disability Discrimination Act (DDA) 1995*. Such needs could include the necessity for medicines during the school day either regularly or in emergencies. *(Staff cannot be required to administer medication though the school **must** make arrangements for it to be administered.)* However, a medical diagnosis or a disability does not necessarily imply SEN.

The four most common conditions that will be encountered in school are asthma, epilepsy, diabetes and anaphylaxis. Depending on the frequency and severity of the condition the pupil may be considered disabled, but none of these conditions will automatically mean that the pupil has SEN; it is the pupil's educational needs that will need to be considered.

Pupils with asthma

You can expect three or four children in each class of 30 to have asthma. Children with asthma must have immediate access to their reliever inhalers

Special Educational Needs and Disabilities

when they need them. Relievers (blue inhalers) are medicines taken immediately to relieve asthma symptoms and are taken during an asthma attack. They are also sometimes taken before exercise.

You should be aware of the signs of an attack - breathlessness and coughing are the easiest symptoms to spot – and encourage them to sit upright or lean forward slightly and breathe deeply. Get them to loosen their clothing and offer water. If the reliever has no effect after 10 minutes an ambulance should be called. Every school needs to have procedures of which all staff are aware.

The National Asthma Campaign has a free school pack:
www.asthma.org.uk/ ***or tel: 020 7704 5888.***
Quick Guides AM4: Helping Children with Asthma.

Pupils with epilepsy

Most teachers, during their careers, will have several pupils with epilepsy in their classes. Although most pupils with diagnosed epilepsy never have a seizure during the school day, you should know what to do if a child has a seizure in your class. If epilepsy is dealt with calmly and reassuringly it helps the child and the rest of the class will develop a healthy and accepting attitude towards epilepsy.

Epilepsy is not an illness. Children with epilepsy have repeated seizures that start in the brain. An epileptic seizure, sometimes called a fit, turn or blackout can happen to anyone at any time. Seizures can happen for many reasons. 5% of people with epilepsy have their first seizure before the age of 20.

As epilepsy is a very individual condition it is unnecessary for teachers to be able to recognise all types of fit. Seizures can take many different forms and a wide range of descriptors are used for the particular seizure patterns of individual children. Schools should have detailed information from parents and health care professionals about each individual. The information should be recorded in an individual health care plan, setting out the particular pattern of an individual child's epilepsy. Class and subject teachers should be aware of the details and what to do, for the particular child, if a seizure occurs. The health care plan should identify clearly the type or types of seizures, including seizure descriptions, possible triggers and whether emergency intervention may be required.

WHAT YOU SHOULD DO if a child has a fit in your classroom:
- Keep calm and reassure the other pupils in the class;
- During a seizure it is important to make sure:
  ◊ the child is in a safe position;
  ◊ not to restrict a child's movements; and
  ◊ to allow the seizure to take its course.
- In a convulsive seizure something soft should be put under the child's head to help protect it. **Nothing** should **ever** be placed in the mouth.
- After a convulsive seizure has stopped, the child should be placed in the recovery position and stayed with, until fully recovered.

Special Educational Needs and Disabilities

Where possible, if a child is having a fit in class there should be an agreed procedure for ensuring that the rest of the class are catered for and are not distressed. One primary school uses a warning system where a teacher sends a child to the next class with a red cotton reel – alerting the teacher to the fact that there is a problem in the next classroom and assistance is required. (The school's emergency plan will depend on the age of the class e.g. in some situations it might be preferable to move very young children out of the situation to avoid any distress.) Schools normally agree a plan of action with the parents and the appropriate health professional, which all teachers should be aware of.

PE and off-site activities
Children with epilepsy can be included in all activities though extra care may be needed in some areas such as swimming, undertaking gymnastic activities at a height or working in science laboratories. Advice should be sought from parents and/or medical adviser.

Epilepsy Action www.epilepsy.org.uk publishes **Epilepsy - a teacher's guide** - http://www.epilepsy.org.uk/info/education/index.html.
The National Society for Epilepsy (NSE) http://www.epilepsysociety.org.uk.
UK Epilepsy helpline, telephone 01494 601 400 (Monday-Friday 10:00 - 4.00 pm).
Epilepsy Wales: Helpline: 08457 413774.
Quick Guides AM5: Helping Children with Epilepsy.

Pupils with diabetes
About 1 in 550 pupils suffers from diabetes, which means that the child cannot naturally control his/her blood sugar levels. Diabetes is either due to a lack of insulin (Type 1 diabetes) or because there is insufficient insulin for the child's needs or the insulin is not working properly (Type 2 diabetes). Each child with diabetes may experience different symptoms and therefore each child will require an individual a health care plan. The majority of children have Type 1 diabetes. They normally need to have daily insulin injections, to monitor their blood glucose level and to eat regularly according to their personal dietary plan. Type 2 diabetes, once known as adult-onset diabetes, is now also found in young adults and children.

Pupils with Type 1 diabetes must be allowed to eat regularly. Schools should have arrangements for this and you should have been told what they are. The diabetes of the majority of children is controlled by injections of insulin each day. Most younger children will be on a twice-a-day insulin regime of a longer- acting insulin and it is unlikely that these will need to be given during school hours, although for those who do it may be necessary for an adult to administer the injection. Older children may be on multiple injections and others may be controlled on an insulin pump. Most children can manage their own injections, but if doses are required at school supervision may be required, and also a suitable, private place to carry it out.

Special Educational Needs and Disabilities

All education staff (including lunchtime supervisors and caretakers and any other staff likely to be on hand if a problem arises) should be aware of the signs of a 'hypo' in a diabetic pupil. These include – hunger, sweating, drowsiness, pallor, glazed eyes, shaking, lack of concentration, headache, mood changes, especially angry or aggressive behaviour and irritability. If these symptoms are ignored the child will rapidly progress to loss of consciousness and a hypoglycaemic coma. If a child has a 'hypo', it is very important that the child is not left alone and that a fast acting sugar, such as glucose tablets, a glucose rich gel, or a sugary drink is brought to the child and given immediately. Slower acting starchy food, such as a sandwich or two biscuits and a glass of milk, should be given once the child has recovered, some 10-15 minutes later. An ambulance should be called if:

- the child's recovery takes longer than 10 -15minutes; or
- the child becomes unconscious.

Some children may experience hyperglycaemia (high glucose level) and have a greater than usual need to go to the toilet or to drink. If the child is unwell, vomiting or had diarrhoea this can lead to dehydration. If the child's breath smells of pear drops or acetone this may be a sign of ketosis and dehydration and the child requires urgent medical attention. Your responsibility is to know the school's policy and how to implement it.

Diabetes UK at www.diabetes. org.uk **Careline: 0845 1202960 (Weekdays 9am to 5pm).**

Quick Guides AM6: Helping Children with Diabetes.

Pupils at risk of allergic reactions

Anaphylaxis is an extreme allergic reaction requiring urgent medical treatment. Causes include nuts, fish and dairy products, wasps and bee stings. Symptoms of a severe allergic reaction can include a metallic taste, itching in the mouth, swelling in the face, throat, tongue and lips, difficulty in swallowing, a flushed complexion, abdominal cramps and nausea, a rise in heart rate, wheezing or difficult breathing, and collapse or unconsciousness.

Schools should bear this risk in mind at break and lunchtimes and in food technology and science lessons. You are not obliged to give injections, but staff who volunteer to give injections in emergencies should be trained to use the pre-loaded adrenaline injection devices which contain one measured dose of adrenaline. The devices are available on prescription for those believed to be at risk. If there is any doubt about the severity of the reaction, or if the pupil does not respond to the medication, an ambulance should be called. You should have training in recognising symptoms and the appropriate response measures. Your school should have procedures known to all staff, pupils and parents.

Quick Guides AM7: Allergic Reactions/Anaphyllaxis.

Managing Medicines in Schools and Early Years Settings DfES 2005 Ref: 1448-2005DCL-EN.

www.teachersnet.gov.uk/ wholeschool/healthandsafety/ medical

Health, Safety, Welfare and Security

Including Me: Managing complex health needs in schools and early years settings
www.ncb.org.uk

Contact a Family www.cafamily.org.uk This site includes an index of specific conditions and rare disorders.

Quick Guides AM7 Allergic Reactions/Anaphylaxis.

H HEALTH, SAFETY, WELFARE AND SECURITY

H1 GENERAL RESPONSIBILITIES

You are expected to act at all times in accordance with your responsibility as a teacher. This was defined in Victorian times as the care that a wise father would take for his sons. Over the years this has been modified by the courts until now it is:

- the action of a prudent parent familiar with the conditions of school life; or
- the actions of a professional, with particular professional knowledge.

For a PE teacher this may mean safe practices in coaching; for a science teacher it may mean carrying out proper risk assessments on experiments and judging whether a particular experiment is appropriate for a particular group of pupils. Both you and your employer also have statutory responsibilities (laws and regulations) for your safety and the safety of other employees.

H2 HEALTH AND SAFETY INFORMATION

Health and Safety Executive

The Health and Safety Executives for England, Wales, Scotland and Northern Ireland are charged with enforcement of legislation (including prosecution of offenders) and providing guidance to those with responsibility of health and safety. *See* www.hse.gov.uk/aboutus and www.hse.gov.uk/enforce.

HSE's Website: www.hse.gov.uk. The Homepage provides access to a wide range of information for those involved in specific industries and health and safety topics. There are also links to:

- *free leaflets* - www.hse.gov.uk/pubns/index.htm.
- *statistics* - www.hse.gov.uk/statistics.
- *research* - www.hse.gov.uk/research/index.htm.
- *HSE Books* - www.hsebooks.co.uk.

Contacting the Health and Safety Executive *HSE's Infoline at:* www.hse.gov.uk/contact. *Infoline* is a public enquiry contact centre, with access to information and expert advice. A multi-lingual service is available for non-English enquiries. It is confidential - you do not have to give your name. *Tel: 0845 3450055: between 8.00am and 6.00pm, Monday to Friday Fax: 0845 4089566.* *email:* hse.infoline@connaught.plc.uk. *Post: HSE Infoline, Caerphilly Business Park, Caerphilly, CF83 3GG.*

Enforcement

HSE's inspectors normally enforce health and safety standards

Health, Safety, Welfare and Security

by giving advice on how to comply with the law. However, sometimes they order people to make improvements by issuing them with a notice, either an Improvement Notice (allowing time for the recipient to comply) or a Prohibition Notice (prohibits an activity until remedial action has been taken). If necessary, HSE may prosecute. www.hse.gov.uk/enforce/ has more detail.

The **Health and Safety Offences Act 2008** increases the maximum fine for certain health and safety offences to £20000. The HSE enforcement policy statement states that prosecution should be in the public interest and where there has been a death caused by a breach of the legislation, reckless disregard or repeated breaches of health and safety requirements.

Safety Policies in the Education Sector (HSE Books) ISBN 978 0 7176 0723 5.
Five Steps to Risk Assessment (Revised 2006) ING163 (rev2) ISBN 978 0 7176 6189 3.
Health and Safety Commission, (HSC). Managing Health and Safety in Schools (HSC) Health and Safety Guidance for School Governors and members of School Boards (HSC). Control of Substances Hazardous to Health (Fifth Edition) Control of Substances Hazardous to Health Regulations 2002. Approved Code of Practice and Guidance (L5 HSE Books).
Managing Work-Related Stress. A Guide for Managers and Teachers in Schools (HSE Books). ISBN 978 0 7176 1292 5.
Reporting School Accidents and Preventing Slip and Trip

Incidents in the Education Sector EDIS2 (HSE Books). Download from HSE website only.
Violence in the Education Sector 1997 (HSE Books). ISBN 978 0 7176 1293 2.
Safety Policies in the Education Sector (HSE) ISBN 978 0 7176 0723 5.
Working Together to Reduce Stress at Work (HSE Leaflet) ISBN 978 0 7176 63439.

Other sources:
DCSF. A Guide to the Law for School Governors 2007. www.governornet.co.uk.
Guidance on Standards for School Premises (ref. DfEE 0029/2000).
DfES/CEDC. Safe Keeping: A good practice guide for health and safety in study support (ref. DfEE 0197/2000).
DfES. Guidance on First Aid for Schools.
DfES. Health and Safety of Pupils on Educational Visits: A good practice guide 1998, and supplements in 2002.
DfES/Home Office. School Security: Dealing with Troublemakers.
Royal Society for the Prevention of Accidents (RoSPA.) Together Safely.
DfES. School Security Website: www.teachernet.gov.uk/wholeschool/healthandsafety/schoolsecurity.
DCSF guides are available free from DCSF publications – 0845 6009506.
British Safety Council 70 Chancellors Road, London W6 9RS:
Tel: 020 8741 1231; fax: 0208 741 4555; email: mail@britsafe.org *Website at* www.britsafe.org.

Health, Safety, Welfare and Security

The Council publishes: *Safety Management - a magazine (11 issues per year).*
British Safety Council Guides on key issues such as: *Communicating the Safety Message; Risk Assessment; Health and Safety in the Office; Fire Safety; Managing Stress.* Contact the Council for a full list. *Order Line: 0208 741231.*
The British Standards Institution (BSI) produces standards relating to the health and safety of machinery, equipment and installations. *Tel: 020 8996 9001: fax: 020 8996 7001: Internet:* www.bsigroup.com *Email:* cservices@bsigroup.com.

Fire Protection Association provides free basic information on workplace safety, but may levy a charge for more detailed searches. Also produces fire safety guidance and videos. *Tel. 01608 812500 and Fax: 01608 812 501: Internet:* www.thefpa.co.uk

Environment Agency Responsible for the majority of environmental legislation in England and Wales. Provides free advice on environmental best practice and free leaflets and booklets. *General Enquiries: 08708 506 506 Free 24-hour hotline for reporting environmental incidents Tel: 0800 807060 Internet:* www.environment-agency.gov.uk.
Health and safety portal for schools on Teachernet: www.teachernet.gov.uk/healthandsafety.
Health and Safety: Responsibilities and Powers (DfES 2001) –

www.teachernet.gov.uk/responsibilities.
HSE free leaflets for the education sector – www.hse.gov.uk/pubns/edindex.htm
HSE free leaflets on risk assessment – www.hse.gov.uk/pubns/raindex.htm
HSE Books has also produced priced documents *Managing Health and Safety in Schools; Contractors in Schools; Safety Policies in the Education Sector* www.hsebooks.co.uk/ *E-mail* hsebooks@prolog.uk.com
HSE Books, PO Box 1999, Sudbury, Suffolk, CO10 2WA.
Quick Guides Management of Health and Safety Division has guidance on the law and model policies.

H3 HEALTH AND SAFETY RESPONSIBILITIES

Schools/colleges are subject to the general requirements of the *Health and Safety at Work etc Act 1974* to make premises reasonably safe for the employees and anyone else on site.

The employer is:
For community and controlled schools - the LA.
For foundation and voluntary aided schools - the governing body.
For independent schools, CTCs, academies and trust schools - the governing body or proprietor/sponsor.
LAs may require community school and controlled school governing bodies to have policies.

Health, Safety, Welfare and Security

What are the employer's duties?
The LA/school/college has the duty to ensure 'as far as reasonably practicable':

- the health, safety and welfare of teachers and other staff in the school;
- the health and safety of pupils in-school and on off-site visits; and
- the health and safety of visitors to schools, and volunteers involved in any school activity.

Schools/colleges as well as LAs must:

- have a health and safety policy and arrangements to implement it;
- must assess the risks of all activities, and introduce measures to manage the risks;
- should review and develop emergency procedures;
- should have appropriate insurance in place; and
- arrange for appropriate training.

In practice, this means that LAs will delegate specific local responsibilities to governing bodies who will delegate the day-to-day management of the policy and risks to the head. They in turn will delegate the identification of risks and management of them to the individuals in charge of the activity. Heads should always remember that although either the LA or governing body must instigate and review policies, ensure assessments of risks are made and maintain an audit track of who is doing what, it is the head's responsibility to ensure that these are implemented in the school. Heads should ensure that procedures are in place for the daily management of the policies.

It is now possible for school staff to claim damages for any injuries or harm caused by the school's breach of the regulations covering health and safety management and fire safety.

Risk assessments
LAs' risk assessments and policies cannot be simply adopted wholesale as a school/college policy. They will have to be adapted and supplemented to take note of the particular circumstances of the school/college - (buildings/facilities/numbers and types of pupil/curriculum/organisation).

In 2008 a council pleaded guilty to breaches of the *Control of Asbestos at Work Regulations* after a school caretaker was twice exposed to asbestos after sweeping the boiler house, unaware that it was contaminated with quarantined asbestos. He had not been told that asbestos was in the boiler house. The first he knew about this was when asbestos removal contractors went in with protective clothing. The regulations require employers to manage asbestos, assessing the risk of asbestos exposure and providing information, instruction and training. For schools this means knowing whether the premises contain asbestos, where it is, what condition it is in and then ensuring that it is managed properly and employees or contractors who may disturb it are told it is there.
In 2009 a former pupil of a school received a six figure payment for fatal mesothelioma caused by exposed to asbestos. The

Health, Safety, Welfare and Security

school had allowed vandalism of ceiling tiles and careless work practices by contractors.

What are your duties as an employee?

You must know the policies and procedures and always act within them. If you 'go off on a frolic of your own' i.e. ignore the policies, you might have to bear the consequences.

You must:

- take reasonable care of your own and others' health and safety;
- co-operate with you employer;
- carry out activities in accordance with training and instructions; and
- inform your school/college of any serious risks.

LAs and schools are required to do what is 'reasonably practicable' to minimise the risks to employees, pupils and visitors.
Health and Safety at Work etc Act 1974.
Health and Safety: Responsibilities and Powers (DfES 0803/December 2001) sets out the legal framework in which employers and employees work.
Management of Health and Safety at Work Regulations 1999 require all schools to assess risks to the health and safety of employees and others on site.
Management of Health and Safety at Work and Fire Precautions (Workplace) (Amendment) Regulations 2003. PE teachers should look at the *Association for Physical Education website:* www.afpe. org.uk.

Quick Guides General Management (GM) Section.

Safety representatives

Employees have a right under the *Safety Representatives and Safety Committees Regulations* to elect a trade union colleague to represent them on health and safety issues. The head can also appoint a representative with delegated responsibility. At the written request of at least two safety representatives, an employer must establish a safety committee, which can study reports, monitor training, and the adequacy of communications about health and safety issues and assist in the development of safe systems.

The guidance booklet *Workplace Health, Safety and Welfare* can be obtained from *The Stationery Office.*www.tsoshop.co.uk
Quick Guides TS2 Teaching Safely: Safety Representatives.

H4 WELFARE OF CHILDREN AND YOUNG PERSONS

Under the *Children Act 2004*, LAs were encouraged to replace their education departments with children's departments.(For a brief period they were described as Children's Service Authorities). Another development was the establishment of Children's Trusts, which are groupings of all those services (including the police and the Primary Care Trust) which are involved with children's welfare. In England LAs were required to have in place a 'Children and Young People's Plan'. This responsibility has moved to the Children's Trust with the passing of the *ASCLA 2009*.

Health, Safety, Welfare and Security

The Plans must set out the improvements to the well-being of children and relevant young people. The improvements relate to:

- physical and mental health and emotional well-being;
- protection from harm and neglect;
- education, training and recreation;
- the contribution made by them to society; and
- social and economic well-being.

These are known as 'the outcomes', first mentioned in the government white paper. **Every Child Matters.**

In addition, the LA must put into the Plan:

- a statement of the authority's vision for children and young people;
- a needs assessment against the outcomes, an outline of the key actions planned to achieve the improvements as they relate to the outcomes;
- a statement about how the authority's budget will contribute to the improvements; and
- a statement as to how the Plan relates to the LA's performance management and review of its services to children and young people.

The regulations also provide for widespread consultation.

Under the **Education and Inspections Act 2006**, schools must have regard to the CYP plan in their work. **Every Child Matters: Government White Paper. The Children's and Young People's Plan (England) Regulations 2005. Education and Inspections Act 2006. Children and Young People's Plan (England) (Amendment) Regulations 2007.**

The Children and Young People's Plan (Wales) Regulations 2007 came into force on 1 September 2007. The regulations required each local authority to publish a YPP for the period 1 August 2008 to 31 March 2011 by 1 September 2008.

H5 DUTY OF CARE

In addition to statutory responsibilities, teachers have a common law duty of care. You have to educate pupils with reasonable care and skill and do what is reasonable to safeguard their health and safety when in your care. For over a hundred years the courts considered teachers to be acting 'in loco parentis' ('in place of parents'). The standard of care has been expressed as that of a 'reasonably careful and prudent parent'. Judges tend now to consider what a reasonable teacher might be expected to do in the circumstances.

The court of appeal held that a teacher in charge of a school group on a skiing visit was not negligent when a pupil was injured, because his actions fell 'within a range of reasonable responses'. You are not expected to second-guess what a judge might think was the proper course of action, so long as what you did was in line with reasonable professional action. You are expected to match up to the

Health, Safety, Welfare and Security

standards currently expected of ordinary, reasonable members of the profession. But some teachers have a 'higher duty of care', because they have extra skills (e.g. PE or science or technology teachers). They will be judged against the reasonable actions of someone with that skill.

In 2007 the Court of Appeal upheld a claim by a 14-year-old schoolboy injured during an inter-school rugby tournament. He was tackled by an over-aged player in an under-15 game. The teacher in charge of the opposition team was not aware the player was over-age. He had not deliberately chosen the over-aged player to give his team an advantage over the opposition. However, the Court ruled he was negligent in selecting the over-aged player.

In 2008 the Court of Appeal overruled the conviction of the owner and headteacher of an independent school who had been fined £12500 for breaches of the **Health and Safety at Work Act.** A 3-year-old pupil suffered head injuries when he jumped down four brick steps in an out-of-bounds area of the playground during morning break. He later died from a hospital-acquired infection. The steps themselves were not dangerous. The Court said 'There is no obligation to alleviate those risks which are merely fanciful.'

In 2009 a judge ruled that a school that put one lunchtime supervisor on a field to supervise over 200 pupils was 'clearly negligent' when a pupil's eye was damaged by a stone thrown by another pupil **(Palmer v Cornwall)**

You must, therefore, apply your professional skill, keep up-to-date, stay within your conditions of employment, make appropriate assessments of any risks you come across and always act in accordance with school policies and procedures. If you fail to do so and a child, or a colleague or a visitor to the school suffers some loss or damage, you could be liable in negligence. In practice it will be the school/LA, which will be sued, as employers are liable for the actions of their employees. However, you may have to face internal investigation and possible disciplinary action if you are alleged to have been negligent.

For all teachers there come moments of doubt and self-questioning. At such times ask yourself, 'if I were the parent of one of these children, would I consider what I am doing or contemplating doing, to be reasonable and prudent in all the circumstances?' The answer to yourself will take into account:

- the nature of the task;
- any hazards that could reasonably be anticipated;
- the steps necessary to avoid or mitigate the risks flowing from the hazards;
- the age, ability, aptitude and special educational needs of the pupils;
- the environment in which the task is to take place; and
- any LA or school procedures that have to be followed.

Health, Safety, Welfare and Security

The law requires a teacher, as a highly trained professional, not to be careless or, at worst, reckless. If it can be shown that you have only acted after due thoughtfulness, it is extremely unlikely that any mishap will occur, and if it does, that the teacher would be considered negligent. However, if you ignore sensible precautions you may face disciplinary action by your employer as well as a threat of legal penalties.

Environment

Employers have a duty to enable employees to work in healthy environments. Schools are regulated by school premises regulations. Exceptionally warm weather in summer sometimes raises the question of maximum working temperatures. There are at present only rules governing minimum temperatures (13°C for strenuous activity; 16°C for general work). There is concern among trades unions that with global warming maximum temperatures should also be set but there are at present no signs of this happening.

Quick Guides Premises (PR) Section has various documents covering environmental issues.

H6 RISK ASSESSMENT

The LA/school/college is required by law to carry out risk assessments. Risk assessment is not some dark mysterious art. You are likely to be doing it every time you step into a classroom. There are basically three types of risk assessment:

- **Generic** - general school policies on leader qualifications; teacher/pupil ratios etc.;
- **Specific** - the assessment that takes place before the visit, when leaders must consider and make plans for all the 'reasonably foreseeable' hazards that might befall the group at each stage of the visit; and
- **On-going** - the continuing risk assessment as the visit progresses and circumstances change.

It is important to consider risks after obtaining:

- all the information about the environment that activities will take place in;
- the qualifications and experience of those in charge; and
- the suitability of equipment, and the age, ability, aptitude and experience of the pupils involved in the activity.

Having assessed the risks it is important to manage the identified risks in such a way as to:

- avoid them if possible; or
- do what is reasonably practicable to minimise their effect.

The legislation suggests that a school will have done what is reasonably practicable if it has considered the following aspects:

- supervision of the pupils;
- protection; and
- training.

Eight steps

Although the HSE recommends five risk assessment steps you might find the following eight steps easier to follow:

1. identify possible risks;

Health, Safety, Welfare and Security

2. consider what needs to be done to minimise the risk;
3. define necessary action to take;
4. identify who should take the action;
5. set a time frame;
6. implement;
7. monitor progress; and
8. review at the end.

The Health and Safety Executive has published helpful advice on Risk Assessment. *HSE: A Guide to Risk Assessment Requirements and Five Steps to Risk Assessment (HSE) INDG163 (rev2) revised 06/06 ISBN 9780717661893 available on the internet at* www.hse.gov.uk *or from HSE Books Tel: 01787 881165.*

Quick Guides Risk Assessment (RAS) Section has examples of model risk assessments and processes, and two risk assessment databases, one covering internal school activities (*RAS 3A*) and one for off-site visits (*RAS3*). The risk assessment documents *RAS2* and *RAS2A* contain a risk assessment template and a version of the HSE's model risk assessment procedure modified to suit the school situation.

There is a sample risk assessment for an office on the **HSE website** www.hse.gov.uk/risk/casestudies/office.htm.

There is a useful HSE leaflet *'Slips and Trips Mapping Tool'* at: www.hse.gov.uk/slips/mappingtool.pdf

The leaflet is aimed at safety representatives.

In 2006 the HSE published a list of principles of sensible risk management.

Sensible risk management is described as being about balancing benefits and risks; reducing real risks; and enabling innovation and learning, not stifling them. It is not about scaring people by exaggerating trivial risks or generating useless paperwork mountains.

School fined for health and safety breach

A secondary school was fined £8000 for breaches to health and safety regulations in 2002, when a 12-year old pupil was badly burned reaching over a candle during a chemistry experiment. The court held that the school had not conformed to the *Management of Health and Safety at Work Regulations 2002*, as it had not conducted suitable and sufficient risk assessments for dangers to pupils and staff. The Crown Court judge also took into account the fact that the school had not ensured that staff had proper health and safety training and, in particular, training in fire precautions. However, the school was acquitted of failing to assess properly the risks to the actual experiment.

There was a serious accident in an art department with plaster of Paris in January 2007. A girl was injured when attempting to make a cast of her hands. She was mixing plaster of Paris with water by hand and she was severely burned losing eight fingers. Plaster of Paris heats up as it hardens. If it is used in thin layers the heat dissipates, but in bulk the temperature can reach up to 60°C. The school

Health, Safety, Welfare and Security

had compounded the problem by using used industrial plaster of Paris and mixing it with hot water. The school was fined £19000 and at the time of writing (January 2010) a civil case for damages is pending. As a result of this accident CLEAPSS, the Schools' Science Advisory Service, issued a guidance leaflet *Using Plaster of Paris in Schools* which advises how to use plaster of Paris safely.

Implications

All areas of the school should have on file 'suitable and sufficient' risk assessments and these should be reviewed from time to time and when any incident occurs that suggests that particular risk assessments need to be revisited. The risks that have to be assessed are those hazards, which the staff consider, in the light of their professional skill and experience to be risks.

Compensation Act 2006

Risk assessments can make people hesitate to run an activity or take a trip. The *Compensation Act* attempts to overcome this by permitting courts to take into consideration that a worthwhile activity might be prevented from taking place if it could only have taken place with safety procedures that would have discouraged anyone from undertaking it. It also allows apologies and expressions of regret to be made without this being able to be produced as proof of guilt.

Quick Guides Management of Health and Safety Division has sections on Negligence and Risk Assessment.

Pregnancy risk assessment

Your school should have on file a generic risk assessment, which can be adjusted to meet the needs of particular pregnant staff, or new mothers. Research carried out by the Equal Opportunities Commission (EOC) as part of the Pregnant and Productive initiative, has revealed that few employers are aware of this requirement. www.equalityhumanrights.com.

Quick Guides RAS7 Risk Assessment for Pregnant Members of Staff.

H7 SAFETY ON WORK EXPERIENCE

LAs and governing bodies are responsible for work experience arrangements and should have policies clarifying their objectives, and clarifying their and their partners' responsibilities. Each placement should be as safe as it is reasonably practicable to make it.

The guidance on Safer Recruitment makes it clear that responsibility for CRB and ISA checks on people in firms supervising work experience lies with schools, not employers. They should be treated as volunteers. The test is that someone has the main or sole responsibility for supervising or training and has this responsibility at least 3 times in 30 days.

In 2006 the DCSF published a guide for employers who host school visits on their sites: www.safevisits.org.uk .

The Right Start – Work Experience for Young People:

Health, Safety, Welfare and Security

Health and Safety basics for Employers. HSE Free leaflet.
Managing Health and Safety on Work Experience: A Guide for Organisers - HSE. A Guide to Health and Safety Good Practice in Work Experience - DCSF Publications.

The HSE produced a video and book ISBN 07176-2351-3 called **Check it Out. Risk Assessment for Young People on Work Placement.** It explains the risks present in workplaces. Identifying hazards and assessing risks are covered. **HSE Books, PO Box 1999, Sudbury, Suffolk, CO10 2WA. Fax 01787 313 995. HSE Books: Tel: 01787 881 165. Website at** www.hsebooks.co.uk.

H8 MANUAL HANDLING

About 38% of all reported three-day injuries at work are caused by manual handling. Within schools manual handling operations are required for SEN pupils to assist them in moving around and with toileting and with physical activities in and outside school, travelling and in the course of emergency procedures. All staff in school are advised to:

- avoid the need for hazardous handling as far as is reasonably practicable;
- carry out risk assessments for manual handling that cannot be avoided; and
- reduce the risks from manual handling as far as possible e.g. using lifting aids.

Manual Handling Operations Regulations 1992.
Health and Safety Matters for SEN: Moving and Handling (HSE Books) ED1S4 (free leaflet).
Health and Safety Matters for SEN: Legal issues including Risk Assessment (HSE Books) ED1S3 (free).
Also for the handling of special needs pupils see: Health and Safety Matters for Special Educational Needs: Moving and Handling Pupils (HSE Guidance EDIS4 www.hse.gov.uk/education.

H9 MEDICAL ROOMS

All **maintained schools** must have a medical room – which could be used for other purposes (other than teaching). It must contain a washbasin and be reasonably close to a bathroom. **Boarding schools** must have at least one sick room and, if more than 40 boarders, an isolation room. There must be associated bathing, washing and toilet facilities. If the pupils are over 8 years old separate rooms and facilities must be provided for boys and girls. In **special schools**, whether maintained or non-maintained, provision must be made for the care and supervision of pupils by an 'appropriately qualified person with relevant experience'.

H10 TRESPASSERS, THREATS AND ASSAULTS

Any person on maintained or independent school premises without lawful authority, who causes or permits nuisance or disturbance to those on the premises, commits an offence.

Health, Safety, Welfare and Security

Abusive or insulting behaviour by a pupil or adult on or off the school premises, which causes you to feel harassed or fear violence (even if you are not actually attacked) could also be an offence. A person who fails to stop this behaviour when warned can be arrested. In some instances one incident alone can be an offence. If you suffer an injury, even if only minor, your assailant could be punished with a fine or imprisonment. This includes psychiatric harm. If there is a racial element it becomes even more serious. You would also be entitled to seek an order restraining the harassment, if necessary. If you sustain a serious injury, the DCSF advises that the school should inform the police.

Father sent to jail for harassing head

A father of a primary school pupil was jailed for 18 weeks by King's Lynn magistrates for harassing and intimidating the head of the school attended by his three children, after she had excluded them from participating in a school football tournament.

Anti-social behaviour

An 'Anti-social Behaviour Order' (ASBO) could be made against anyone ten years old or more, who has acted in an antisocial way, which has caused or is likely to cause harassment or distress. The Order lasts for a minimum of two years. Your LA/school/college should know how to apply for such an order.

Prompt action

You should inform the head, and your union, of any harassment that concerns you. By taking immediate and effective action LAs/schools/colleges can combat the growth of this kind of unacceptable behaviour.

Trespassing

Anyone, including parents, excluded pupils and ex-pupils (and neighbours with their dogs), who come into school without authority can be asked to leave. If they do not leave, and cause a nuisance or disturbance, they commit an offence. The police and 'authorised members of staff' can use 'reasonable force' to remove a person who can reasonably be expected to commit an offence. The head should ensure that all authorised staff are trained in effective ways of exercising this authority and all staff should know who is authorised.

As a further support to schools, LAs in England can now close or divert rights of way across school premises, in order to protect pupils or staff from possible violence, harassment, alarm or distress or any other risk to health and safety arising from unlawful activity.

Three contrasting responses to attacks on teachers

A 4-month evening curfew and 180 hours community service (plus payment of £60 costs) were meted out to a parent by a district judge, after the parent admitted assaulting a head. Apparently he had come to the school to protest against the lack of action against bullying of his son, but had ended up head-butting the head and pinning him to the wall in front

Health, Safety, Welfare and Security

of pupils. It appears that the head's defence of himself had prevented serious injury for which a custodial sentence on the parent would have been likely.

In the second case a parent was jailed for causing actual bodily harm to his son's headmaster, by hitting him on the jaw and punching him several times, during an exclusion hearing.

In a third case a parent was jailed for three months by Sheffield magistrates for assaulting her child's teacher, who was pregnant at the time. The impetus for the assault was an argument about the cost of a school visit.

Staff authorised to deal with trespassers:

Carrying weapons

It is an arrestable offence to carry an offensive weapon in public without lawful authority, or to carry in public any article with a blade or which is sharply pointed without good cause (other than a small pocket knife). An 'offensive weapon' in law is an item designed, adapted or intended to be used to harm someone. Examples are respectively: a gun; a bottle broken to form a weapon; and a paper-weight picked up to club with or throw. It is an offence to carry an offensive weapon or knife on school premises,

whether maintained school or independent school. The police have the power to enter school premises to search for an offensive weapon.

Searching for weapons

Heads, and those authorised by heads, have the statutory power to search their pupils in school, or elsewhere when on authorised school activities, for offensive weapons, drugs and alcohol. **You should not take it upon yourself to search a pupil unless you are authorised and you may refuse to do so if asked to by someone else.**

There are various conditions:

- the pupil may not be required to remove any clothing during the search except for 'outerwear';
- heads cannot 'require' most of the school staff to conduct the searches, only 'authorise' them to do so. But they may 'require' staff employed for security purposes to carry out searches;
- the searches can only be carried out if the searcher is of the same sex as the pupil, and the searcher must be accompanied by a second member of staff of the same sex;
- a pupil's possessions may not be searched under the statutory arrangements without a second member of staff present, which means that a class teacher working on his/her own cannot require a pupil to empty a school bag under s550AA though the common law provisions may still apply to other searches under section 45 (13); and

Health, Safety, Welfare and Security

- if a search reveals any 'offensive weapons' or knives, or 'evidence in relation to an offence' the school MUST call the police in. The school has no discretion in this, not even if the head or anyone else on the staff wanted to resort solely to internal discipline procedures.

S45 of the Violent Crime Reduction Act 2006 as amended inserts a s550AA into the Education Act 2006 to this effect.

DCSF Guidance: School Staff: Screening and Searching Pupils for Weapons www.teachernet. gov.uk.

Violent Crime Reduction Act 2006.

The Public Order Act 1986.

s547 Education Act 1996 (removing trespassers).

S20 of the Education Act 2002 (with Schedule 20) (gives powers to non-maintained schools).

S9 Criminal Justice Act 1988 deals with minor injuries caused in a common assault.

S29 Crime and Disorder Act 1998 covers assaults with a racial element.

The Protection from Harassment Act 1997 (the anti-stalking legislation).

S154 Criminal Justice and Public Order Act 1994 makes it an offence to cause harassment, alarm and distress on or off school premises.

Countryside and Rights of Way Act 2000 (protecting staff and pupils on paths across school sites).

The Offensive Weapons Act 1996.

Apprenticeships, Schools, Children and Learning Act 2009.

General information about school security can be found on the Department website at www.dcsf.gov.uk/schoolsecurity.

DCSF - Toolkit for Schools. Legal Remedies for Preventing and Responding to Violence against Members of the School Community: gives guidance on risk assessment, and provides model letters and incident form. The school can get from the DCSF a poster for display at the school, stating that 'violent and threatening or abusive behaviour will not be tolerated and culprits will be removed from the premises'.

Home Office and DCSF – School Security: Dealing with Troublemakers.

Protecting Pupils and Staff 1997: gives advice on steps to discourage trespassing on school premises:

- posting notices, making clear the terms on which people enter e.g. visitors should report to a specified reception point and suppliers/deliverers of goods should follow specific instructions; and
- introducing signing in and badge systems.

The former DfEE published in 1996 *Improving School Security in Schools* which gives practical advice on security issues. www.tsoshop.co.uk

Quick Guides S8 Security: Diverting Rights of Way to Protect Schools; S2 Security: Dealing with Trespassers: Model Policy.

Health, Safety, Welfare and Security

Contact details of LA health and safety officer:

Names of school's health and safety representatives:

H11 LOSS OF OR DAMAGE TO PERSONAL PROPERTY

If any of your personal property is lost or damaged in the course of your school duties, it is normal for the school to compensate you, even though neither the school nor LA may be legally liable. If the LA or school/college takes out insurance you will normally be offered the amount proposed by the insurance company. Where neither the LA nor school/college carries appropriate insurance, the normal practice would be to make you an ex gratia payment. It would not necessarily follow that this would be the replacement value of the article. Account might have to be taken of any wear and tear.
The Conditions of Service for School Teachers in England and Wales. (The Burgundy Book).
Quick Guides LD1 Loss of or Damage to Personal Property.

H12 NEGLIGENCE

The last few years have shown a considerable increase in the number of cases of alleged negligence brought by parents against schools and LAs for a wide range of perceived injuries – from accidents on schools trips to the long term effects of a failure to detect specific learning difficulties.

What constitutes negligence?
To succeed in an action for negligence, a claimant has to show:
- that the school owed a duty of care to them;
- that the duty had not been discharged, or not been discharged properly; and
- that as a result they have suffered some loss or damage.

For the purpose of quantifying this loss, courts, like insurance companies, use a scale of damages, which enables judges to put a price on most injuries whether financial, physical, emotional or psychological.

Standard of proof
In negligence actions the consequences of the negligence must be shown to have been **foreseeable** and not be so remote that no one could have reasonably forecast the consequences. The defendant will attempt to show that his/her reactions to the circumstances were within a range of reasonable responses.

An action in the civil courts is not directly concerned with guilt or innocence. The claimants want some redress for their injury. In these cases the level of proof necessary is that of the '**the balance of probability**' i.e. which side has the most convincing argument. Gross negligence can sometimes amount to a criminal offence. In these cases the prosecution has to prove the guilt of the accused '**beyond reasonable doubt**'. A court might

Health, Safety, Welfare and Security

inflict a fine or prison sentence in such cases.

Contributory negligence

Where the claimant, by some failure of action of his/her own, has contributed to his/her damages, appropriate liability can be apportioned between claimant and defendant according to the contribution each made to the injury. It would clearly be difficult to argue this in the case of damage to a young child.

Damages

It is for the court to decide, on the facts in the particular case, whether a duty of care exists and whether it has been breached and how the claim for damages should be apportioned.

Compensation Act 2006

The Compensation Act (see also H6) contains sections designed to assist schools and others involved in activities which themselves involve risk e.g. education outside the classroom. Negligence cases often turn on whether certain steps should have been taken to reduce risk. Under this Act courts must now 'have regard' to whether a requirement to do so would 'prevent a desirable activity from being undertaken at all, to a particular extent, or in a particular way', and/or 'discourage persons from undertaking functions in connection with a desirable activity.' A further provision is that 'an apology, an offer of treatment or other redress shall not of itself amount to an admission of negligence or a breach of statutory duty.' *Quick Guides Negligence (NE) Section.*

A school had to pay damages when a cleaner tripped over a plastic basket used to hold lunchboxes in a classroom. The bright blue object was 'staring her in the face' in the words of the judge but she won her case, as the school had breached its statutory duty to keep floors and surfaces clear. However, the court reduced the cleaner's damages by 50% for 'not keeping a proper lookout.' Statutory duty is statutory duty and contributory negligence does not remove that liability, said the judge.

Implications for schools

This case emphasises the need for schools to make proper risk assessments right across the school. You will need to be aware of the importance not only of generic risk assessment (probably carried out at senior management or department level) but also of on-going risk assessments, which all staff should be trained to do. In this case the school should have recognised the hazard.

An 8-year-old pupil fell down stairs in a school, having been given permission to go to the toilet. It appeared that he had been trying to slide down the banister. He suffered severe injuries and sought damages. In holding the school not liable the judge pointed to the fact that the staircase had been there since 1936, and no similar accident had been reported. Since the accident the school had installed studs in the banister, but this, according to the judge was a 'belt and braces' reaction not an admission

Health, Safety, Welfare and Security

of liability. Although such an accident had been foreseeable it was 'not particularly likely', and the school had given proper warnings to the pupils in order to secure good behaviour when using the staircase. Finally, the 8-year-old had made a 'substantial percentage of contributory negligence', as he clearly knew what he was doing.

Implications

All cases of negligence rest on their own facts. Similar cases to the one above have gone against schools. Courts will look carefully at what you actually did to try to avoid, or minimise the risk of an accident, where the possibility of someone injuring themselves was 'reasonably foreseeable'.

Corporate manslaughter

Where it is proved beyond reasonable doubt that a death is caused by acts or omissions that are reckless then a criminal charge of manslaughter may be brought. Until recently this could in practice only be brought to bear on firms which were small enough for a 'controlling mind' to be identified. The **Corporate Manslaughter and Corporate Homicide Act 2007** makes it possible for action to be successful against a company if the way that the company is conducted and staff are supervised creates a situation where recklessly negligent behaviour can take place. Schools which are properly conducted should not be at risk and you are expected to act in accordance with school policies.

H13 TEACHERS FALLING DOWN

The **Working at Height Regulations 2005** have now, after long consultation, been made acceptable to those who work at height in leading and training people for leisure activities such as climbing and potholing. This will be a relief to those who use outdoor activities centres. But teachers and others working in schools have also been prone to falling down in school as well as off-site. The HSE have issued guidance.

In 2007 the HSE published a survey on falls in classrooms. The survey showed that:

- schools do not see falls from height as a major issue; and
- teachers and assistants see themselves as professionals.

Their main concern is the education of pupils. They are prepared to take risks (they see these risks as no more than they take at home) to get the job done.

In 2008 a school caretaker was awarded compensation for injuries after falling 6ft off a step ladder. He was 69 at the time. The High Court ruled that the employee's training to use step ladders safely was deficient and so he was not aware of the extent of the danger posed by going on the top platform of the ladder. As an experienced and intelligent man he still needed direct training on using a step ladder. His compensation was reduced by 25% to reflect contributory negligence.

Health, Safety, Welfare and Security

Keeping safe when working at height: advice for teachers and classroom assistants (HSE).
Two posters are also available:
More at: www.hse.gov.uk/falls
Working at Height Regulations 2005. Preventing slip and trip incidents in the education sector (HSE) 2006 (EDIS2) contains a list of slip and trip controls for pupils and school staff. *HSE: Working at Height Guidance for Schools 2008.*
Quick Guides Negligence (NE) Section.

H14 FIRE

Although schools do not have to have a fire certificate they do have to comply with the fire precautions legislation. The new fire regulations of 2006 made persons who are responsible for premises responsible also for ensuring the safety of both the premises and occupants. Schools must have a comprehensive fire safety system based on relevant risk assessments. You may face disciplinary action if you do something that breaches fire regulations – for example, propping a fire door open on a regular basis.

Schools should have in place policies that aim to:
- keep the risk of fire to a minimum;
- safeguard means of escape;
- limit the spread of fire;
- specify who is responsible for what;
- ensure that there are at least two fire drills per year; and
- ensure that the lessons from fire drills are assessed and reviewed.

The head and governors must ensure that fire safety policies are known and implemented. A senior member of staff should be responsible for fire safety. Duties will include:
- training and fire drills (for staff and pupils);
- checking and maintenance of equipment; and
- record-keeping.

What teachers should know and do:
- how to raise the alarm;
- action to be taken on discovering a fire;
- evacuation procedure;
- assembly area and checking of pupils;
- location and use of fire-fighting equipment; and
- location of escape routes.

It is important that new teachers are also trained in these procedures and all staff have revision training from time to time.

Name of school fire officer:

Dates of fire drills:

Regulatory Reform (Fire Safety) Order 2005.
Fire Safety. Published by the DCSF in 2000 as part of the Managing School Facilities series.
Fire Safety Risk Assessment: Educational Premises. (Department for Communities and Local Government 2006.)

Health, Safety, Welfare and Security

www.communities.gov.uk/fire/firesafety/firesafetylaw/aboutguides.
Quick Guides F1 Fire Safety: Points of Law.

H15 UNDER STRESS

Stress is considered to be the adverse reaction people have to excessive pressure. It is not a disease but it can lead to mental and physical ill health. It is the employer's duty to make sure that employees are not made ill by their work. Schools like other employers do not have to prevent ill health caused by stress outside work e.g. domestic or financial worries. However, since these can cause problems at work the school should be sympathetic. If you are off school with stress, or think that your condition might force you to be absent sick, you should inform the head as soon as possible. It is part of the school's duty of care to support an employee who has been off with stress and to ensure that reasonable arrangements are made on return. The school must ensure that the arrangements are implemented and followed. Just showing consideration for an employee is not sufficient. There has to be appropriate action.

Standards
The Health and Safety Executive (HSE) has published guidance on the standards that schools and other organisations can use as a yardstick to assess their stress management procedures.

Target
Demands: staff indicate they can cope with job demands;

Control: staff indicate that they are able to have a say in how they do their work;

Relationships: indicate that they are not being subjected to unacceptable behaviour at work;

Change: indicate that the school engages them when undergoing organisational changes;

Support: indicate that they receive adequate information and support from colleagues and superiors.

In a leading school case in 2002, the Court of Appeal said that employers were entitled to assume that employees can cope with the 'normal pressures of the job', unless the employer was aware of some particular problem or vulnerability attaching to that employee. In one case the applicant, who was on anti-depressants sent a note to his superiors saying 'I need some help'. No additional support was forthcoming and he eventually suffered a nervous breakdown. Although more flexible arrangements were then put in place on his return to work these did not last, and he went sick again. He won his claim for damages for a breach of the employer's duty of care.

In another case a Mrs Vahidi had had a 'breakdown' but then returned to school. When she had another breakdown she sued. The judge ruled against her. She appealed. The Court of Appeal dismissed the appeal. It was not up to the school to dismiss her in her own interests when she had wanted to return. The school had supported her by allowing a gradual return, initially on a part-time basis,

Health, Safety, Welfare and Security

and had held three support meetings. It was reasonable for the school to have accepted the claimant's assurances about her health and not to have questioned her further which would have been intrusive and suggested that she was dishonest. If the school had suggested that the claimant left her job it might have been perceived as hostile and this could also have led to a relapse.

In 2004, however, a secondary school maths teacher was awarded over £70000 damages by the House of Lords, which held that the school management had failed to help him even though they were aware that he was suffering from a stress-related illness. The Lords felt the teacher had not been treated well by the school. The Lords confirmed the circumstances in which damages for work-related stress can be awarded:

- the teacher has told the school that he/she is suffering ill health through stress, or thinks he/she is about to; or
- the school must be aware that the teacher has suffered a previous mental breakdown.

Sometimes compensation for injury can be paid without a case reaching a court. In 2004 a deputy head accepted £200000 from a LA after being bullied by her school's governing body. Although she was reinstated to the school, she found it impossible to return because of stress.

Generally, however, the courts have become concerned about claims for stress which are incurring legal costs in excess of any possible award. They are advising mediation rather than legal action.

In a case that is at the time of writing (January 2010) still subject to appeal a headteacher received an award of £387778.22 which included the sum of £25000 for pain, suffering and loss of amenity because the local authority failed to intervene effectively to protect her from persecution by two governors. **Connor v Surrey County Council (2009)**

Implications for schools

The HSE has published guidelines on stress for school employers. Any evidence that an employee is under stress should be taken seriously. The employee should seek medical support and the school should be informed of the medical opinion and prognosis. Appropriate action and support should be considered and implemented. If necessary a second medical opinion could be sought with the employee's agreement. It would be reasonable for the school not to allow an employee back to work without being signed off by a doctor. It is also reasonable to allow an employee to return gradually, and to set time limits for this. Schools are strongly advised to ensure that colleagues have access to a counselling service, and to ensure that where there appears to be a problem, the colleague is recommended to use the service. The fact that a colleague finally cannot cope will not be held against the school if help is given.

Health, Safety, Welfare and Security

Dealing with trauma

There have been in the past, and doubtless always will be, tragedies on school trips and loss of life following road traffic accidents and illness etc. Schools are large communities and in situations like these, or indeed major worldwide tragedies like 9/11, the Asian tsunami and the London bombings in 2005, the whole school will feel the loss or be emotionally affected. It is important that schools have a clear strategy for coping with trauma and that all staff are aware of this. *Wise before the event – Coping with Crises in Schools. Ref. 1993 ISBN 0 903319 667 – Gulbenkian Foundation.*
Quick Guides CP14 Child Protection: Guidance on handling grief amongst pupils.

Termination of contracts on the grounds of ill-health

Your contract could be terminated if you are unable to return because of your medical condition, but this can only happen when there is no alternative. While there is an alternative solution available (i.e. any reasonable adjustment that a school could make) then it is a matter for you to decide whether or not to leave before your condition makes you unfit for the work you were doing. At this point there can be a conflict between your desire to continue working and the school's responsibility to terminate that contract in your own interests.

In **Coxall v Goodyear Great Britain Ltd 2002** the Court of Appeal held that even though the applicant chose to remain at work, knowing that work in a paint shop was detrimental to his asthmatic condition, it was the duty of the employer to move him, or, in the last resort, to dismiss him.

It seems to be the nature and extent of the risk to the individual employee that should determine whether he/she should be dismissed or not. If you find yourself in this position expert help and advice is crucial.

Summary of action points:

- there is a duty for all schools to carry out risk assessments on employees under the *Management of Health and Safety at Work regulations 1999*;
- if you are concerned about your medical condition consider what might be done to alleviate the condition, and inform the school about your stress or potential vulnerability;
- it would also be appropriate to inform your union of your situation;
- the head, or other senior person on the staff, should discuss the issue with you, with a view to determining the best way forward;
- the school/LA should enable you to consult a counselling service about any work-related stress. You would be well advised to make use of such a service;
- the school might also suggest obtaining an expert assessment of your condition and advice on what reasonable adjustments might be made by the school to help you, (the head should listen to your views on what might be done and any requests you make). The school must

Health, Safety, Welfare and Security

consider its responsibilities under disability legislation and its equality policy. The school must make a full assessment of your situation and do what is reasonably practicable to adjust your working arrangements on return to work;

- the school must ensure that those arrangements are implemented and followed, but you should help the school to do this; and
- ultimately the head or governing body must decide what steps to take.

HSE's guidance on preventing stress is:

For large organisations:

Managing the causes of work related stress: a step-by-step approach using the management standards ISBN 9780717662739. Working Together to reduce stress (HSE Leaflet) ISBN 9780717661200.

For small organisations:

Work-related stress: a short guide, INDG281rev1. Single copies free; also available in packs, *ISBN 0 7176-2137- 5. The Dept. of Education and Dept. of Health* published guidance in 2001 *- Obtaining Occupational Health Advice on Fitness to Teach.*

The Teacher Support Network (TSN) is the leading independent organisation providing practical and emotional support for teachers. *Teacher Support Line*, the flagship service, offers telephone information, support and counselling, for all teachers, including trainees, in England. Staffed by trained counsellors with education experience,

the service is 24-hour, free and confidential. *The number to call is 0800 562561.*

Teachers in Wales can call Teacher Support Line Cymru on 0800 0855088.

Quick Guides Absence Through Ill-Health (AB) Section has a full model absence through ill health policy and examples of procedures and letters that could be used in cases of absence through ill health.

Local information:

Occupational Health Service:

School's medical adviser (doctor):

H16 SUN SAFETY

The Health Education Authority recommends all schools to have a sun safety policy. Schools should also carry out risk assessments on how long pupils are exposed to sun on a daily and weekly basis, and when outdoor activities are scheduled. Steps should be introduced to reduce any risks. You will need to be aware of this when planning or supervising an activity.

Sun Safety Guidelines for Schools(1998); HEA. The Use of Sunscreens in Schools: a good practice guide (1999); Go to www.nice.org.uk

Health, Safety, Welfare and Security

H17 DEALING WITH DRUGS

Problems occur with the use of drugs that have no accepted medical purpose, or medicinal drugs which are misused. It is an offence to possess, supply or produce a dangerous drug. It is also illegal for the occupier or someone concerned in the management of premises to knowingly permit on those premises the smoking of cannabis, or the production, attempted production, supply or attempted supply or offering to supply any controlled drug. There are three classes of controlled drugs:

- **Class A:** cocaine, crack, heroin, LSD, ecstasy or E, magic mushrooms;
- **Class B:** cannabis, amphetamines, barbiturates; and
- **Class C:** tranquillisers.

(Some anabolic steroids are now on the controlled list).

Cannabis was re-classified as a Class B drug in view of the government view that there was evidence of increasingly potent varieties of cannabis and evidence of cannabis-induced psychosis. This was contrary to the view of the government's scientific advisers but is now the law. Even under the former classification it was still illegal and young people aged 17 or under found with it could be arrested. It is illegal to possess it or supply it in or near a school. The Act does not cover solvent abuse. Glue sniffing is not an offence, but someone who supplies a solvent to a young person under 18 could be committing an offence.

What can teachers do?

As a teacher you would be permitted to take temporary possession of a substance suspected of being a controlled drug for the purpose of protecting a pupil from harm and from committing the offence of possession. But you must hand the substance to the police and should not attempt to analyse or taste an unidentified substance. Your school should have a procedure for sealing up and securing suspicious substances. Under the common law schools have not been obliged to inform the police when illegal drugs are found on a pupil. But s45 in the *Violent Crime Reduction Act 2006* obliges schools to inform the police if a search for an offensive weapon reveals 'evidence in relation to an offence'. It would be wise for schools to have a policy that made this clear to all relevant staff.

Searches

Heads, and those authorised by heads, have been given the statutory power to search their pupils in school, or elsewhere when on authorised school activities, for offensive weapons, drugs and alcohol. Staff also may have a common law power to search pupils' desks and lockers if they have reasonable suspicion that they might contain illegal drugs. If such a search reveals any 'evidence in relation to an offence' the school **MUST** call the police in. The school has no discretion in this, not even if the head or anyone else on the staff wanted to resort solely to internal discipline procedures. Where pupils are suspected of concealing drugs about their

Health, Safety, Welfare and Security

persons, every effort should be made to persuade the pupil to produce the substance voluntarily e.g. they can be asked to empty their pockets. However, if the pupil refuses, the police should be called. Teachers should not physically search a pupil. *Violent Crime Reduction Act 2006. Apprenticeships, Skills, Children and Learning Act 2009.*

Police powers

A police officer can search a pupil if he/she has 'reasonable grounds' for suspecting that he/she is in possession of a controlled drug and can seize anything which seems to be evidence of an offence. The police have their own codes of practice. A police officer should only interview pupils away from the school. If the pupil is under 17 the interview should be in the presence of a parent, adult friend, and/or social worker. Pupils may be interviewed on school premises with the head's agreement, provided that efforts have been made to inform the pupil's parents.

Co-operation with the police

Schools have a legal duty to co-operate with the police. But police have no right of access to the classroom, although any representation made by a local chief police officer about curriculum matters must be considered by the governing body and head. Most schools now have arrangements for police liaison.

```
Police contact details:




```

Confidentiality

You cannot guarantee confidentiality to a pupil who wishes to discuss with you drugs he/she is taking. The most you can do is to tell the pupil that the only person you will tell is the 'named teacher' responsible for child protection in the school.

Drugs policy

There is no statutory requirement for schools to have a drugs policy, but all schools are required to consider the need to have one. Most schools recognise the pressing need to have a policy, known to staff, parents and pupils. It should spell out clearly what will happen to pupils caught in possession or supplying banned drugs. The policy should also enable staff to manage drugs in schools consistently and confidently.

Disciplinary action

The DCSF has published guidance on how to handle drugs cases. The recommendation is that pupils should not be excluded for a first offence of possession. In a recent case the court ruled that although a school could have a zero tolerance policy it would have to justify departing from government guidance. *Misuse of Drugs Act 1971. Violent Crime Reducation Act 2006. Drugs: Guidance for Schools 2004. Drugs: Guidance for Schools - summary for Heads and Governors.*

Health, Safety, Welfare and Security

The national **Drugs Helpline** is open 24 hours a day **Tel: (free) 0800 77 66 00. Website at** www.ndh.org.uk.

The Qualification Curriculum Authority (QCA) developed exemplar drug, alcohol and tobacco curriculum materials for Key Stages 1-4. To access these materials go to **QCA Schemes of Work for Drug Alcohol and Tobacco at KS3 and 4,** which is on the DCSF Standards site.

A pack produced by the government's drug-awareness campaign focuses specifically on vulnerable groups, including school excludees and truants, young offenders, the homeless, young people in care and children of substance-misusing parents. These young people are among those most likely to become problematic drug users and, as such, are most in need of support. **Vulnerable Young People Making the Difference** highlights the key issues that they face and outlines practical action points: **There is detailed guidance from DCSF in Drugs: Guidance for Schools. More information at** www.talktofrank.com.
Quick Guides HE3 Model Drugs Education and Prevention Policy;HE2 Misuse of Drugs: Points of Law and Guidance.
There is also guidance for a drugs policy on the government's website at www.teachernet.gov.uk

LA contacts:

Schools must have adequate first aid provision. All staff should know what the provision is. Schools must appoint a person to take charge of first aid and the first aid equipment. Such a person could be a teacher or member of the support staff.

First aid boxes

Boxes should contain a 'sufficient quantity of suitable first aid materials and nothing else'. It is intended to be used by untrained persons until skilled help arrives. Travelling first aid kits should be available for school visits. None of the kits should contain any medicines or painkillers. If you are in charge of a first aid kit make sure you check the contents against the inventory regularly.
DCSF document Guidance on First Aid for Schools: a good practice guide. More information at http://www.teachernet.gov.uk/wholeschool/healthandsafety/firstaid.
Available from the HSE are two invaluable First Aid posters. They do not replace formal training but could be a memory jog to help first-aiders:
Basic First Aid at Work: includes information on how to resuscitate a casualty, deal with severe bleeding, broken bones, burns and eye injuries.
ISBN 9780717661954. Electric Shock – First Aid Procedures: advises on breaking the contact between an electrical source and a casualty, making the area safe before administering first aid. **ISBN 9780717662036. To order: Tel: 01787 881165 or Fax: 01787 313995. More**

Health, Safety, Welfare and Security

information at website: www.
hsebooks.co.uk
*Quick Guides AM2 First Aid in
Schools: Points of Law.*

H19 ADMINISTERING MEDICINES

School staff have no legal obligation to administer medicines to pupils unless they have been specifically contracted to do so. It is generally accepted, and stated in LA policies, that all staff are acting voluntarily. You may volunteer to assist in administering medicines to pupils but should be given training and guidance. The headteacher should be satisfied that the member of staff has the confidence and competence to carry out the task. Normally employees who volunteer to assist with any form of medical procedure are deemed to be acting within the scope of their employment and are indemnified by the school/LA against legal action over an allegation of negligence.

Parents should normally administer medicines, but this is not always practicable without seriously impairing the child's education Some children with medical needs are protected from discrimination under the **Disability Discrimination Act (DDA) 1995**. Such needs could include the necessity for medicines during the school day either regularly or in emergencies. Any child, for whom regular or emergency medication during the school day is essential, in that it would be detrimental to the child's health if the medicine were not administered, is likely to fall within the legal definition of disability. Schools should draw up healthcare plans for these pupils that follow LA guidelines and make sure that all staff are aware of the situation and what the school's procedures are. No medicine should be administered unless clear written instructions to do so have been obtained from the parents or legal guardians and the school has indicated that it is able to do so.

Children who are acutely ill and who require a short course of medication, such as antibiotics, will normally remain at home until the course is finished. If it is felt by a medical practitioner that the child is fit enough to attend school, the dosage can usually be adjusted so that it can be taken before school, after school and at bedtime. Medicines should be administered by a named individual member of staff, with specific responsibility for the task, in order to prevent any errors occurring. Children who require medication during school hours should have clear instructions where and to whom they report. Parents or legal guardians must take responsibility for updating the school of any changes but schools must only act on the instructions of the prescriber (doctor, dentist or nurse consultant) or the instructions as provided by the dispensing pharmacist. All medicines should be in their original container as dispensed, and with the prescriber's instructions and child's name clearly labelled. Parents must also be responsible for maintaining an in-date supply of the medication. Any unused

Health, Safety, Welfare and Security

or time-expired medication must be handed back to the parents or legal guardians for disposal. Most medicines should be kept in a secure place, although emergency items, such as inhalers, must be available at all times; for example at the sports field or swimming pool. The school should make sure that you know of any medical problems in groups you take. If you have any questions or concerns You should contact the school nurse or school doctor for advice.

Aspirin

Government guidance advises against administering any over the counter medicines including analgesics such as paracetamol; and that aspirin should <u>never</u> be administered to pupils under 16 unless prescribed by a doctor or nurse consultant.

DCSF Guidance

In March 2005, the DCSF updated its guidance on medicines, advising schools on developing medicines policies, dealing with medicines safely and drawing up health care plans for pupils with special medical needs. There is advice on dealing with medical emergencies and practical advice on four common conditions, asthma, epilepsy, diabetes and anaphylaxis.
Managing Medicines in schools and early years settings Ref 1448-2005 DCL-EN DCSF Guidance: Make sure you use the updated version of November 2007. http://www.teachernet.gov.uk/wholeschool/healthandsafety/medical/

The document, *Medicines Standard of the National Service Framework (NSF) for Children* includes a recommendation about the prescription of medicines for children. It recommends that medicines should normally be taken out of school. For example, medicines that have to be taken more than three times per day could be taken in the morning before school, after school and then at bedtime. Schools are recommended never to accept medicines that have been taken out of the original container and not to accept any parental instruction to change any dosage.

LA Advice

If an LA, or governing body, instructs the head, or gives advice, on the administration of medicines, the instructions or advice must be adhered to.

Parental consent for treatment

A pupil over 16 can give consent to any medical treatment. For pupils younger than 16 only a person with parental responsibilities (usually the mother or father) may give consent. When the parents withhold their consent, usually for religious reasons, (e.g. when a pupil is about to go on a school journey) the school has to decide in the circumstances whether it is reasonable to allow the pupil to participate, or whether it is likely to unreasonably affect the safety of the other pupils and/or to put the group leaders into unacceptable legal jeopardy.

The decision is likely to depend on the kind of treatment and healing that is acceptable to the parents and whether this would be available on the visit.

Health, Safety, Welfare and Security

A secondary school refused to allow a pupil suffering from a diabetic condition to join a school visit because none of the accompanying staff were prepared to take the responsibility for overseeing the administering of necessary medicines. A court ruled that the school was out-of-order in that it had discriminated against the disabled pupil. Schools must try to take reasonable steps and, make reasonable adjustments, to enable disabled pupils as much access to the curriculum as other pupils enjoy.

School staff authorised to administer medicines:

School first-aiders:

Quick Guides AM1 Administration of Medicines: Points of Law.

H20 HEALTHY EATING

As a result of the *Education and Inspections Act 2006* schools may no longer sell unhealthy drinks and snacks.

The government has announced new standards for all food sold or served in schools. There are three parts which were to be phased in by September 2009. *The Education (Nutritional Standards for School Lunches) (England) Regulations 2000. School Food Trust, Eat Better Be Better – a guide to the Government's new food-based*

standards for school lunches. Education and Inspections Act 2006.

In Wales the *Healthy Eating Measure 2009* makes provision for the promotion of healthy eating and drinking by pupils in maintained schools .

Quick Guides HE1 Nutritional Standards in Schools; HE1A Guidance on Nutritional Standards for School Lunches.

H21 SECURITY

Schools have a duty to keep staff, pupils and visitors as secure as reasonably practicable. All schools should review their security arrangements periodically. All staff should know what measures have been taken and so should pupils and visitors as far as this is reasonably possible. Many schools have locked entrances with codes and a signing-in and labelling system for visitors; some have CCTV; some have security lighting. It is important for you, as a teacher, to participate in making people and equipment as safe as is reasonably possible. The union safety representatives or staff safety committee can play a constructive part in this, working with the school's management at all levels.

H22 KEEPING PUPILS AND STAFF SAFE ON THE INTERNET

All schools are urged to have their own internet policy, which is communicated clearly to pupils, staff and parents. The Home Office has a standing Task Force on Child Protection - government, police, industry and charities

Health, Safety, Welfare and Security

working together to tackle the danger posed to children by online paedophiles. Following recommendations from the Task Force the Home Office has established a website providing information to teachers and parents, to help them to advise children on how to chat safely online. A booklet has also been published providing additional tips - which can be downloaded from the site.

It is important that schools give advice to staff as to how to keep themselves safe and have regard to their duties to their staff if staff are subject to internet or mobile phone attack by pupils. The school can use the provisions of the **Education and Inspections Act 2006** to take disciplinary action against pupils who harass staff in cyberspace. **The Computer Misuse Act 1990** makes it an offence for a person to access computer material without authorisation.

The booklet is **Keeping your child safe on the Internet. See** http://bit.ly/5v7a1X

The internet filtering company **Surfcontrol** has a guide to safe internet access at school and in the home with advice to teachers and suggestions for other resources. www.websense.com **Tel: 01260 296 200. Fax: 01260 296 201.**

The Becta site is www.becta. org.uk. The Becta website has a link aimed at school leaders and their responsibilities with regard to health and safety in school, in this case internet safety and good practice. It covers questions such as: what is the internet used for? what is an acceptable use

policy (AUP) in relation to home/ school agreement and/or internet policy?

The Child Exploitation and Online Protection Centre (CEOP) is the body charged with protecting children online. They actively police the net and also offer training to those involved in child protection. **Child Exploitation and Online Protection Centre, 33 Vauxhall Bridge Road, London SW1V 2WG** ceop.gov.uk/contact.

H23 USE OF EQUIPMENT

Whiteboards
Safety issues on the use of interactive whiteboards are highlighted on both the Becta and DCSF websites, based upon HSE guidelines. The sites outline simple measures to take to ensure that the equipment is being used in a safe and appropriate manner. All LAs have been given appropriate guidance material.

All suppliers of interactive whiteboards must provide health and safety advice regarding the safe use of projectors.

It is recommended that health and safety notices are posted adjacent to interactive whiteboards. Although the content or posting of such notices is not a requirement under law, it should be considered as best practice.

All staff using whiteboards should be given good guidance and training as soon as the equipment is installed.

Display screens
The HSE advises that computer projectors, which are used in the

Health, Safety, Welfare and Security

classroom to show presentations or to illuminate interactive whiteboards, can expose the eye to levels above one of the exposure limits. Although such exposure limits are not statutory, the HSE provides guidance on good practice. It is a legal requirement for schools to ensure that they do everything reasonably practicable to prevent staff and pupils developing pains and illnesses from overuse or misuse of display screen equipment. *See the HSE leaflet (available online): Working with VDUs (INDG36) at* www.hse.gov.uk/pubns.

Mobile phones

Schools should have a policy about pupils' use of mobile phones in school. You should ensure the policy is carried out. This should include clear rules prohibiting cyberbullying or harassment of other students or school staff, directly or indirectly.

School staff should take note of DBERR's warning about the use of mobile phones in vehicles. The regulations stipulate that no person must drive a vehicle (including a school minibus) on the road if he/she is using a hand-held phone. Hands-free phones are not prohibited provided the device is not held at any point. You are strongly advised to ensure that your own mobile phone is kept inaccessible to pupils at all times and is security enabled. It is particularly important that the camera function is protected.

The use of mobile phones by pupils at school and on school trips is a potentially contentious issue. Schools should have firm guidelines which all pupils and parents understand.

H24 SUPERVISION

You are required to take care of the pupils in your charge. The responsibility for ensuring that you are given a reasonable number of pupils to supervise rests with your employer. However, if you believe that you are being asked to supervise pupils in a situation where either you cannot see them all or there are too many to supervise you should bring this to the attention of your employer (through your line manager and/or your union representative). You must always bear in mind the age, aptitude, ability and any special educational needs when deciding on particular courses of action with your classes. You should try not to leave a class unsupervised, but if you have to leave the room for any reason, you must consider the general nature of the class, the expected time away and the proximity of other teachers before deciding whether the class can be left alone for a few minutes.

In the case mentioned in H5 where the head and owner of an independent school was initially fined £13000 for breaching the *Health and Safety at Work Act 1974* by failing to ensure, so far as is reasonably practicable, the health and safety of pupils, there was one member of staff on playground duty supervising 59 pupils aged 3 to 11 years. Some areas of the playground, including the steps, were out of view. **The Court of Appeal nevertheless overturned the conviction** saying 'there is no obligation to alleviate those risks which are merely fanciful'. Steps were a normal hazard that a child might have been

Health, Safety, Welfare and Security

expected to come across without supervision.

However, in another case where one supervisor who was looking after Year 7, 8, and 9 pupils on the field admitted that she was hardly looking at the Year 9s and 10s, and a pupil was struck in the eye by a stone, the court found:

'First, to have one dinner lady supervisor who would be stretched to supervise over 150 pupils in Years 7 and 8, only glancing occasionally at Years 9 and 10, was in my view clearly negligent. Second, since the purpose of appropriate supervision is to deter children from taking part in dangerous activities, as well as to stop dangerous activities if they do occur, a court should not be too ready to accept that the dangerous activity would have happened anyway. Third, where as here the recorder found witnesses called by the appellant were telling the truth, there was no reason not to accept their evidence that if a supervisor had been near they would not have thrown stones because they knew that stone throwing was prohibited.'

In 2000 a secondary school pupil suffered an eye injury by an eraser thrown by another pupil when the teacher had left the room for a few minutes. Both the lower court and Appeal court rejected the pupil's claim for damages. The court's view was that teachers have to exercise care and forethought, having regard to the children's age and propensity for high spirits, but fault could only be established if the incident was more likely to happen while the teacher had been absent for a while. The judges considered that such an incident as this was not unusual in classroom life and could have occurred if the teacher was there and his/her back was turned.

Duties before and after school

You are required to supervise for reasonable periods before and after school sessions. There is no definition of 'reasonable' in this context, but a period of 10 to 15 minutes before and after school has long been considered normal and presumably would be upheld by the courts. The amount required by the school must be part of the 1265 hours that teachers are required to work under the direction of the head. Heads also have the duty to ensure that the number of teachers on duty is adequate for the purposes.

All parents should be notified of the official school opening time, but if pupils tend to arrive earlier, the issue should be dealt with by the head. The courts have made it clear that just because pupils arrive early does not mean that schools have to provide supervision. Apart from organised school visits and off-site activities, you should not supervise pupils beyond the school gates. But if you see a group of pupils immediately outside the school gates acting in such a way as to cause a risk to themselves or others, you would have a duty to intervene. There is no contractual requirement to supervise a young pupil, say an infant, waiting for

Health, Safety, Welfare and Security

an older sibling or parent to pick them up. The head would have to do it him/herself or rely on voluntary help, or to advise the parents to make their own arrangements. If the parents fail to do so the matter should go to the education welfare officer.

Schools can release pupils from school early for good reason, but must inform the parents (and LA) if intending to do so. (This has usually happened during strike action, but has also been known as a reward for well-behaved classes). In one case the release of a class early resulted in a child being knocked down by a car, resulting in an action for damages against the LA for negligence.

In the case **Bradford-Smart v West Sussex** where a child had been bullied to and from school, the judge ruled that 'normally' the responsibility of the school ended at the school gates. However, he did state that there might be circumstances where the responsibility of the school might extend further and some lawyers believe that this is opening the way to a wider responsibility for schools. At present, however, the position is as stated above.

Stopping traffic
A teacher has no authority, nor duty, to stop traffic to allow children to cross a road. Where there is a requirement to cross a road outside a school then the LA, or governing body, should provide wardens, if the school perceives a risk. If you have to take a group outside school (say to a swimming pool) you should plan the route via zebra crossings

and ensure there are sufficient accompanying staff. If there is no zebra crossing enlist police help. The school will need to make a generic risk assessment of such activities. If you are in charge, you will have to make a risk assessment of the specific activity and the specific group.

Midday supervision
If you work in a maintained school, you are under no obligation to supervise pupils during the midday break. The school management has to make the supervision arrangements both for the eating of lunch and otherwise. You may, however, volunteer to do lunchtime activities, or you may supervise on a separate contract. If you remain on the school site you are legally required to assist the head in any action to prevent risks to pupils, if asked to do so. If you want a complete break you should leave the school during the midday break.

Other breaks
Your contract obliges you to participate in the school's roster of duties during other breaks in the school sessions.

My duty roster:

H25 ACCIDENTS

To staff:
The LA/school has to do everything reasonably practicable to safeguard your health, safety

Health, Safety, Welfare and Security

and welfare. If you are involved in an accident a first-aider should be available, with appropriate equipment. The accident must then be reported in accordance with the school's procedures and in the case of a major injury there is a statutory procedure, *(see below: Reporting Accidents in School H26).*

An accident at school counts as an industrial injury entitling you to claim disablement benefit. This is assessed on a percentage basis. To qualify you must be assessed as at least 14% disabled. You may also be entitled to compensation from insurers e.g. for injuries on a school visit. You should always check the personal injury cover and conditions in any insurance policy for a school visit. *See the advice on insurance in the Department's Health and Safety on School Visits: a good practice guide 1998.*

If you sustain an injury as a result of someone else's criminal activity e.g. you are assaulted, you can make a claim to the Criminal Injuries Compensation Authority (as well as claim damages from your assailant). Your union will help you – seek their advice.

In 2007 a council was fined £12000 for a breach of Section 2 of the *Health and Safety at Work Etc Act 1974* by failing to ensure, so far as is reasonably practicable, the health and safety of its employees. A technician working in a design technology department suffered serious hand lacerations from an unguarded circular saw blade. An investigation revealed that the member of staff who used the saw before the technician had removed the guard to adjust the blade height but had not replaced the guard. Neither of them had received any recent training in the use and maintenance of woodworking machinery. The LA had failed to impose, monitor and enforce a uniform safe system of work and minimum levels of training, and the HSE also served an Improvement Notice on the LA to correct the shortfalls.

To pupils:

By virtue of your conditions of service and your common law duty of care, you are required to do what is reasonably practicable to safeguard the health and safety of pupils in your charge. If you act with gross recklessness you will be held liable and may face criminal charges. You will be normally indemnified by the LA or governing body for civil actions brought against you for alleged negligence, so long as the act took place when you were on authorised school duties and you were acting within the scope of your employment. In practice LAs and governing bodies have supported teachers financially even when the teacher, in the quaint legal phrase, 'went off on a frolic of their own' i.e. acted outside the school's/LA's policies and procedures. But teachers should not rely on this. It is sound advice to always act in accordance with LA/school policies.

If you take on added responsibilities e.g. as a head of department or as a first-aider, you are expected to carry these out with the necessary skill. You should ensure that you are appropriately trained. The

Health, Safety, Welfare and Security

school must have a reporting procedure for accidents, which you must keep to. In the case of major accidents there are statutory procedures **see below in H26.** You must not discuss the circumstances of any accident with possible claimants, nor should you give any information about the accident to anyone other than the persons named in the school's procedures.

Addresses: Criminal Injuries Compensation Authority, Tel: 0800 358 3601. www.cica.gov.uk *Quick Guides NE3 Accidents.*

To other visitors:
As occupiers of premises, schools have responsibilities for the safety of visitors to the site. As well as ensuring that the site is safe and hazards are sign-posted, where, for example, a PTA is running an event on the site, the school should make sure that the organisers are clear about their legal responsibilities and that they act accordingly. This is particularly the case where potentially dangerous equipment (e.g. bouncy castles) is in use. It is also important to make it clear if you volunteer to assist at such events whether you are, or are not, acting in the course of your duties or in an activity closely connected with your duties, which will involve the school in vicarious liability for any negligent act of yours.

H26 REPORTING ACCIDENTS IN SCHOOL

Schools must report two types of work-related accidents to the Health and Safety Executive (HSE)

See: The Reporting of Injuries, Diseases and Occurrences Regulations 1995. SI 1995 No.3163.

Accidents to employees
- accidents resulting in death or major injury;
- fractures, except to fingers, thumbs, toes;
- amputations;
- dislocation of shoulder, hip, knee or spine;
- loss of sight (temporary or permanent);
- chemical or hot metal burn to an eye or a penetrating injury to an eye;
- injury from electric shock or electric burn leading to unconsciousness, or requiring rescue, or hospitalisation; or
- any other injury leading to hypothermia, heat-induced illness or unconsciousness; or requiring resuscitation; hospital for more than 24 hours; loss of consciousness; acute illness from exposure to biochemical agent; any ill health which is diagnosed as an occupational disease.

All such incidents must be reported to the HSE within 10 days on Form 2508. The HSE must be notified of fatal and major injuries without delay (e.g. by telephone), with a follow-up report.

Accidents to pupils and visitors
Any accident resulting in death or hospitalisation which arises out of or in connection with work at the school must be reported to the HSE without delay, with a follow-up report, on Form 2508 within 10 days. Accidents are reportable if attributable to:

Health, Safety, Welfare and Security

- work organisation (e.g. supervision of a field trip);
- plant and substances (e.g. experiments); or
- condition of the premises;

(Playground accidents are not reportable unless they arise out of or in connection with work (e.g. level of supervision, or condition of equipment)).

The Incident Contact Centre

All cases are now reported to a single point - the Incident Contact Centre (ICC). Incident reports can be by telephone, fax, the internet, or by post. You can still report directly to your local HSE office or LA. Maintained schools would normally report to their LA.

Records

Schools also have to keep a record of reported incidents, which must be available for inspection by visiting HSE inspectors. If you use the internet or telephone the school will be sent a copy of the report to give the school a chance to correct any errors.

Reports

Postal Reports go to: Incident Contact Centre, Caerphilly Business Park, Caerphilly, CF83 3GG.
For internet reports at http://www.hse.gov.uk/riddor.
By telephone (charged at local rate): 0845 300 9923;
By email: riddor@connaught.plc.uk.
A Guide to RIDDOR '95 (HSE Books) (updated 2008).

Safety Management - a magazine published by the *British Safety Council, 70 Chancellors Road, London W6 9RS: Tel: 0208*

7411231; fax: 020 8741 4555; email: mail@britsafe.org.
Website at www.britsafe.org.
Incident Reporting in Schools (HSE free)
Quick Guides GM5 Reporting Accidents.

H27 SAFETY IN LABORATORIES AND WORKSHOPS

Science teachers, by virtue of their training and experience, are expected to have a clearer view of the likely results of their acts than the ordinary teacher. They owe what is known as a 'higher duty of care'. Science teachers and support staff should have frequent safety training to keep their knowledge and skills up-to-date.

Safe practice

Teachers in charge of labs and workshops must ensure that:

- safe practices are known and implemented by all staff;
- pupils know the safety rules and are trained in safe practices as appropriate to their age, ability and aptitude, and in accordance with the requirements of the national curriculum;
- appropriate fire-fighting equipment is in place;
- fire exits are marked and free from obstruction;
- evacuation procedures are known;
- adequate first aid kits are in place;
- the safety requirements of specific machinery are known to all staff;

Health, Safety, Welfare and Security

- statutory and local safety regulations are readily available;
- regular checks are made on the equipment;
- all isolating switches are clearly marked; and
- all staff are trained in their safety responsibilities.

You should ensure that you always wear the correct protective gear and that pupils do too. You should know the manufacturer's operating instructions for all equipment.

A young chemistry teacher gave a lesson to a class of 15-year-olds on the reaction of oxides of zinc, aluminium and tin to caustic soda. After his demonstration the class worked in pairs and he warned them of the dangers of playing about with chemicals. There was apparently some horseplay and one boy, who was taking some test tubes from the back of the class to the front, was squirted with caustic soda by a girl firstly in his ear and then in his eye. He claimed damages. The judge was satisfied that there was no inherent danger in such a lesson for 15-year-olds, and that the fact that the bottle with the caustic soda was unlabelled was irrelevant, as there was no other liquid being used that day. The case hinged on whether in the circumstances of the lesson and the pupils it was right for the teacher to allow pupils from the back to come up to the front. On the evidence the claim that the horseplay amounted to a lack of responsibility was not made out and the claim failed.

But in another case, where a boy filled a syringe with sulphuric acid from an unlabelled beaker in the absence of the teacher and scarred another boy with it, the judge was not satisfied that the teacher had taken sufficient care. He thought that the warning given by the teacher about the acid was insufficient. It should have been more graphic, particularly when the acid was not labelled. It amounted to a departure from the high standards demanded of science teachers.

Portable Appliances Testing (PAT)

All portable electrical appliances must be well maintained and fit for use at all times. All electrical appliances in the school, whether owned by the school or privately owned, must be periodically tested (i.e. PAT) under the **Electricity at Work Regulations 1989**. It is commonly believed that all such equipment must be tested once per year, but this is not so. The equipment must be safe whenever used. This means that the testing depends on such factors as:

- the type;
- age;
- frequency of use;
- environment used in;
- the nature of the design, and
- the manufacturer's advice.

Quick Guides EL1 Electrical Portable Appliance Testing (PAT).

H28 NOISE

The safety rules on noise in the workplace are unlikely to affect you unless you are working in

Health, Safety, Welfare and Security

a laboratory or workshop and possibly music studios. The rule of thumb is that if you cannot hear someone two metres away because of noise in the area, then ear protection is needed.

Quick Guides PR9 Environmental Issues covers the **Noise at Work Regulations 2005.**

The Education Service Advisory Committee (ESAC) of the Health and Safety Commission (HSC) publishes guidance on safety in educational premises.

British Standard codes of practice: Recommendations for Health and Safety in Workshops of Schools and Colleges (BS4163).

Safety in Science Laboratories. No.2. DES Safety Series.

Safeguards in the School Laboratory, Association for Science Education (ASE), College Lane, Hatfield, AL10 9AA. Tel: 01707 283 000. Fax: 01707 266 532.

Dept of Health, Richmond House, 79 Whitehall, London SW1A 2NS.

Website: www.dh.gov.uk

Royal Society for the Prevention of Accidents Website: www.rospa.com.

H29 VOICE CARE

Evidence shows that teachers are particularly at risk of developing voice problems. Female voices are vulnerable and some subjects, e.g. PE, music and technology are more risk to the voice than others. Environmental factors can contribute to voice strain. In schools these can include:

- class size;
- class layout and design;
- noise;
- acoustics;
- chalk dust, fumes, irritants; and
- uncomfortable temperature, poor ventilation.

Research also indicates that since the voice influences the listener's reaction, the teacher's voice quality can affect pupil learning.

Voice Care Network

Voice Care Network (VCN) provides care for teachers and other voice professionals. It has 100 tutors in the UK who are voice teachers and speech therapists. They provide individual support, information, seminars and workshops. VCN promoted the Year of the Teacher's Voice, September 2005 to July 2006 to draw attention to the importance of teachers' voices. There were a series of conferences, seminars and workshops. VCN gives 7 tips for speaking to any group of listeners:

1. plan attention-getting routines;
2. feel secure, let the territory you stand on be yours;
3. find opportunities for ease, poise and stillness in addressing your listeners;
4. use the visual message of your body language;
5. consider how your tone of voice creates relationships;
6. use muscular energy in key words instead of loudness; and
7. allow pause and silence to strengthen your meaning.

VCN UK, Office No 2, 10 Station Road, Kenilworth CV8 1LA. Tel/Fax: 01926 864000. Email: info@voicecare.org.uk, *website* www.voicecare.org.uk.

Educational Visits

Quick Guides GM11 Voice Care; RAS10 Risk Assessment for Voice Care.

H30 SMOKING

The anti-smoking regulations were implemented from July 2007. These regulations put an end to the legal use of cigarettes anywhere in the public areas of any school. Your LA may have a policy of 'no smoking on Council premises'. If not, it will be up to each school to determine whether it wishes to accommodate smokers in other ways, or to apply further restrictions. It is an issue that may affect in particular schools with residential staff.

Quick Guides HE4 No Smoking 2007 Regulations; HE4A No Smoking Policy

J EDUCATIONAL VISITS

The government has published new draft guidance on educational visits and all learning outside the classroom. It is expected that the guidance will replace the current guidance 'Health and safety on Educational Visits (HASPEV) 1998' in the summer of 2010. It will be known as Health and Safety of Learners Outside the Classroom (HASLOC). HASLOC has a wider audience across all children's services (not just schools). It sets out the enabling nature of sensible risk management and how to reduce 'red tape'. It flags up the lessons learned from serious incidents. HASLOC also sets out how and why staff can expect to be treated fairly if a participant is injured despite their care. In general HASLOC works at a high level and leaves most of the detail to the operational parts of the learning outside the classroom council's website - http://www.lotc.org.uk which carries downloadable material.

Quick Guides Educational Visits (EV) Section.

Name of the School EVC:

Name of the LA's OEA:

Learning outside the classroom - SEN and disabled pupils

All pupils benefit substantially and in a variety of ways from learning outside the classroom through educational visits and extended school activities. Schools **must** make reasonable adjustments to include children with disabilities. Practical measures should be in place so that all young people with special educational needs, disabilities or medical conditions can be involved in the activities wherever that is possible. They should have the same learning opportunities as the others in their group. But the activity can be adjusted for individual participants' needs. Risk assessments should be carried out and the management of any risks should incorporate enabling measures.

Educational Visits Co-ordinators (EVC) and Learning Outside the

Educational Visits

Classroom Co-ordinators (LOtC) should consider, as an integral part of risk assessment, whether one-to-one supervision, which may suffice in the classroom or during less complex activities outside the classroom may be insufficient during more complex activities. Two-to-one supervision may be advisable when, for example, a participant has a history of wandering or otherwise leaving the area of supervision. An adult assigned to the supervision or care of one particular participant should not be included in the ratio for the group as a whole.

As part of risk assessment, EVCs/LOtCs should seek advice from any support staff who look after an individual child in the classroom on a one-to-one basis. They will have an informed opinion as to what ratio of supervision the child will need for learning outside the classroom. It is important to inform and remind parents that learning outside the classroom will take place, but you don't always need parental consent. Consent for medical treatment should be part of overall consent where that is advised. You can and should omit someone from the activity if such consent is withheld. First aid suppliers and first-aiders should always be available on learning outside the classroom.

J1 POLICIES AND PROCEDURES

LAs/schools/colleges must set standards of competence for staff leading each type of visit. They must develop appropriate policies and provide clear guidance for staff, including guidance on supervision and ratios and advising how staff should be deployed. They should also ensure that staff are trained in their health and safety responsibilities and that they are competent to carry out their health and safety duties, especially risk assessment.

The DCSF guidance strongly recommends all schools/colleges appoint an Educational Visits Co-ordinator (EVC), and for each LA to have an Outdoor Education Adviser (OEA) to liaise with the school EVCs, help to train staff and to provide generic risk assessments to schools. EVCs and group leaders must take into account the DCSF guidance and LA policies. The EVC does not have to be one person. The duties could be shared.

The general functions of an EVC are:

- to liaise with the Outdoor Education Adviser to ensure compliance with requirements;
- support head and governors;
- assign competent leaders to groups;
- organise training and induction;
- check CRB disclosures;
- help to gain parental consent;
- organise emergency arrangements;
- keep records of visits, including accident reports; and
- review system and monitor practice.

See DCSF Guidance: Standards for LEAs in Overseeing Educational Visits and A Handbook for Group Leaders. Published by the DCSF, they offer detailed advice on the

Educational Visits

practicalities of leading school groups, including supervision, on-going risk assessment, emergency procedures and specific activities. **Contact DCSF publications on Tel: 0845 6022260 or go to:** www.teachernet.gov.uk/wholeschool/healthandsafety/visits.

Guidance has also been issued by the DCSF on the role of support staff on educational visits: *Guidance on roles of school support staff beyond the classroom.* www.schoolcall.com is a site dedicated to helping parents find out about the visit their children are on.

The government has published an **Education outside the Classroom Manifesto**, which among other things expresses the government's support for schools and LAs so that they can better manage safety on educational visits. **See the full manifesto on** www.teachernet.gov.uk.

In Wales *Educational Visits - a safety guide for learning outside the classroom* an all Wales Guidance was published in 2008. In Wales this comprehensive document incorporates and supersedes previous guidance Health and Safety of Pupils on Educational Visits (HASPEV). *Quick Guides Educational Visits (EV) Section.*

Name of the School EVC: Name of the LA's OEA:

There is no regulation about staff/pupil ratios, but the DCSF gives some guidance in **Health and Safety of Pupils on Educational Visits (HASPEV)**.

The rule is that each visit must be accompanied by the number of trained staff, depending on the nature of the visit and the age and aptitude of the pupils. Each school should have a policy on staff ratios and the level of training and experience required. LA outdoor education advisers will be able to advise on this. There is no reason not to use support staff in supervising pupils, so long as they have the necessary competence and training.

Volunteer adults can also be used so long as they are not asked to do anything beyond their competence and the limits of their authority are clearly defined to staff and pupils. **A Handbook for Group Leaders (DCSF).**

Quick Guides PEG3 Use of Volunteers and Paid Coaches in Physical Education and School Sport.

Charging for educational visits

Most schools will be aware that since 1996 pupils whose parents receive certain prescribed benefits or allowances are entitled to have free board and lodging on residential educational visits. New regulations have up-dated the scheme in both England and Wales. Maintained schools are not allowed to charge for school visits that take place in

Educational Visits

school time, or are connected with the curriculum taught in the school. You may, however, ask for voluntary contributions towards the cost of the visit, so long as those who do not volunteer to pay are not penalised. There are complicated rules covering residential visits that are in and out of school time and for the remission of some charges. All maintained schools should have charging and remission policies and you should stick strictly to these.

Collecting money

You are not required to collect money from pupils. However, if you choose to do so, you should never put money collected from pupils into your own bank account, even for a short time. There should be school procedures for collecting and accounting for monies as well as specifically designated accounts for particular activities and trips. All money received from pupils/parents should be acknowledged with a written receipt.

Incompetent handling of money

During 2002, the General Teaching Council told a teacher that he can only teach so long as he does not handle money. He had mislaid cheques and used funds for subsequent trips to cover losses in the accounts. It was an open and shut case, as he had admitted his misdemeanours and his inability to keep records. But often in these financial irregularity cases the facts are more complex.

Ss 451, 456, 457 Education Act 1996; Schedule 30 School Standards and Framework Act 1998. Charging for Education Residential Trips (Prescribed Tax Credits) (England) Regulations 2003 and Remission of Charges Relating to Residential Trips(Wales) Regulations 2003.
Circular 2/89: Education Reform Act 1988, Charges for School Activities.
Quick Guides GOV13 Charging for Education: Points of Law.

J4 ADVENTURE ACTIVITIES

The government is keen to promote safe outdoor activities, including those of a more hazardous nature and has published its outdoor education manifesto, *Education outside the Classroom.*
For more information go to: www.lotc.org.uk.
Quick Guides EV23 The Learning Outside the Classroom Manifesto.

Licensing and badging

The Adventure Activities Licensing Authority, renamed the Adventure Activities Licensing Service (AALS) in 2007 inspects on behalf of the government the safety management systems of commercial centres, which have been granted licences. The regulations concerning adventure activity centres only cover centres in the UK and do not cover all activities or the voluntary sector or teacher-led trips.
Teachers leading their own parties away from centres do not have to be licensed. They should however, ensure that they are competent in the activity

which they are leading. The fact that they do not fall within the scope of the regulations does not exempt them from their existing legal duty of care. Also, if the activity is one organised by the school for curricular purposes, the LA or board of governors, as employers, are subject to the provisions of the **Health and Safety at Work Act** and the **Management of Health and Safety at Work Regulations**. They require employers to assess the risks to teachers and pupils of any of their activities and to have in place measures to control these risks.

The licensing duties of AALS were taken over by the HSE during 2006-7. A number of pilot non-statutory inspection schemes are being tried out to complement the statutory schemes. In addition, the Educational Visits Advisory Council (EVAC) is consulting in England on the introduction of a robust system of safety accreditation badges across the range of school visits. The Royal Geographical Society (RGS), in conjunction with the British Standards Institution (BSI), are also co-operating in providing training for EVCs.

A Greater Manchester school was fined £3500 after two pupils had fallen down a cliff, one of them suffering a hairline fracture of his skull during a privately-organised school expedition to Snowdonia. Five more pupils aged 12-14 were left in danger when the group became separated in appalling weather after their teacher fell and broke his leg. An RAF helicopter eventually rescued them, one of them reportedly hanging by his fingertips from a muddy rock. It was only because passing hikers were able to alert emergency services that the group was rescued, said the Health and Safety Executive. The court found that the school had failed to ensure the safety of its pupils, as a result of poor planning, preparation and supervision. The school admitted the charges and paid costs as well as the fine.

Implications for schools

The Health and Safety Executive after the trial urged schools not to be deterred from running school visits for fear of legal action, but stressed that organisers must be aware of their duty to properly plan, prepare and manage the events.

In 2002 a pupil drowned in Glenridding Beck, Lake District. The teacher in charge was convicted of manslaughter and sentenced to 12 months in prison. Although conditions were unsuitable, there was no alternative activity planned for the group; no emergency procedure or safety equipment. The HSE identified as the causes the inappropriate actions of the leader and the failings of a management system which allowed an unsuitable leader to be in charge in such conditions.

Activities Centres (Young Persons' Safety) Act 1995. New regulations were made under the Act in 2004. *(DCSF for England and Scotland, and WAG for Wales).*

Educational Visits

Circular 22/94 **Safety in Outdoor Activity Centres** – gives extensive guidance and lists other helpful documents. See the website of the **British Activity Holidays Association (BAHA)** at www.baha.org.uk.

J5 FARM VISITS

The DCSF **Handbook for Group Leaders 2002** now includes advice on the precautions schools should take when taking groups on farm visits. The farm accreditation scheme was launched in summer 2003. Farms wishing to host groups must meet health and safety standards. The scheme is a self-accreditation one but there will be independent inspection. **Further details from Farms for Schools** www. farmsforschools.org.uk.

J6 GROUP SAFETY AT WATER MARGINS

DCSF and CCPR guidance, Group Safety at Water Margins, published in 2003, is available on the DCSF website. It covers learning activities near or in water, but it does not cover swimming or other activities, which require water safety or rescue qualifications. It includes 'Top Tips' for leaders. Swimming outside of supervised swimming pools is a hazardous activity. Pupils on any school trip should not be allowed to go swimming unless this has been included in the programme and agreed with parents beforehand. No swimming should ever take place without proper supervision.

Swimming trips

In 2006 a 17-year-old boy was drowned during a Duke of Edinburgh's Award expedition to South America. He disappeared whilst swimming in the Rio Anzu in Ecuador. The trip was well prepared by the school and the usual consent forms were used. In relation to swimming, it appears the consent form asked for confirmation that the pupil could swim 50 metres.

There were two teachers on the trip, two leaders from the adventure activity company and those four, along with a local guide, were supervising the swimming activity. Their evidence was that they had no concerns either about the water conditions or about the pupils' swimming ability. Another pupil had got into difficulties in the river and had to be rescued. It was during a head count after that incident that it was noticed there was a pupil missing.

At the inquest the coroner recommended that pupils going on adventure holidays should have to pass swimming tests before being allowed to take part in water activities. As yet there is no specific instruction from the Duke of Edinburgh Award Scheme as to the level of competence in swimming that should be expected.

Quick Guides EV12 Summary of DCSF Guidance on Group Safety at Water Margins.

Educational Visits

J7 USING REPUTABLE TOUR OPERATORS

Before undertaking their own organisation of any hazardous visit all schools should ask themselves why they are not using external providers, the best of whom are vastly experienced in safety management. They will take on much of the responsibility for the detail of risk assessment and minimising risk, while the ultimate responsibility will remain with the school to ensure that the arrangements, personnel and equipment are of the required standard.

Look out for the following:
- reliability: the company should have an appropriate programme, and have demonstrated its reliability over a number of years;
- acceptable booking conditions: scrutinise any limitations of liability, the cancellation terms and the insurance package;
- financial security: is your money secured to your satisfaction e.g. through ABTA or ATOL bonding schemes;
- suitable safety procedures: ensure that the safety management system is thorough and conforms to your expectations;
- the right price;
- a relevant programme; and
- appropriate supporting literature.

Member companies of the School Travel Forum (STF) are committed to ensuring that all reasonable measures are taken so that their clients are assured of a high level of safety throughout their tour.

STF expects member companies to ensure that minimum standards are met by their individual safety management system. *See the School Travel Forum (STF) website for further details:* www. educationaltravel.org.uk.
The British Activity Holidays Association (BAHA) at www. baha.org.uk has specific details about activity centres.
Tour operators who are members of STF adhere to a Code of Practice which can be accessed on their website.

The LOtC Council Quality Badge

You are now able to select a tour operator or activity provider who holds the LOtC Council Quality Badge. The badge gives reasonable assurance of both good and safe learning with this provider. So you do not need to do any further risk assessment other than checking that the provider and venue are suitable for your group. There is no need to send a risk assessment form to a quality badge holder.

The scheme is voluntary. You are also free to use a non-badged provider, but you will then have to do your own risk assessment and check what accreditation the provider holds. *For details go to:* www.lotcqualitybadge.org. uk .
Quick Guides EV1 Planning an Educational Visit with a Tour Operator.

J8 MINIBUSES

Many schools have their own minibuses. There are rigorous rules governing their use. You must make sure that you

Educational Visits

implement the school's policy and hold the correct licence. Driver assessment and training is essential. The school should have rules about drivers' hours in the working day and about rest breaks.

The school has overall responsibility for providing a safe service, but every driver is personally responsible for ensuring that the vehicle is roadworthy before taking it out.

Minibus driving licences

Drivers of a minibus with 9-16 seats normally require a Category D1 PCV driving entitlement. However, drivers who passed their ordinary Category B (eight or fewer seats) before 1 January 1997 were also given a restricted D1 entitlement to drive minibuses 'not for hire and reward' and retain this right when driving permit buses. New drivers passing their tests after 1 January 1997 do not get an automatic D1 entitlement but are covered by a relaxation of the European Driving Licence Directive adopted by the UK, which allows them to drive a minibus if:

- it is used by a non-commercial body for social purposes;
- they are over 21 and have held a full licence for 2 years;
- they are a volunteer; and
- the vehicle does not exceed 3.5 tonnes excluding an allowance of 750kg for a tail lift.

Teachers might not be volunteers because they are paid for their work in school, but the government takes the view that so long as teachers and support staff are 'incidental' drivers, then they will not need to have a D1

licence. They should, however, be appropriately trained. You should ensure that there is nothing in your local contract with the school or LA that obliges you to drive and that you receive appropriate training. *For DCSF guidance see note on:* www.teachernet.gov.uk/wholeschool/healthandsafety/visits.

The Motor Vehicles (Driving Licences) Regulations 1999 as amended in 2007.

Quick Guides EV8 School Minibuses: Points of Law.

J9 INSURANCE

Your school/college/LA should already hold cover for you, as a group leader or assistant for public liability, so long as the visit is an authorised school visit. As standard practice the school should set out in its educational visits policy what other insurance is necessary. Adequate cover is required for all the activities and eventualities, including specific cover for any high risk activities, personal accident to all members of the party, medical, damage and loss to belongings, transport and other arrangements in an emergency, compensation for cancellation and delay, legal aid and failure of the tour operator. You will find that most 'holiday/activity' policies contain the same headings; it is the amount of cover on offer that you need to check, especially if you are taking a group to the USA. You will need specialist advice on this.

LA Outdoor Education Advisers (OEAs) should be able to give guidance.

Quick Guides EV14 Insurance for School Visits.

RED KITE

The UK's Leading Supplier
of School Minibuses

Driving Education Further

The very latest range of stylish 9 - 17 seat minibuses from all the leading manufacturers
All new minibuses have a 36 month manufacturers warranty
All pre-owned minibuses have our exclusive Red Kite 12 month 'no-quibble' warranty
Comprehensive choice of specialist mobility options if required
Flexible finance plans including Outright Purchase, Contract Hire and Lease Purchase,
designed to suit your schools budget
Prompt nationwide service and support

FREE Sat Nav on all orders quoting ref LPB0210. Ask for details

Call 01202 827678

Red Kite Vehicle Consultants Ltd, 3 Haddons Drive,
Three Legged Cross, Wimborne, Dorset BH21 6QU
Fax: 01202 821720 Email: sales@redkite-minibuses.com

Photograph Courtesy of Castle Court School

visit our new website
www.schoolminibuses.com

Educational Visits

J10 GUIDANCE

The new guidance **'Health and Safety of Learners Outside the Classroom (HASLOC)'** applies to schools (including independent schools), local authorities, statutory youth clubs and any other setting for children's services. It is not statutory guidance, but it sets out good practice and will help activity organisers to meet their legal duties. It does not cover: work experience; sporting activities; PE; or play. Until this guidance is issued in its final form you should refer to the good practice guide **Health and Safety of Pupils on Educational Visits 1998 (HASPEV)** which has been supplemented by an update, which is split into three parts, covering:

- Standards for LAs in overseeing educational visits;
- Standards for adventure;
- A handbook for group leaders.

The website host is the Council for Learning Outside the Classroom www.lotc.org.uk.n It carries generic forms and checklists, and gives details of the quality badge system **(see J7 above)**.

Group Safety at Water Margins was published in the summer of 2003. You can get copies of all the DCSF guidance by contacting **DCSF publications on Tel: 0845 6009506, or go to:** www.teachernet.gov.uk/wholeschool/healthandsafety/visits/ - to download DCSF guidance documents.

The Protection of Young People in the Context of International Visits. Guidelines for Organisers. Published by City of Edinburgh

Education Dept. (Education Dept.) Tel. 0131 469 3328. Quick Guides Educational Visits (EV) Section.

Useful Organisations
Adventure Activities Licensing Service (AALS); Tel: 0292075 5715. More information at www.aals.org.uk.
British Activity Holidays Association (BAHA) www.baha.org.uk.
British Canoe Union: www.bcu.org.uk.
Duke of Edinburgh's Award Scheme: www.dofe.org.
Mountain Leader Training Board: www.mlte.org.
Royal Lifesaving Society: www.lifesavers.org.uk.

K USEFUL INFORMATION

Many references and contact details are included in the text. Here are some others you might find useful.

K1 DCSF, TeacherNet, WELSH ASSEMBLY, GTC, LSC

- The **DCSF** provides information and resources for schools and colleges.
- **TeacherNet** brings people who work in schools comprehensive guidance, tools and information. Sections of the website include teaching and learning, professional development, whole school issues, management, research and education overview. There

Useful Information

is also a popular-questions database and a community area for sharing ideas and debating education issues, www.teachernet.gov.uk.

- **Teachers magazine** offers the latest education news, resources, real-life teaching examples and practical advice to support people who work in schools. The magazine is published six times per year, with dedicated editions for primary and secondary, and subscription is free. You can receive a copy at work or home or view the latest edition online. To subscribe, or to obtain free back copies of *Teachers magazine (primary or secondary editions)* www.teachernet.gov.uk/teachers.
- **Governornet** provides comprehensive information and guidance on school governance issues. The site features a discussion board and an interactive year planner, www.governornet.co.uk.
- **Governors newsletter** comes out termly and aims to keep governors up to date with the latest developments in education policy. To subscribe to *Governors newsletter* email your name and address to govnews@prolog.uk.com or call *Prolog on 0800 035 1464*, www.governornet.co.uk/governorsnewsletter.
- **Spectrum** keeps you updated with the latest news about DCSF publications. Read it online on TeacherNet. www.teachernet.gov.uk/spectrum.

A selection of the information available online from TeacherNet includes:

www.teachernet.gov.uk/wholeschool/behaviour - *all the latest on behaviour and attendance, including information about bullying, drugs and exclusion.*

www.teachernet.gov.uk/management/atoz/ - *the A to Z of school leadership contains over 100 must-know policy summaries for school leaders and managers.*

www.teachernet.gov.uk/community – *this interactive area contains forums where you can swap ideas with other professionals, take part in hot seat discussions or watch webcasts.*

www.teachernet.gov.uk/professionaldevelopment/careers/vacancies - *links to thousands of teaching vacancies currently listed online, plus articles on researching and applying for jobs and hints for jobseekers and recruiters.*

www.teachers.tv - *information on Teachers' TV, the first digital channel designed for teachers and education professionals.*

www.teachernet.gov.uk/management/payandperformance/pay - *information on teachers' pay policy and conditions.* www.teachersnet.gov.uk/management/staffingandprofessionaldevelopment/pensions - *the latest information and guidance for members of the Teachers' Pension Scheme.*

www.teachernet.gov.uk/management/schoolfunding - *information for schools and LAs on all aspects of school*

Useful Information

funding, financial planning and management.

www.teachernet.gov.uk/wholeschool/supportstaff - *news and resources for teaching assistants and school support staff.*

www.teachernet.gov.uk/wholeschool/sen - *information for teachers and heads working with children with special educational needs.*

www.teachernet.gov.uk/emergencies/ - *a complete guide to drawing up an emergency plan.*

www.teachernet.gov.uk/pshe - *resources and a tool to help identify your PSHE knowledge gaps (and fill them).*

www.teachernet.gov.uk/faq - *a large searchable collection of FAQs as well as a list of the top ten most popular questions for teachers.*

TeacherNet's Online publications for schools service allows you to browse, download or order publications and have these delivered to your work or home address. You can also sign up to receive regular email updates from the DCSF. *Register at* http://publications.teachernet.gov.uk.

The Learning and Skills Council (LSC) Responsible for funding and planning post 16 education and training in England: www.lsc.gov.uk.

National Assembly for Wales

Following the 2007 election whereupon a coalition government was formed between Labour and Plaid Cymru, the Assembly government has ten ministries, one of which is the Department of Children, Education, Lifelong Learning and Skills (DCELLS) It has four main divisions. The Department's four groups are responsible for policy, planning, funding, and monitoring services in their respective areas.

- **Children, Young People and School Effectiveness Group** – learner support, schools management, educational effectiveness and children's and young people's strategy.
- **Qualifications, Curriculum and Learning Improvement Group** – the content of the school curriculum, assessment arrangements, practitioner development, the regulation of qualifications and support for Welsh-medium teaching.
- **Skills, Higher Education and Lifelong Learning Group** – post-16 education and training, including HE, and skills development.
- **Business Improvement and Resource Investment Group** – corporate services, knowledge management, and the management and delivery of DCELLS funding to learners and providers.

In addition the department has teams operating in the following four regions:
- South East Wales;
- South-West & Mid Wales;
- South Wales; and
- North Wales .

Each area team assists the department in its relationship with local stakeholders and providers, and provides a source of local knowledge relevant to planning and to the configuration of provision.

The final element of the department is the DCELLS Strategy Unit, which has a pan-

Useful Information

DCELLS remit focusing on strategy, horizon-scanning and strategic policy development, and the strategic positioning of DCELLS both inside and outside of the Welsh Assembly Government.
National Assembly for Wales, Cardiff Bay, Cardiff CF99 1NA. Tel: 029 20 825111.
Department for Children, Education, Lifelong Learning and Skills email:
education.training@wales.gsi. gov.uk.
www.new.wales.gov.uk - *The National Assembly for Wales website.*

General Teaching Councils:
The General Teaching Council for England (GTCE): www.gtce. org.uk.
The General Teaching Council for Wales (GTCW): www.gtcw. org.uk.

K2 TEACHER AND LECTURER UNION CONTACT DETAILS

ASCL - Association of School and College Leaders: www.ascl. org.uk.
ATL - Association of Teachers and Lecturers: www.atl.org.uk.
NAHT - National Association of Headteachers: www.naht.org.uk.
NASUWT - National Association of Schoolmasters and Union of Women Teachers: www.nasuwt. org.uk.
NATFHE - National Association for Teachers in Further and Higher Education: www.ucu.org.uk.
NUT - National Union of Teachers: www.teachers.org.uk.
VOICE - www.voicetheunion.org. uk.

UCAC - Undeb Cenedlaethol Athrawon Cymru: www.athrawon. com.

K3 PROFESSIONAL ASSOCIATIONS AND ORGANISATIONS

Adventure Activities Licensing Service (AALS): www.aals.org.uk.
Advisory, Conciliation and Arbitration Service (ACAS): www.acas.org.uk.
Association of Colleges: www. aoc.co,uk.
Association for Citizenship Teaching (ACT): www. teachingcitizenship.org.uk.
Association for Language Learning: www.all-languages.org. uk.
Association for Physical Education: www.afpe.org.uk.
Association of Science Education (ASE): www.ase.org. uk.
Association of Teachers of Mathematics (ATM): www.atm. org.uk.
Association of Workers for Children with Emotional Difficulties: www.sebda.org.
Basic Skills Agency: www.niace. org.uk.
British Educational Communications and Technology Agency (Becta): www.becta.org.uk - the government agency leading the drive to ensure effective and innovative use of technology throughout learning.
British Educational Research Association (BERA): www.bera. ac.uk.
British Association of Teachers of the Deaf (BATOD): www. batod.org.uk.

Useful Information

British Dyslexia Association (BDA): www.bdadyslexia.org.uk.

Centre for Languages (CiLT): www.cilt.org.uk.

Child Exploitation and Online Protection Centre (CEOP): 33 Vauxhall Bridge Road, London SW1V 2WG www.ceop.gov.uk/contact.

Department for Business, Innovation and Skills (BIS) : www.berr.gov.uk.

Design and Technology Association (DATA): www.data.org.uk.

Development Education Association (DEA): www.dea.org.uk.

Duke of Edinburgh Award: www.dofe.org.

Estyn: Her Majesty's Inspectorate for Education and Training in Wales: www.estyn.gov.uk.

Equality and Human Rights Commission: www.equalityhumanrights.com.

First-Tier Tribunal (SENDIST) www.sendist.gov.uk.

Foundation and Aided Schools National Association (FASNA): www.fasna.org.uk.

Geographical Association: www.geography.org.uk.

Health and Safety Executive (HSE): www.hse.gov.uk.

The Historical Association: www.history.org.uk.

Institute of Physics: www.iop.org.

Institution of Occupational Safety and Health: www.iosh.co.uk.

Learning and Skills Network: www.lsnlearning.org.uk.

Lifelong Learning UK: www.lluk.org.

Local Government Employers: www.lge.gov.uk.

Institute for Learning: www.ifl.ac.uk.

Mathematical Association: www.m-a.org.uk.

National Association of Advisers for Computers in Education (naace): www.naace.co.uk.

National Association for the Teaching of English: www.nate.org.uk.

National Association of Careers Guidance Teachers (NACGT): www.guidance-research.org.

National Association of Music Educators: www.name2.org.uk/home/P1.php.

National Association for Special Educational Needs (nasen): www.nasen.org.uk.

National Confederation of Parent/teacher Associations (NCPTA): www.ncpta.org.uk.

National Institute of Adult Continuing Education (NIACE): www.niace.org.uk.

National Society for Education in Art and Design (NSEAD): www.nsead.org.

National College (formerly NCSL): http://www.nationalcollege.org.uk.

Office for Standards in Education (Ofsted): www.ofsted.gov.uk.

Qualifications and Curriculum Development Authority (QCDA): www.qcda.org.uk

SEN Tribunal for Wales (SENTW): www.sentw.gov.uk

Social, Emotional and Behavioural Difficulties Association (SEBDA): www.sebda.org.

Training and Development Agency for Schools (TDA): www.tda.gov.uk.

Times Educational Supplement (TES): www.tes.co.uk.

Teachers' Pensions (TP): www.teacherspensions.co.uk.

UK Skills: supports the teaching of skills and organises the British team for the Skills Olympics: www.ukskills.org.uk

University for Industry: www.ufi.com

Welsh Assembly Government: http://new.wales.gov.uk/.

K4 EXAMINATION BODIES

AQA www.aqa.org.uk.
City and Guilds www.cityandguilds.com.
Edexcel www.edexcel.com.
OCR www.ocr.org.uk.
WJEC www.wjec.co.uk.

Other Examination bodies can be found at www.qcda.gov.uk.

K5 INITIALS UNRAVELLED

ADD Attention Deficit Disorder
ADHD Attention Deficit with Hyperactivity Disorder
ASCL Act (ASCLA) Apprenticeships, Skills, Children and Learning Act
ASD Autistic Spectrum Disorder
AST Advanced Skills Teacher
BESD Behaviour, Emotional and Social Difficulties
BSL British Sign Language
CEO Chief Education Officer (less used now than previously)
CPD Continuing Professional Development
CSA Children's Services Authority
DCS Director of Children's Services
DCSF Department for Children, Schools and Families
EHRC Equality and Human Rights Commission
EVC Educational Visits Co-ordinator
FASNA Foundation and Aided Schools National Association

GNVQ General National Vocational Qualification
GTP Graduate Teacher Programme
IEP Individual Education Plan
INSET In-service Training
ITT Initial Teacher Training
LA Local Authority
LPSH Leadership Programme for Serving Heads
NOF New Opportunities Fund
NPQH National Professional Qualification for Headship:
NQT Newly Qualified Teacher
OEA Outdoor Education Adviser (at LA Level)
Ofsted Office for Standards in Education, Children's Services and Skills
Ofqual Office of the Qualifications and Examinations Regulator
PGCE Post Graduate Certificate of Education
PRU Pupil Referral Unit
QCDA Qualifications and Curriculum Development Authority
QTS Qualified Teacher Status
RTP Registered Teacher Programme
SATs Statutory Assessment Tests
SENCO Special Educational Needs Co-ordinator
SENDIST Special Educational Needs and Disabilities Tribunal (now replaced by First Tier tribunal (see above)
SENTW Special Education Needs Tribunal for Wales
SSP Statutory Sick Pay
STRB School Teachers' Review Body
STPCD School Teachers' Pay and Conditions Document
TDA Training and Development Agency for Schools
UPS Upper Pay Spine
VOICE The Union for Education Professionals (formerly PAT)

Useful Information

K6 WHAT ARE THESE?

Burgundy Book: containing those **Conditions of Service of School Teachers in England and Wales** in schools where the Local Authority is the employer, agreed between teacher unions and LAs, which are not contained in the **School Teachers' Pay and Conditions Document** issued by the DCSF.

Excellence in Cities (EiC): part of the government School Improvement programme, intended to bring additional resources to address the needs of core urban areas in England, increasing the diversity of provision for pupils but at the same time encouraging schools to co-operate to raise standards. Now superseded www.standards. dcsf.gov.uk/sie.

Extended School: One that provides a range of services and activities often beyond the school day to help meet the needs of its pupils, their families and the wider communities (England only). **Documents can be viewed on:** www.teachernet.gov.uk.

First-Tier Tribunal (Special Educational Needs and Disability): a tribunal which sits in different parts of the country to hear appeals from parents unhappy with LA decisions about their child's special educational needs and parental claims against responsible bodies in respect of disability discrimination: www. sendist.gov.uk.

First Wave Partnerships: a government initiative aimed at preventing low achievement, reducing crime and improving health. Ofsted report on progress: **Children's Fund First Wave Partnerships.** Available from

Ofsted Publications Centre: Tel: 07002 637 833. or www.ofsted. gov.uk.

ICT in Practice Awards: organised by Becta for models of best practice.

Implementation Review Unit (IRU): a DCSF unit designed to reduce the effect of government policies on workload, and to which you can report any excessive bureaucracy. http://iru. mood.levle.co.uk

Leading Edge Schools: a government scheme to get some schools in England to work in partnership with others, with one school being designated to lead the local group. Intended to create a system-wide reform through teachers developing and sharing innovative and best practice. Interested schools have to approach the DCSF: www.standards.dcsf.gov.uk/ Leadingedge.

Multiple Intelligence: Howard Gardner postulates that the human mind is capable of at least eight different ways of knowing the world. See his book, **Frames of Mind - The Theory of Multiple Intelligence.**

National College for Leadership of Schools and Children's Services: set up by the government to provide school leadership training: www. nationalcollege.org.uk.

The Parent Centre: a website to answer parents' questions about how their children are being educated. Will form part of a cross-government portal. www. theparentcentre.co.uk.

Playing for Success: a government scheme linking sports clubs and local communities. Reported in NFER research to improve numeracy scores of both primary

Useful Information

and secondary pupils. www.dcsf.gov.uk/playingforsuccess.

Private Finance Initiative (PFI): a government scheme allowing private companies to fund and manage public sector building projects.

Skills Funding Agency (SFA) – body to be set up under the **ASCLA 2009** to oversee funding for adult education outside higher education.

Specialist Schools and Academies Trust (SSAT): promotes the development of specialist colleges and academies and supports them, www.ssatrust.org.uk.

Success for All: the government's agenda for post-16 education and training: www.successforall.com.

Young People's Learning Agency (YPLA) a body to be set up under the **ASCLA 2009** to fund 16-19 education.

K7 THE TEACHING AWARDS

The Teaching Awards, established in 1998, publicly acknowledge and celebrate the crucial role that teachers play in the lives of our children and our future as a nation.

The categories of award for 2010 are:
- The SSAT award for outstanding new teacher of the year
- The National College award for headteacher of the year in a secondary school
- The DCSF award for enterprise
- The Becta award for next generation learning
- The TDA award for teaching assistant of the year
- The RAF award for teacher of the year in a primary school
- The RAF award for teacher of the year in a secondary school
- The DCSF award for governor of the year
- The DCSF award for sustainable schools
- The award for outstanding school team of the year
- The WAG award for the promotion of the Welsh language in a school – Wales
- The Ted Wragg award for lifetime achievement
- The Henry Winkler teaching award for special needs

Information can be found at: www.teachingawards.com. Nominations can be made on that site, too. *You can also telephone: 0207 7762340.*

Teachers of Primary Science and Teachers of Physics Awards: Institute of Physics; Tel: 020 7470 4800. Fax: 020 7470 4848. www.iop.org/activity/awards/index.html.

K8 SCHOOL LEAVING DATE

The official leaving date for Year 11 leavers is usually the last Friday in June.

K9 CONFERENCES AND EXHIBITIONS

The British Educational Technology Trade Exhibition (BETT) takes place every January at Olympia. *Check the website:* www.bettshow.com for current dates.

The Education Show at the NEC, Birmingham is an annual event taking place in March. *Check the*

Useful Information

website: www.education-show.com

The Teaching Exhibitions website is at: www.teachingexhibitions.co.uk

Other occasional conferences can be found on the Teachernet site: www.teachernet.gov.uk.

K10 NATIONAL TARGETS

Key stage targets (England)

The targets are set as part of the Comprehensive Spending Review. The current targets come from CSR O7.

Key stage 1

There are no targets for key stage 1.

Key stage 2

- All children (except SEN) to reach level 2.
- All children to advance by 2 levels on their KS1 level.
- No child failing to improve by one level.
- 45% who achieved level 1 at the end of KS1 to achieve level 4 or above in English and maths.
- SEN to achieve 2 levels of improvement if appropriate.

Key stage 3

- All level 4 in English or maths.
- All improve 1 level at least.
- English: 40% of pupils achieving level 3 at KS2 to achieve level 5, most to gain level 6.
- Maths: 50% of pupils achieving level 3 at KS2 to achieve level 5, most to achieve level 6.

Aim: all children to improve by 2 levels in English and maths on KS2 level. SEN to achieve 2 levels of improvement if appropriate.

Key stage 4

- All pupils achieving Level 6 in English and maths at KS3 to achieve 5 or more A* - C .
- 30% of pupils achieving level 5 in English and maths at KS3 to achieve 5 or more A* - C.
- All those achieving level 6 at KS3 to improve by 2 levels in English and maths.
- Majority of those achieving level 5 at KS3 to improve by 2 levels in English and maths (A* = level 8; G = below level 2 etc.).

Low attaining schools

Low attaining schools to achieve:
- 65% level 4 in English and maths (KS2).
- 50% Level 5+ in English and maths (KS3).
- 30% 5 A* - C including English and maths.

In October 2006 the Education Minister launched the document, *The Learning Country: Vision into Action* which updated The Learning Country 2001 and set out a revised programme based on research from the last five years. Some of the original education targets were the subject of consultation in the document, *The Learning Country: Delivering the Promise* which set out the educational agenda for Wales to transform education and lifelong learning.

Education and training are at the heart of the Welsh agenda and the document *The Learning Country: Vision into Action* outlines the key outcomes in six areas which are:
1. Strong foundations. Early Years and inclusion.
2. Schools and learning.

Useful Information

3. 14-19 Learning Pathways and beyond.
4. Supporting practitioners.
5. Beyond compulsory education; skills, further education and lifelong learning.
6. The future of higher education.

Two important policies that follow from *The Learning Country Vision* into action and complement its contents are *Transforming Education and Training Provision in Wales; Delivering Skills that Work for Wales*. The aim is to form geographic and sectoral learning partnerships to integrate the work of schools, FEI's, HEI's and other post-16 providers to transform the ways in which education and training provision is delivered.

The other policy is *School Effectiveness Framework*. In the Welsh Assembly Government publication *The Learning Country: Vision into Action (2006)* acknowledgment is made to the internationally-recognised knowledge relating to school effectiveness and improvement. *School Effectiveness Framework* applies this knowledge in the particular circumstance in Wales. *PISA* (Programme for International Student Assessment) provides the international benchmark for the performance of our school system in Wales.

School Effectiveness Framework sets out the vision and implementation schedule for putting school effectiveness based on tri-level reform into action; that is tri-level reform in the whole of the education, community (schools, local authorities, and WAG) working together

collaboratively. The framework describes the key characteristics required to build on existing good practice and improve on young people's learning and well being throughout Wales. The school, local authority and WAG contribute to that agenda.

For the year 2009-2010 the Welsh Assembly Government has piloted this programme in almost a hundred schools in Wales and after an independent evaluation it is to be rolled out across Wales. The earlier phase of the *School Effectiveness Framework* established the programme in each of the four local authority consortia in Wales. Each consortium identified pilot schools in their area to include primary, secondary and special schools. The framework will continue to encourage further collaboration between the three partners' schools, local authorities, and assembly government, to tackle low standards and narrow the gap between school performances. Over the next year the respective partners will plan the implementation of this national policy and its roll out across Wales from September 2010.

This programme will form part of a more coherent approach to assessing and monitoring quality and driving up standards in education and training in Wales. It is aimed as a flagship policy to which all other policies will be aligned. This is a key factor. The policy will have to be aligned to the new Estyn inspection system which is due to come into operation for a new six-year cycle from September in 2010. It will

Useful Information

link with the **Skills that work for Wales** commitment to the new **Quality and Effectiveness Framework** to support continued improvements in the quality of post-16 learning. **The School Effectiveness Framework** has its own website http://www.sefwales.co.uk and produces its own newsletter.

School absence
To reduce the level of school absence by 8% on the 2002/2003 figure.

Road accidents
Almost 20% of child pedestrian accidents happen to and from school, between 7am and 9am and 3pm and 6pm. Human behaviour is cited by the Royal Society for the Prevention of Accidents (RoSPA) as a factor in 95% of cases. The government is aiming to reduce child deaths and serious injuries by 50% by 2010.

RoSPA's book **School Assembly Plans Using Road Safety Themes** (made up of plans for 4-7s, 7-11s, 11-14s, and 15s plus) helps schools to make children more road safety conscious. All road safety officers have free copies. It can also be downloaded from the **RoSPA website:** www.rospa.com

K11 PROFESSIONAL DEVELOPMENT OPPORTUNITIES

See www.teachernet.gov.uk/professionaldevelopment for recommended Continuous Professional Development opportunities in England.

See www.gtcw.org.uk for continuous professional development opportunities in Wales.

66 *Excellence is in the details.*
Give attention to the details
and excellence will come 99 *

CORE

Core Publications Limited
66 Barton Road, Barton Seagrave
Kettering, Northants NN15 6RX

t: 07814 786 409
e: mail@corepublicationslimited.co.uk

Index

Index

Index

Index

Index

Index

Index

Notes

Notes

Notes

Notes